The Gospel of John

Verse-by-Verse
The Expository Bible Study and Commentary

Chapter 8 to 14

VOLUME 2

DR. MAXWELL SHIMBA

Shimba Publishing, LLC
Printed in the United States of America

Table of Contents

The Gospel of John Overview

The Gospel According to John, often referred to simply as the Book of John, is the fourth Gospel in the New Testament of the Bible. Written by the apostle John, the book is distinct in its theological emphasis, presenting a unique perspective on the life, teachings, and significance of Jesus Christ. Here's an overview of the key themes and characteristics of the Book of John:

1. Theological Emphasis:
- John's Gospel is distinguished by its theological depth and emphasis on the divinity of Jesus Christ. It explores profound concepts such as the pre-existence of Christ, His relationship with God the Father, and the significance of faith.
2. Purpose of Writing:
- John explicitly states the purpose of his Gospel: "But these are written that you may believe that Jesus is the Messiah, the Son of God, and that by believing you may have life in his name" (John 20:31, NIV). The Gospel is written to inspire faith in Jesus as the Son of God.
3. Unique Content:
- John's Gospel contains material not found in the synoptic Gospels (Matthew, Mark, and Luke). It includes seven "I am" sayings of Jesus, such as "I am the way, the truth, and the life" (John 14:6), and seven miraculous signs, including the turning of water into wine and the raising of Lazarus from the dead.
4. The Word Became Flesh:
- The prologue of John's Gospel (John 1:1-18) is a poetic and theological masterpiece. It introduces the concept of the "Word" (Logos) as both divine and incarnate, identifying Jesus Christ as the eternal Word who became flesh and dwelt among humanity.
5. Signs and Miracles:
- John's Gospel highlights seven miraculous signs performed by Jesus. These signs serve as more than mere wonders; they are symbolic and reveal deeper spiritual truths. The Gospel also includes

a series of "I am" statements in which Jesus discloses His divine nature.

6. Encounters and Dialogues:

- The Book of John features extended dialogues and encounters, such as the conversation with Nicodemus (John 3), the woman at the well (John 4), and the discourse on the Bread of Life (John 6). These interactions provide profound insights into Jesus' teachings.

7. The Farewell Discourse:

- In John 13-17, Jesus delivers the Farewell Discourse, a significant portion of the Gospel. This discourse covers themes of love, the role of the Holy Spirit, and Jesus' impending departure. It concludes with the high priestly prayer of Jesus.

8. Passion Narrative:

- John's account of the passion narrative (the events leading to Jesus' crucifixion and resurrection) is distinct from the synoptic Gospels. It emphasizes Jesus' control over the events and His voluntary sacrifice.

9. Resurrection and Commission:

- The Gospel of John provides a detailed account of Jesus' resurrection, including His appearances to the disciples. It concludes with Jesus commissioning Peter and reaffirming the importance of faith.

The Book of John stands as a profound theological testimony, inviting readers to a deeper understanding of the identity and mission of Jesus Christ. Through its unique narrative style, symbolic language, and emphasis on belief, John's Gospel continues to inspire and challenge readers in their faith journey.

Who is Apostle John?

St. John, also known as John the Apostle or John the Evangelist, was one of the twelve apostles of Jesus and the author of the Gospel of John, as well as the letters of 1, 2, and 3 John, and the Book of Revelation. He was the son of Zebedee and the brother of James, also apostles. John is often referred to as the "beloved disciple" or the "disciple whom Jesus loved" in the Gospel of John, indicating a close relationship with Jesus.

The Gospel of John is traditionally believed to have been written towards the end of the first century AD, likely between 90-110 AD, which would make it one of the later books of the New Testament to be written. John wrote his gospel while living in Ephesus, a prominent city in the Roman province of Asia (modern-day Turkey).

John's Gospel emphasizes the divinity of Jesus Christ more explicitly than the other Gospels. He presents Jesus as the eternal Word (Logos) who was with God in the beginning and was God (John 1:1). Through a series of "I am" statements and miraculous signs, John highlights Jesus' divine nature and identity. John includes unique teachings and events not found in the other Gospels, such as the extended discourses of Jesus and the high priestly prayer in John 17, which further illuminate Jesus' divine status and mission.

John's Gospel also emphasizes the concept of belief in Jesus as the Son of God and the source of eternal life. John includes several testimonies and signs that point to Jesus' identity and invites readers to believe in Him (John 20:30-31). The Gospel of John serves as a theological and spiritual reflection on the significance of Jesus' life, death, and resurrection, highlighting His divine nature and the salvation He offers to all who believe in Him.

An Adulteress Faces the Light of the World

John 8:1 (King James Bible): "Jesus went unto the mount of Olives."

Interpretation and Commentary:

This verse marks a transition in the narrative, showing Jesus' movement to the Mount of Olives. While seemingly simple, this action carries symbolic and theological significance.

Key Points:

1. Symbolism of the Mount of Olives: The Mount of Olives is a location with spiritual and prophetic significance in the Bible. It's associated with prayer, reflection, and future eschatological events. Jesus going to this place may indicate a moment of prayer, solitude, or divine connection.

2. Teaching through Action: Jesus often used His actions to convey profound meanings. Moving to the Mount of Olives could be a deliberate act to impart spiritual lessons, signaling the importance of seeking God in moments of solitude and prayer.

3. Foreshadowing: The Mount of Olives is later associated with significant events, including Jesus' agony, arrest, and ascension. This early mention could foreshadow the unfolding of these crucial events in the later chapters of the Gospel.

References:
- The Mount of Olives is a significant location in various biblical events, including Zechariah 14:4 and Matthew 24:3.

Key Takeaway:
This verse sets the stage for deeper spiritual insights, signaling Jesus' intentional move to a place with symbolic meaning. It invites

readers to consider the significance of this action in the broader context of Jesus' ministry and the unfolding narrative.

John 8:2 (King James Bible): "And early in the morning he came again into the temple, and all the people came unto him; and he sat down, and taught them."

Interpretation and Commentary:

This verse depicts Jesus returning to the temple early in the morning to teach. It highlights both the consistency of Jesus' ministry and the eagerness of the people to hear His teachings.

Key Points:

1. Consistency of Jesus' Teaching: The phrase "came again into the temple" emphasizes Jesus' regular presence in places of worship and instruction. His commitment to teaching reflects the importance of imparting spiritual wisdom to the people.

2. Accessibility to the People: The fact that "all the people came unto him" underscores the widespread appeal of Jesus' teachings. His messages were not confined to a select group but were accessible to everyone, demonstrating His inclusive approach to sharing the Gospel.

3. Symbolism of Sitting Down: In the cultural context, a teacher often sat down while teaching. Jesus sitting down could symbolize authority, a posture of readiness to impart knowledge, and a desire to engage with His audience on a personal level.

References:
- The act of Jesus teaching in the temple is consistent with His ministry (Matthew 21:23; Mark 14:49).

Key Takeaway:
This verse showcases the continued dedication of Jesus to teaching and the responsiveness of the people. It emphasizes the

accessibility of His message and the significance of His role as a teacher in the spiritual guidance of the community.

John 8:3 (King James Bible): "And the scribes and Pharisees brought unto him a woman taken in adultery, and when they had set her in the midst."

Interpretation and Commentary:

This verse introduces a scene where the religious authorities, the scribes and Pharisees, bring a woman caught in the act of adultery to Jesus, placing her in the center of attention. This sets the stage for a significant encounter and challenges Jesus with a moral dilemma.

Key Points:

1. Scribes and Pharisees' Action: The scribes and Pharisees, known for their strict adherence to the law, present a woman caught in adultery. This action might be an attempt to test Jesus' response to a situation that involves a clear violation of Mosaic Law, which prescribed severe consequences for adultery.

2. Dramatic Setting: Placing the woman "in the midst" suggests a dramatic and public confrontation. The intention may be to force Jesus into a difficult position, either endorsing the stoning required by the law or challenging it.

References:
- The severity of consequences for adultery under Mosaic Law (Leviticus 20:10; Deuteronomy 22:22).

Key Takeaway:
This verse marks the beginning of a confrontation between Jesus and the religious authorities, testing His wisdom and compassion in handling a situation that involves moral and legal complexities. It sets the stage for one of the well-known episodes in the Gospel narratives.

John 8:4 (King James Bible): "They say unto him, Master, this woman was taken in adultery, in the very act."

Interpretation and Commentary:

In this verse, the scribes and Pharisees address Jesus, referring to him as "Master." They provide additional information, emphasizing that the woman was caught in the very act of adultery. This detail adds a sense of immediacy and urgency to their accusation.

Key Points:

1. Acknowledgment of Jesus as Master: The use of the term "Master" reflects a form of address that acknowledges Jesus as a respected teacher or authority figure. However, the context suggests that their intent might be more to test Him than to genuinely seek His guidance.

2. Emphasis on the Act of Adultery: By stating that the woman was taken "in the very act," the accusers highlight the gravity of the situation. This detail reinforces their accusation and puts pressure on Jesus to respond in accordance with Mosaic Law.

References:
- The seriousness of adultery under Mosaic Law (Leviticus 20:10; Deuteronomy 22:22).

Key Takeaway:
The scribes and Pharisees, by addressing Jesus as "Master" and emphasizing the immediacy of the woman's caught-in-the-act adultery, intensify the challenge they present to Him. The stage is set for Jesus' response to this complex moral and legal scenario.

John 8:5 (King James Bible): "Now Moses in the law commanded us, that such should be stoned: but what sayest thou?"

Interpretation and Commentary:

In this verse, the scribes and Pharisees refer to the Mosaic Law, stating that Moses commanded that individuals caught in adultery should be stoned. They present this as a challenge to Jesus, asking for His response to the situation.

Key Points:

1. Appeal to Mosaic Law: The religious leaders are invoking the authority of Moses and the Mosaic Law, which prescribed stoning as the punishment for adultery. This reflects their attempt to test Jesus and potentially find grounds to accuse Him of contradicting the Law.

2. Testing Jesus' Authority: By asking, "but what sayest thou?" the accusers are challenging Jesus to provide His stance on the matter. They are putting Him in a position where His response could be used against Him or in favor of the woman.

References:
- The Mosaic Law's prescription for stoning in cases of adultery (Leviticus 20:10; Deuteronomy 22:22).

Key Takeaway:
The scribes and Pharisees strategically use the Mosaic Law to test Jesus, seeking to expose any inconsistency or disagreement with established religious regulations. Their question sets the stage for Jesus' response to the delicate matter at hand.

John 8:6 (King James Bible): "This they said, tempting him, that they might have to accuse him. But Jesus stooped down, and with his finger wrote on the ground, as though he heard them not."

Interpretation and Commentary:

The religious leaders, having presented a woman caught in adultery to Jesus, were attempting to test Him and find grounds for accusation. In response, Jesus stoops down and writes on the ground, seemingly ignoring their challenge.

Key Points:

1. Tempting Jesus: The Pharisees' question about stoning the woman was not a sincere inquiry but a trap set to test Jesus. They sought to find fault in His response.

2. Jesus' Response: Instead of directly answering their question, Jesus stoops down and writes on the ground, an action that reflects deep thought and deliberation. The content of what He wrote is not specified in the text.

3. Ignoring Provocation: By not immediately responding to their challenge, Jesus demonstrates composure and avoids falling into the trap they set for Him.

References:
- No direct references in this verse, but the concept of testing or tempting Jesus is consistent with other Gospel narratives.

Key Takeaway:
Jesus responds to the Pharisees' attempt to trap Him with calm and deliberate action, choosing not to engage immediately in their provocative question. This sets the stage for a profound and unexpected turn in the encounter.

John 8:7 (King James Bible): "So when they continued asking him, he lifted up himself, and said unto them, He that is without sin among you, let him first cast a stone at her."

Interpretation and Commentary:

As the Pharisees persist in questioning Jesus about the fate of the woman caught in adultery, Jesus responds by challenging them to introspection. He invites anyone among them who is without sin to be the first to cast a stone at the woman.

Key Points:

1. Persistence of the Pharisees: Despite Jesus' initial response of writing on the ground, the Pharisees continue pressing Him for an answer, hoping to catch Him in a dilemma.

2. Jesus' Challenge: Jesus, in response, elevates the moral tone of the conversation. By inviting those without sin to cast the first stone, He directs attention to the hypocrisy and self-righteousness of the accusers.

3. Call for Self-Examination: Jesus' words challenge the Pharisees to reflect on their own shortcomings before passing judgment on others. It emphasizes the importance of humility and self-awareness.

References:
- No direct references in this verse, but the idea of sin and judgment is consistent with broader biblical teachings.

Key Takeaway:
Jesus shifts the focus from the woman's sin to the sinfulness of the accusers, prompting a call for self-examination and humility in the face of moral judgment. This encounter underscores the theme of mercy and the need for a just and introspective approach to judgment.

John 8:8 (King James Bible): "And again he stooped down, and wrote on the ground."

Interpretation and Commentary:

In this verse, after Jesus challenges the crowd with the statement about casting the first stone, he stoops down once more and writes on the ground. The exact content of what he wrote remains unknown, as the Bible doesn't specify. However, this action signifies a deliberate pause, allowing the weight of his previous statement to settle and giving the accusers time for self-reflection.

Key Points:

1. Reiteration of Writing: Jesus repeats the action of writing on the ground, maintaining a composed and reflective posture. This repetition adds emphasis to the gravity of the moment.

2. Symbolism of Writing: The act of writing on the ground is symbolic and holds significance, although the specific message is not revealed. It might represent a divine message, a moment of pause, or a call to introspection.

References:
- The act of writing on the ground in this context has no direct reference in other parts of the Bible.

Key Takeaway:
The repetition of Jesus writing on the ground emphasizes the solemnity of the moment, allowing for contemplation and self-reflection among the accusers. It adds a layer of mystery and invites readers to ponder the deeper meaning behind this symbolic act.

John 8:9 (King James Bible): "And they which heard it, being convicted by their own conscience, went out one by one, beginning at the eldest, even unto the last: and Jesus was left alone, and the woman standing in the midst."

Interpretation and Commentary:

In this verse, the crowd, upon hearing Jesus' words and being convicted by their own consciences, begins to leave one by one, starting with the eldest. This powerful scene illustrates the impact of Jesus' wisdom and challenges on the accusers. Their departure signifies a recognition of their own wrongdoing and an acknowledgment of Jesus' authority.

Key Points:

1. Conviction by Conscience: Jesus' words penetrate the hearts of the accusers, causing them to confront their own conscience. This internal conviction leads to a transformative response.

2. Orderly Departure: The crowd leaves in an orderly manner, beginning with the eldest. This orderly departure may reflect a sense of reverence or a recognition of the authority and wisdom displayed by Jesus.

3. Jesus and the Woman: As the crowd disperses, Jesus is left alone with the woman who was caught in adultery. This highlights Jesus' compassion and willingness to engage with individuals in moments of vulnerability.

References:
- This scene is unique to the Gospel of John, and there are no direct references to a similar event in the other Gospels.

Key Takeaway:
The departure of the crowd, starting with the eldest, showcases the transformative power of Jesus' words on individual consciences. It emphasizes the personal and internal nature of conviction, leading to a moment of solitude between Jesus and the woman caught in adultery.

John 8:10 (King James Bible): "When Jesus had lifted up himself, and saw none but the woman, he said unto her, Woman, where are those thine accusers? hath no man condemned thee?"

Interpretation and Commentary:

In this verse, Jesus, having lifted Himself up after the crowd had dispersed, addresses the woman who was caught in adultery. He asks her about the whereabouts of her accusers and whether anyone has condemned her. This moment is marked by Jesus' compassion and an invitation for the woman to reflect on her situation.

Key Points:

1. Jesus' Posture: Jesus, after the departure of the crowd, takes a position of attention and addresses the woman. His act of lifting

Himself up may symbolize His authority and readiness to engage with the woman.

2. Personal Inquiry: Jesus directs a question to the woman, acknowledging her presence and inviting her to consider the absence of those who accused her. This reflects Jesus' concern for individuals and His focus on their personal experiences.

3. Absence of Condemnation: By asking whether anyone has condemned her, Jesus creates an opportunity for the woman to realize that she is not facing condemnation in that moment. This highlights the transformative nature of Jesus' interactions, emphasizing mercy over judgment.

References:
- This account of Jesus and the woman caught in adultery is found only in the Gospel of John (John 8:1-11).

Key Takeaway:
Jesus' compassionate inquiry and the absence of condemnation provide a significant moment for the woman to experience mercy and grace. It underscores Jesus' mission to bring salvation and forgiveness to those in need.

John 8:11 (King James Bible): "She said, No man, Lord. And Jesus said unto her, Neither do I condemn thee: go, and sin no more."

Interpretation and Commentary:

In this verse, the woman caught in adultery responds to Jesus' question, affirming that no one has condemned her. Jesus, in turn, declares that He does not condemn her either. However, He adds the instruction to "go, and sin no more." This encounter reflects Jesus' balance of mercy and a call to repentance.

Key Points:

1. Acknowledgment of Sin: The woman acknowledges her situation and the absence of condemnation from those around her. This honest admission sets the stage for Jesus' response.

2. Jesus' Mercy: Jesus, in a powerful display of mercy, declares that He does not condemn her. This moment encapsulates the forgiving nature of Jesus and His willingness to extend grace to those who repent.

3. Call to Repentance: While showing mercy, Jesus also instructs the woman to "go, and sin no more." This is a call to a transformed life, emphasizing the importance of turning away from sin and walking in a new direction.

References:
- The phrase "go, and sin no more" is a powerful teaching of Jesus found only in the Gospel of John (John 8:11).

Key Takeaway:
This encounter illustrates the profound combination of Jesus' mercy and His call for a changed life. It emphasizes the transformative power of forgiveness and the opportunity for individuals to turn away from sin under the guidance of Christ.

John 8:12 (King James Bible): "Then spake Jesus again unto them, saying, I am the light of the world: he that followeth me shall not walk in darkness, but shall have the light of life."

Interpretation and Commentary:

In this verse, Jesus declares Himself as the "light of the world." This metaphorical language signifies that Jesus is the source of spiritual illumination and guidance. Those who follow Him will not walk in darkness but will experience the light of life.

Key Points:

1. Metaphor of Light: Jesus uses the metaphor of light to convey spiritual truth and understanding. Light symbolizes purity, knowledge, and the absence of darkness or ignorance.

2. Exclusive Claim: Jesus' statement is exclusive, emphasizing that He is the unique source of spiritual enlightenment. This aligns with other "I am" declarations in the Gospel of John, highlighting His divinity.

3. Freedom from Darkness: Followers of Jesus are promised freedom from spiritual darkness. By adhering to His teachings and following Him, they will experience the transformative light of truth and life.

References:
- This "I am" saying is one of several in the Gospel of John, where Jesus uses this formula to make profound statements about His identity (John 8:12).
- In the Gospel of John, Jesus uses similar "I am" statements, such as "I am the bread of life" (John 6:35) and "I am the way, the truth, and the life" (John 14:6).

Key Takeaway:
Jesus' proclamation as the "light of the world" signifies His role in dispelling spiritual darkness and leading people into the truth. It calls for followers to align themselves with Him to experience the profound and life-changing illumination He provides.

John 8:13 (King James Bible): "The Pharisees therefore said unto him, Thou bearest record of thyself; thy record is not true."

Interpretation and Commentary:

In this verse, the Pharisees challenge Jesus, questioning the validity of His testimony because He bears witness to Himself. The Pharisees, adhering to legal principles, suggest that self-testimony is not trustworthy or valid.

Key Points:

1. Legal Challenge: The Pharisees, known for their strict adherence to legal principles, challenge Jesus on the grounds that self-testimony is not considered reliable in their legal tradition.

2. Jesus' Unique Testimony: Jesus often made unique claims about His identity and relationship with God, which stirred opposition and skepticism among religious leaders. The Pharisees' response here reflects their doubt and desire for external validation.

3. Foreshadowing Opposition: This episode foreshadows the increasing opposition Jesus faces from religious authorities who question His teachings and claims.

References:
- The Pharisees' challenge echoes the legal principle found in the Old Testament, where a matter is established by the testimony of two or three witnesses (Deuteronomy 19:15).

Key Takeaway:
The Pharisees' challenge underscores the tension between Jesus and the religious leaders. It sets the stage for further debates and challenges to Jesus' authority and claims, illustrating the growing opposition to His teachings.

John 8:14 (King James Bible): "Jesus answered and said unto them, Though I bear record of myself, yet my record is true: for I know whence I came, and whither I go; but ye cannot tell whence I come, and whither I go."

Interpretation and Commentary:

In response to the Pharisees' skepticism about His self-testimony, Jesus asserts the truthfulness of His witness. He emphasizes His unique knowledge of His divine origin and ultimate destination, contrasting it with the Pharisees' lack of understanding.

Key Points:

1. Self-Testimony Validated by Knowledge: Jesus defends the validity of His self-testimony by pointing to His intimate knowledge of His divine origin and destiny. Unlike ordinary witnesses, His testimony is grounded in a deep understanding of His divine nature.

2. Divine Origin and Destination: Jesus claims a unique connection with the heavenly realm, knowing both His divine origin and the ultimate purpose of His mission. This points to His divine nature and the fulfillment of a divine plan.

3. Contrast with Pharisees: Jesus highlights the Pharisees' inability to comprehend His origin and mission, suggesting a spiritual blindness or lack of understanding on their part.

References:
- Jesus' claim to know where He came from and where He is going aligns with His divine identity and mission (John 13:3, John 16:28).
- The Pharisees' lack of understanding echoes themes of spiritual blindness and rejection found throughout the Gospel of John (John 1:10-11, John 9:39-41).

Key Takeaway:
Jesus asserts the truth of His self-testimony based on His unique knowledge of divine matters. This claim sets the stage for a deeper exploration of Jesus' identity and mission, emphasizing the Pharisees' spiritual blindness in contrast to His divine insight.

John 8:15 (King James Bible): "Ye judge after the flesh; I judge no man."

Interpretation and Commentary:

Jesus addresses the Pharisees, criticizing their limited, worldly judgment based on external appearances. Unlike human judgments influenced by worldly standards, Jesus, in His divine capacity, refrains from passing final judgment on individuals at this moment.

Key Points:

1. Judging After the Flesh: Jesus contrasts the Pharisees' mode of judgment, which is often influenced by external, worldly criteria, with a higher, divine standard. Human judgments are often superficial and lack the depth of understanding inherent in divine judgment.

2. Divine Non-Judgment: Jesus emphasizes that, at this particular moment, He refrains from rendering final judgment on individuals. This statement does not negate the concept of judgment entirely but highlights a specific context or timing in which He, as the divine Judge, defers this role.

References:
- Jesus encourages righteous judgment in other contexts (John 7:24), emphasizing a discernment that goes beyond superficial appearances.
- The concept of divine judgment is explored in other parts of the New Testament, underscoring God's role as the ultimate and just Judge (Romans 2:16, 2 Timothy 4:1).

Key Takeaway:
Jesus challenges the Pharisees' earthly, superficial judgment, presenting a contrast with His divine understanding. While asserting the appropriateness of righteous judgment, Jesus, at this moment, indicates a withholding of final judgment, leaving room for further revelation and the unfolding of God's plan.

John 8:16 (King James Bible): "And yet if I judge, my judgment is true: for I am not alone, but I and the Father that sent me."

Interpretation and Commentary:

In this verse, Jesus asserts the reliability and truthfulness of His judgment, emphasizing the divine partnership between Himself and the Father. The collaborative nature of His judgment ensures its accuracy and righteousness.

Key Points:

1. Divine Collaboration: Jesus affirms that He is not alone in His judgment; He collaborates with the Father. This unity underscores the divine nature of Jesus and highlights the coherence between the Father and the Son in their purposes and judgments.

2. Truthful Judgment: Jesus declares that if He does judge, His judgment is true. This emphasizes the reliability and righteousness of His discernment. Unlike human judgments, Jesus' judgment is not flawed or influenced by sin but is grounded in divine wisdom.

References:
 - The concept of the Father and Son working in unity is consistent with the broader theological understanding of the Trinity (John 10:30, John 14:9-11).
 - Jesus' claim to truthful judgment aligns with His earlier statements about being the way, the truth, and the life (John 14:6).

Key Takeaway:
Jesus asserts the accuracy and reliability of His judgment, emphasizing the divine partnership between Himself and the Father. This collaboration ensures that His discernment is grounded in truth and righteousness, setting it apart from human judgments influenced by sin and fallibility.

John 8:17 (King James Bible): "It is also written in your law, that the testimony of two men is true."

Interpretation and Commentary:

In this verse, Jesus refers to a legal principle from the Mosaic Law that establishes the reliability of testimony when given by two witnesses. This concept emphasizes the importance of collaboration and agreement in establishing truth.

Key Points:

1. Legal Principle: Jesus alludes to a legal principle found in the Mosaic Law, which states that the testimony of two men is considered true. This principle underscores the significance of multiple witnesses in verifying the truthfulness of a statement.

2. Application to His Testimony: By referencing this legal principle, Jesus may be indirectly asserting the validity of His own testimony. He often presented Himself as a witness to the truth of His identity and mission, and here, He draws attention to a well-known legal concept to support the credibility of His words.

References:
- The principle of two witnesses is found in the Old Testament, such as in Deuteronomy 17:6 and Deuteronomy 19:15. It was a safeguard to prevent false accusations or judgments.

Key Takeaway:
Jesus uses a legal principle from the Mosaic Law to emphasize the credibility of testimony when supported by two witnesses. This may serve as an indirect affirmation of the reliability of His own testimony, aligning with His broader claims about His divine mission and identity.

John 8:18 (King James Bible): "I am one that bear witness of myself, and the Father that sent me beareth witness of me."

Interpretation and Commentary:

In this verse, Jesus acknowledges that He bears witness to Himself, but He also highlights the additional testimony provided by the Father who sent Him. This dual testimony serves to establish the validity and truth of Jesus' claims.

Key Points:

1. Self-Testimony: Jesus asserts that He testifies about Himself. While self-testimony might be viewed with skepticism, Jesus, being the Son of God, carries unique authority and truthfulness.

2. Divine Confirmation: Jesus goes further by stating that the Father who sent Him also bears witness of Him. This divine confirmation adds a layer of authority and credibility to Jesus' claims, reinforcing His divine mission.

References:
 - This concept aligns with the broader theme in the Gospel of John, emphasizing the divine nature of Jesus and His close relationship with the Father (John 5:19-23).

Key Takeaway:
Jesus combines His own testimony with the divine confirmation from the Father, presenting a dual witness to the truth of His identity and mission. This reinforces the unique authority and divine nature of Jesus as the Son sent by the Father.

John 8:19 (King James Bible): "Then said they unto him, Where is thy Father? Jesus answered, Ye neither know me, nor my Father: if ye had known me, ye should have known my Father also."

Interpretation and Commentary:

The religious leaders question Jesus about His Father, likely expecting Him to reveal the location of His earthly father. However, Jesus responds with a deeper truth, emphasizing their lack of understanding. He asserts that knowing Him is intricately linked to knowing the Father, highlighting the inseparable connection between Himself and God the Father.

Key Points:

1. Misunderstanding Jesus: The question about Jesus' Father reveals a misunderstanding on the part of the religious leaders. They

were thinking in earthly terms, missing the profound spiritual reality of Jesus' identity.

2. Profound Connection: Jesus stresses that knowing Him is equivalent to knowing the Father. This statement underscores the intimate and inseparable connection between Jesus and God, emphasizing their shared divine nature.

References:
- This aligns with Jesus' earlier statement in John 14:9, where He declares, "He that hath seen me hath seen the Father," emphasizing the unity of the Father and the Son.

Key Takeaway:
In this response, Jesus redirects the focus from an earthly understanding of His Father to a deeper recognition of His divine identity. Knowing Jesus is the key to knowing the Father, highlighting the profound unity and connection between the two.

John 8:20 (King James Bible): "These words spake Jesus in the treasury, as he taught in the temple: and no man laid hands on him; for his hour was not yet come."

Interpretation and Commentary:

Jesus speaks these words in the treasury, a part of the temple where offerings were collected. Despite teaching openly in the temple, no one seizes Him because His appointed time for crucifixion had not yet arrived.

Key Points:

1. Teaching in the Temple: Jesus boldly teaches within the temple complex, including the treasury. His words, likely provocative to the religious leaders, are spoken in a significant and public place.

2. Divine Timing: The phrase "for his hour was not yet come" emphasizes the divine timing of events in Jesus' life. It suggests that

Jesus' crucifixion and arrest will happen at the appointed time determined by God.

References:
- This verse echoes similar statements about the timing of Jesus' death, emphasizing the fulfillment of divine purposes (John 7:30; John 2:4).

Key Takeaway:
In this moment, Jesus continues to teach openly despite the potential threat to His life. The mention of the specific location and the divine timing of events underscores the sovereignty of God's plan in the unfolding narrative of Jesus' ministry and sacrifice.

John 8:21 (King James Bible): "Then said Jesus again unto them, I go my way, and ye shall seek me, and shall die in your sins: whither I go, ye cannot come."

Interpretation and Commentary:

Jesus forewarns the people that He is leaving, and they will seek Him but won't be able to follow. He associates this separation with the consequence of dying in their sins, indicating the significance of accepting Him.

Key Points:

1. Jesus' Departure: Jesus speaks of "going His way," signaling a departure. This could refer to His eventual return to the Father or the impending events leading to His crucifixion.

2. Seeking in Vain: Those who seek Jesus will not find Him. This could imply a missed opportunity for repentance and acceptance of His message.

3. Dying in Sins: Jesus links their inability to follow Him with the consequence of dying in their sins. Rejecting Him leads to spiritual death and separation from God.

4. Inability to Come: The phrase "whither I go, ye cannot come" underscores the exclusivity of the path to the Father through Jesus. Without acceptance of Christ, they won't share in His destination.

References:
- This echoes themes of Jesus as the way, truth, and life (John 14:6). The idea of dying in sins is a serious consequence highlighted elsewhere in the New Testament (Romans 6:23).

Key Takeaway:
Jesus emphasizes the urgency of accepting Him, portraying Himself as the exclusive way to the Father. The gravity of dying in sins underscores the importance of responding to Jesus' message during the time of His earthly ministry.

John 8:22 (King James Bible): "Then said the Jews, Will he kill himself? because he saith, Whither I go, ye cannot come."

Interpretation and Commentary:

The Jews, misunderstanding Jesus' words about His departure, speculate whether He plans to take His own life. They are puzzled by His reference to a destination they cannot reach.

Key Points:

1. Misinterpretation: The Jews struggle to comprehend the spiritual nature of Jesus' departure and assume a literal understanding, questioning if He plans self-harm.

2. Spiritual Disconnect: Their confusion highlights the spiritual gap between Jesus and those who reject His message. They cannot grasp the divine dimension of His mission.

References:

- This incident foreshadows Jesus' later assertion that those who reject Him are of a different spiritual lineage (John 8:44). It also aligns with the theme of spiritual blindness (John 9:39-41).

Key Takeaway:
The Jews' misunderstanding reflects their spiritual blindness and inability to grasp the profound nature of Jesus' mission. It sets the stage for Jesus to further clarify His identity and the consequences of rejecting Him.

John 8:23 (King James Bible): "And he said unto them, Ye are from beneath; I am from above: ye are of this world; I am not of this world."

Interpretation and Commentary:

Jesus responds to the Jews, emphasizing the stark contrast between Himself and them. He declares that while they are of earthly origin and belong to this world, He is of heavenly origin, not bound by the limitations of this world.

Key Points:

1. Origin and Nature: Jesus asserts His divine origin, highlighting the heavenly nature of His being. This statement underscores His unique identity as the Son of God.

2. Worldly vs. Divine: The distinction between "from beneath" and "from above" emphasizes the difference in spiritual origin. Jesus is not confined by the limitations of earthly existence; His origin is divine.

References:
- This statement aligns with the prologue of John's Gospel, emphasizing the Word becoming flesh (John 1:14) and the concept of Jesus as the pre-existent Son of God (John 1:1-3).

Key Takeaway:

Jesus' words emphasize His divine nature, highlighting the stark contrast between His heavenly origin and the earthly origin of those who reject Him. This sets the stage for a deeper exploration of His identity and the consequences of unbelief.

John 8:24 (King James Bible): "I said therefore unto you, that ye shall die in your sins: for if ye believe not that I am he, ye shall die in your sins."

Interpretation and Commentary:

In this verse, Jesus delivers a solemn warning to the people. He declares that without believing in Him, they will die in their sins. The phrase "I am he" is a significant affirmation of His identity as the Messiah and the Son of God.

Key Points:

1. Critical Belief: Jesus emphasizes the essential nature of belief in Him. Failure to recognize His divine identity will lead to spiritual consequences, namely, dying in sins.

2. Messiahship: The use of "I am he" echoes the divine self-revelation in the Old Testament (Exodus 3:14). Jesus claims to be the promised Messiah, and acknowledging Him as such is crucial for salvation.

References:
- This warning aligns with the broader biblical theme of salvation through faith (Ephesians 2:8-9) and the exclusivity of Christ as the way to the Father (John 14:6).

Key Takeaway:
Jesus underscores the critical importance of recognizing Him as the Messiah and Son of God for salvation. The consequences of unbelief are severe, highlighting the centrality of faith in Christ for eternal life.

John 8:25 (King James Bible): "Then said they unto him, Who art thou? And Jesus saith unto them, Even the same that I said unto you from the beginning."

Interpretation and Commentary:

In response to Jesus' warning about dying in sins without belief, the people question His identity. Jesus, in his reply, reaffirms that He is the same person He claimed to be from the beginning of their interaction.

Key Points:

1. Consistency: Jesus emphasizes the consistency of His identity and message. He doesn't waver or change; He remains true to what He declared from the outset of His ministry.

2. Divine Authority: By asserting that He is the same as He said from the beginning, Jesus implies a divine authority. His identity and purpose are unchanging, reflecting the eternal nature of God.

References:
- This echoes Jesus' earlier statements about His identity, such as "I am the light of the world" (John 8:12) and "Before Abraham was, I am" (John 8:58).

Key Takeaway:
Jesus, in His response, underscores the unwavering nature of His identity and message. His consistency emphasizes the divine authority behind His claims, reinforcing the importance of recognizing Him for who He truly is.

John 8:26 (King James Bible): "I have many things to say and to judge of you: but he that sent me is true, and I speak to the world those things which I have heard of him."

Interpretation and Commentary:

Jesus acknowledges that He has much to say and judge concerning the people, but He emphasizes the truthfulness of the One who sent Him. His words are a direct reflection of what He has heard from the Father.

Key Points:

1. Abundance of Wisdom: Jesus possesses a wealth of divine wisdom and insight. His understanding surpasses human comprehension, allowing Him to discern and judge matters with divine accuracy.

2. Divine Source: Jesus attributes the truthfulness of His message to the One who sent Him, signifying the divine origin of His teachings. He aligns His words with the absolute truth of God.

References:
 - This statement echoes Jesus' earlier assertion that He speaks only what the Father has taught Him (John 8:28).

Key Takeaway:
In expressing the abundance of His wisdom and the divine source of His message, Jesus establishes the authority and truthfulness of His teachings. He highlights the connection between His words and the divine will, emphasizing the authenticity of His mission.

John 8:27 (King James Bible): "They understood not that he spake to them of the Father."

Interpretation and Commentary:

The people listening to Jesus were unable to grasp the full significance of His words, particularly when He spoke about the Father. Despite Jesus' attempts to communicate spiritual truths, the crowd struggled to comprehend the depth of His message, indicating a spiritual blindness or lack of receptivity.

Key Points:

1. Spiritual Understanding: Jesus often conveyed profound spiritual truths, but the listeners' limited spiritual understanding hindered them from fully comprehending His teachings about the Father.

2. Divine Revelation: The failure to understand Jesus' reference to the Father underscores the need for divine revelation. Without spiritual insight, the depth of Jesus' message remains veiled.

References:
 - This verse reflects a recurring theme in the Gospel of John, emphasizing the importance of spiritual understanding and the role of divine revelation in comprehending Jesus' teachings.

Key Takeaway:
The people's inability to understand Jesus' reference to the Father highlights the crucial role of spiritual insight in grasping the deeper meanings of His words. It prompts reflection on the need for divine revelation and an open heart to fully comprehend the truths Jesus imparts.

John 8:28 (King James Bible): "Then said Jesus unto them, When ye have lifted up the Son of man, then shall ye know that I am he, and that I do nothing of myself; but as my Father hath taught me, I speak these things."

Interpretation and Commentary:

In this verse, Jesus refers to His impending crucifixion, stating that when they lift up the Son of Man (a reference to His crucifixion), they will come to know His true identity. Jesus emphasizes that His words and actions are in complete harmony with the Father's teachings, reinforcing the divine nature of His mission.

Key Points:

1. Foretelling Crucifixion: Jesus alludes to His future crucifixion, using the phrase "when ye have lifted up the Son of man." This hints at the redemptive purpose of His death on the cross.

2. Revelation of Identity: The lifting up of the Son of Man is linked to a revelation of Jesus' true identity. It suggests that the events surrounding His crucifixion will bring a deeper understanding of who He is.

3. Dependency on the Father: Jesus affirms that He does nothing of Himself, highlighting His complete dependence on the Father. His words and actions are a direct reflection of the teachings He has received from the Father.

References:
- This verse connects with the broader theme in John's Gospel, emphasizing Jesus' sacrificial mission, His unique identity, and His close relationship with the Father.

Key Takeaway:
Jesus, in foretelling His crucifixion, points to a profound revelation of His identity. The verse underscores His complete alignment with the Father's teachings, highlighting the divine nature of His mission and the redemptive significance of the cross.

John 8:29 (King James Bible): "And he that sent me is with me: the Father hath not left me alone; for I do always those things that please him."

Interpretation and Commentary:

In this verse, Jesus affirms his close relationship with the Father and declares that the One who sent Him is always with Him. The profound unity between Jesus and the Father is emphasized, highlighting the divine support and approval of Jesus' actions.

Key Points:

1. Divine Unity: Jesus asserts a profound unity with the Father, indicating their inseparable connection. This unity underscores the divine nature of Jesus as the Son of God.

2. Divine Approval: The statement "the Father hath not left me alone" reflects the continuous divine presence and approval of Jesus. It suggests that Jesus' actions align perfectly with the will of the Father.

3. Obedience to the Father: Jesus states that He always does those things that please the Father. This underscores Jesus' perfect obedience and adherence to the divine will, setting an example for believers.

References:
- This verse aligns with the broader theme in the Gospel of John, emphasizing Jesus' divine nature, unity with the Father, and obedient fulfillment of the Father's will.

Key Takeaway:
Jesus' declaration emphasizes the divine unity between Him and the Father, highlighting the approval of His actions by the Father. It serves as a model of obedience and underscores the significance of aligning one's life with the divine will.

John 8:30 (King James Bible): "As he spake these words, many believed on him."

Interpretation and Commentary:

In this verse, we witness a response to Jesus' words as many among the audience believe in Him. The significance lies in the transformative power of Jesus' teachings, prompting faith among those who were present.

Key Points:

1. Impactful Words: Jesus' words have a profound effect, leading to belief. This emphasizes the persuasive and transformative nature of His teachings.

2. Faith in Action: Believing in Jesus is not just a passive acknowledgment but an active response to His message. The listeners are moved to faith by the content and authority of His words.

References:
- This verse aligns with the Gospel theme of belief and faith as essential responses to Jesus' teachings. It also sets the stage for further discussions on faith and discipleship.

Key Takeaway:
The verse highlights the power of Jesus' words to inspire belief. It serves as a reminder of the dynamic impact His teachings had on the hearts and minds of those who were present, foreshadowing the role of faith in the unfolding narrative.

John 8:31 (King James Bible): "Then said Jesus to those Jews which believed on him, If ye continue in my word, then are ye my disciples indeed."

Interpretation and Commentary:

Jesus addresses those who have already expressed belief in Him, emphasizing that true discipleship involves a continued adherence to His teachings. Mere belief is a starting point, but a genuine disciple is characterized by an ongoing commitment to the principles and truths found in Jesus' words.

Key Points:

1. Conditional Discipleship: Jesus sets a condition for true discipleship – a consistent and enduring commitment to His words. It's not just about a one-time belief but an ongoing, transformative relationship.

2. Authentic Discipleship: The authenticity of discipleship is linked to a steadfast adherence to Jesus' teachings. It involves a continuous alignment of one's life with the principles laid out by Him.

References:
- This statement aligns with the broader biblical theme that true discipleship requires more than a superficial acknowledgment. It echoes the idea that faith should manifest in a life lived in accordance with God's Word.

Key Takeaway:
This verse underscores the dynamic nature of discipleship. It's not a static status but an evolving relationship marked by a sustained commitment to living out the principles and teachings of Jesus.

John 8:32 (King James Bible): "And ye shall know the truth, and the truth shall make you free."

Interpretation and Commentary:

Jesus declares a profound truth, emphasizing that knowledge of the truth leads to freedom. This statement goes beyond mere intellectual understanding; it speaks to a transformative knowledge that liberates individuals from the bondage of sin, ignorance, and falsehood.

Key Points:

1. Transformative Knowledge: The knowledge Jesus refers to is not just informational but transformative. It has the power to bring about a profound change in the individual.

2. Freedom through Truth: The truth Jesus speaks of isn't just a set of facts but the embodiment of divine principles. Embracing this truth liberates individuals from the chains of sin and falsehood.

References:

- This statement aligns with the broader biblical theme of the liberating power of God's truth. Throughout the Bible, truth is depicted as a force that brings freedom.

Key Takeaway:
The verse emphasizes the liberating impact of genuine, transformative knowledge of the truth. It's an invitation to a profound understanding that leads to freedom from the entanglements of sin and deception.

John 8:33 (King James Bible): "They answered him, We be Abraham's seed, and were never in bondage to any man: how sayest thou, Ye shall be made free?"

Interpretation and Commentary:

The response of the people reflects a misunderstanding of Jesus' spiritual message. Claiming descent from Abraham, they assert never having been in bondage. However, Jesus is addressing spiritual freedom from sin, not physical slavery.

Key Points:

1. Misinterpretation of Freedom: The people misunderstand Jesus, equating freedom with physical liberation. Their focus on lineage (Abraham's seed) blinds them to the spiritual bondage of sin.

2. Spiritual Bondage: Jesus aims to liberate them from the spiritual bondage of sin. This freedom is not about political or social independence but a profound transformation of the soul.

References:
- Throughout the Gospels, Jesus emphasizes spiritual truths over superficial, worldly perspectives. His teachings challenge conventional thinking about freedom and salvation.

Key Takeaway:

This verse highlights the contrast between earthly and spiritual perspectives on freedom. Jesus seeks to free them from the deeper bondage of sin, a liberation that goes beyond political or social conditions.

John 8:34 (King James Bible): "Jesus answered them, Verily, verily, I say unto you, Whosoever committeth sin is the servant of sin."

Interpretation and Commentary:

Jesus emphasizes a profound truth about sin and its enslaving nature. Anyone engaging in sin becomes a servant to it, highlighting the spiritual bondage that sin creates. Jesus' "verily, verily" underscores the seriousness of this statement.

Key Points:

1. Sin as a Master: Jesus uses the analogy of servitude to describe the relationship between a sinner and sin. Sin becomes a dominating force, enslaving the one who commits it.

2. Spiritual Slavery: The emphasis is on spiritual liberation. Jesus' teachings consistently address the deeper, eternal aspects of human existence, focusing on freedom from sin's entanglement.

References:
- Throughout the Gospels, Jesus teaches about the transformative power of spiritual freedom. This aligns with the broader biblical theme of liberation from sin.

Key Takeaway:
In this verse, Jesus underscores the enslaving nature of sin and the need for spiritual liberation. The call to break free from sin echoes throughout his teachings, emphasizing a profound shift in one's spiritual state.

John 8:35 (King James Bible): "And the servant abideth not in the house for ever: but the Son abideth ever."

Interpretation and Commentary:

In this verse, Jesus draws a distinction between a servant and a son, using it to convey a deeper spiritual truth. A servant, in the context of the time, had a temporary position in the household, but a son had a lasting and permanent relationship.

Key Points:

1. Temporal Nature of Servitude: Jesus implies that a servant's stay in the house is temporary. This could be seen as an allegory for the limited nature of the bondage to sin that he mentioned earlier.

2. Eternal Abiding of the Son: In contrast, the Son, referring to himself, has an everlasting presence. This points to the eternal nature of the relationship between Jesus and those who become children of God through faith.

References:
- The concept of sonship and adoption into God's family is prevalent in the New Testament, emphasizing a profound and enduring relationship with God.

Key Takeaway:
Jesus uses the analogy of a servant and a son to highlight the temporary and limited nature of a life bound by sin, contrasting it with the eternal relationship offered through faith in Him. This reinforces the transformative and enduring nature of the spiritual freedom Jesus brings.

John 8:36 (King James Bible): "If the Son, therefore, shall make you free, ye shall be free indeed."

Interpretation and Commentary:

In this powerful statement, Jesus asserts that true freedom comes through Him. He links freedom to the Son, emphasizing a liberation that goes beyond physical or societal constraints to a profound spiritual emancipation.

Key Points:

1. Source of True Freedom: Jesus positions Himself as the source of genuine freedom. This freedom extends beyond external circumstances to the innermost being, addressing the bondage of sin.

2. "Free Indeed": The repetition of "free indeed" emphasizes the completeness and authenticity of the freedom that Jesus offers. It is not just a partial or temporary liberation but a transformative and lasting one.

References:
 - This concept aligns with the broader biblical theme of liberation from sin and the redemptive work of Christ.

Key Takeaway:
Jesus declares Himself as the ultimate source of true and enduring freedom. His liberating power goes beyond external circumstances, providing a profound and authentic freedom from the bondage of sin. This verse encapsulates a central theme of Christian theology—the transformative power of Christ's redemption.

John 8:37 (King James Bible): "I know that ye are Abraham's seed, but ye seek to kill me, because my word hath no place in you."

Interpretation and Commentary:

In this verse, Jesus acknowledges the physical lineage of the people He is addressing, affirming that they are descendants of Abraham. However, He points out a stark contradiction: despite their ancestry, they harbor intentions of killing Him because His words find no reception in their hearts.

Key Points:

1. Physical vs. Spiritual Lineage: Jesus recognizes the heritage of Abraham in the people He addresses, highlighting their physical connection to the patriarch. This acknowledgment sets the stage for a deeper spiritual discussion.

2. Rejection of His Word: The core issue lies in the rejection of Jesus' words. Despite their lineage, the people are resistant to His teachings, indicating a spiritual misalignment.

3. Hostility Toward Jesus: The extreme response of wanting to kill Jesus reveals the depth of the conflict. This hostility arises from an internal resistance to His message.

References:
- This aligns with the recurring theme in the Gospels where Jesus faces opposition, especially from those who, despite their heritage, reject His teachings.

Key Takeaway:
Jesus emphasizes the importance of receiving His words, indicating that spiritual lineage goes beyond physical descent. The rejection of His message results in hostility, illustrating the profound impact of accepting or rejecting the teachings of Christ.

John 8:38 (King James Bible): "I speak that which I have seen with my Father: and ye do that which ye have seen with your father."

Interpretation and Commentary:

In this verse, Jesus draws a sharp contrast between Himself and the people He addresses. He asserts that He speaks what He has witnessed in the presence of His Father, indicating a divine source for His teachings. In contrast, He implies that the actions of the people align with a different "father."

Key Points:

1. Divine Authority: Jesus claims a unique authority for His teachings, emphasizing a direct connection with God the Father. This reinforces the divine origin of His words.

2. Contrast of Fathers: By stating, "ye do that which ye have seen with your father," Jesus introduces a metaphorical contrast between His heavenly Father and another, suggesting a spiritual lineage distinct from God.

3. Spiritual Allegiance: The reference to different fathers implies a distinction in spiritual allegiances. This sets the stage for a deeper exploration of the nature of their actions and beliefs.

References:
- This echoes Jesus' earlier statements about His oneness with the Father and the authority derived from that unity (John 5:19, John 5:30).

Key Takeaway:
Jesus highlights the divine source of His teachings, emphasizing a connection with God the Father. The contrasting reference to another "father" lays the groundwork for a more profound exploration of spiritual allegiances and the implications of following different sources of authority.

John 8:39 (King James Bible): "They answered and said unto him, Abraham is our father. Jesus saith unto them, If ye were Abraham's children, ye would do the works of Abraham."

Interpretation and Commentary:

In this verse, Jesus engages with the people who claim Abraham as their father. He challenges their assertion by stating that if they were truly children of Abraham, their actions would reflect the righteous deeds of Abraham.

Key Points:

1. Claim to Lineage: The people assert their lineage to Abraham, likely referring to their physical descent. This claim might carry cultural and religious significance.

2. Deeper Meaning: Jesus challenges the superficial claim by emphasizing that true lineage is not merely physical but involves a spiritual and moral dimension. He implies that being a child of Abraham involves embodying Abraham's righteous actions.

3. Works of Abraham: Jesus establishes a connection between one's lineage and the manifestation of character through actions. He suggests that true children of Abraham would exhibit the same virtuous deeds as Abraham.

References:
- This aligns with the biblical understanding that true lineage and identity are not solely based on physical descent but also on spiritual and moral alignment (Romans 9:6-8, Galatians 3:7).

Key Takeaway:
Jesus challenges the notion of identity based solely on physical lineage, emphasizing the importance of spiritual and moral alignment. He introduces the concept that genuine descendants of Abraham would exhibit the righteous deeds characteristic of their claimed ancestor.

John 8:40 (King James Bible): "But now ye seek to kill me, a man that hath told you the truth, which I have heard of God: this did not Abraham."

Interpretation and Commentary:

In this verse, Jesus points out a sharp contrast between the actions of his listeners and the character of Abraham. He accuses them of seeking to kill him, despite his truthful teachings received from God. This behavior, Jesus implies, is entirely contrary to the righteous conduct of Abraham.

Key Points:

1. Intent to Kill: Jesus accuses his listeners of harboring murderous intentions towards him. This highlights the escalating tension and hostility between Jesus and certain religious leaders.

2. Bearer of Truth: Jesus emphasizes his role as a messenger of truth, stating that what he speaks is what he has heard from God. This underscores the divine authority behind his teachings.

3. Abraham's Example: Jesus contrasts the violent intentions of his audience with the nonviolent and faithful example of Abraham. This suggests that their actions are inconsistent with the legacy of the revered patriarch.

References:
- This aligns with Jesus' consistent claim throughout the Gospels that his teachings are directly from God (John 7:16-18, John 12:49-50).
- The accusation of seeking to kill Jesus becomes a recurring theme in the narrative (John 5:18, John 7:1, John 8:37, John 8:59).

Key Takeaway:
Jesus confronts his audience with the sharp contrast between their violent intentions and the righteous example set by Abraham. He reinforces his divine authority and the disconnect between their actions and their claimed spiritual lineage.

John 8:41 (King James Bible): "Ye do the deeds of your father. Then said they to him, We be not born of fornication; we have one Father, even God."

Interpretation and Commentary:

This verse reveals a confrontation between Jesus and his audience. Jesus suggests that their actions align with a different spiritual lineage, and they retort by claiming God as their Father, denying any illegitimacy in their heritage.

Key Points:

1. Deeds and Lineage: Jesus implies a misalignment between the deeds of his audience and the true identity of their spiritual father. This challenges their claim to be children of God.

2. Denial of Illegitimacy: The response of Jesus' audience indicates an understanding of his insinuation. They vehemently deny any wrongdoing in their spiritual lineage, asserting that God is their Father.

References:
- This exchange reflects a recurring theme in the Gospel of John where Jesus challenges the religious leaders' understanding of their relationship with God (John 1:12-13, John 8:44).
- The accusation of fornication may be a metaphorical expression pointing to spiritual unfaithfulness rather than a literal accusation (Jeremiah 3:8-9, Ezekiel 16:15-22).

Key Takeaway:
The dialogue intensifies as Jesus suggests a misalignment between the deeds of his audience and their claimed spiritual lineage. Their denial and assertion that God is their Father set the stage for a deeper exploration of their spiritual identity and allegiance.

John 8:42 (King James Bible): "Jesus said unto them, If God were your Father, ye would love me: for I proceeded forth and came from God; neither came I of myself, but he sent me."

Interpretation and Commentary:

In this verse, Jesus challenges his audience, asserting that if God were truly their Father, they would recognize and love Him. He emphasizes his divine origin, declaring that he came from God and was sent by Him.

Key Points:

1. Love as a Sign: Jesus connects the recognition of God as a Father with love for Himself. This implies that genuine divine parentage is reflected in a deep love for Jesus as the one sent by God.

2. Divine Origin: Jesus emphasizes his unique relationship with God, stating that he didn't come of his own accord but was sent by God. This underscores his divine mission and origin.

References:
- This aligns with the broader theme in the Gospel of John where Jesus repeatedly emphasizes his divine origin and mission (John 3:17, John 5:23, John 10:36).
- The concept of love as an expression of true discipleship is recurrent in Jesus' teachings (John 13:34-35, John 14:15).

Key Takeaway:
Jesus challenges his audience to reflect on their relationship with God by pointing to the love they should have for Him if God were truly their Father. This reinforces the central theme of recognizing Jesus' divine identity and mission.

John 8:43 (King James Bible): "Why do ye not understand my speech? even because ye cannot hear my word."

Interpretation and Commentary:

In this verse, Jesus addresses the crowd's inability to understand His words. He attributes their lack of comprehension to an inherent resistance or incapacity to truly hear and grasp the profound meaning of His teachings.

Key Points:

1. Spiritual Deafness: Jesus suggests that the root cause of their lack of understanding is a spiritual impediment, symbolized by an inability to "hear" His words. This implies a deeper, spiritual deafness rather than a mere intellectual challenge.

2. Resistance to Truth: The question posed by Jesus implies a sense of frustration or disappointment. He highlights the disconnect between his message and their capacity to comprehend, pointing to a resistance to the truth He is conveying.

References:
- The theme of spiritual deafness and blindness is recurrent in the Bible, emphasizing the need for receptive hearts to understand spiritual truths (Isaiah 6:9-10, Matthew 13:15, Mark 8:18).
- Jesus often uses parables and figurative language, requiring listeners to engage spiritually for true comprehension (Matthew 13:13-15).

Key Takeaway:
This verse underscores the importance of spiritual receptivity in understanding Jesus' teachings. It suggests that the lack of comprehension is not due to a deficiency in Jesus' communication but rather a spiritual resistance or incapacity to grasp the profound truths He imparts.

John 8:44 (King James Bible): "Ye are of your father the devil, and the lusts of your father ye will do. He was a murderer from the beginning, and abode not in the truth because there is no truth in him. When he speaketh a lie, he speaketh of his own: for he is a liar, and the father of it."

Interpretation and Commentary:

In this verse, Jesus confronts a group of opponents, accusing them of having the devil as their spiritual father. He attributes their actions to the devil's influence and characterizes the devil as a murderer, a liar, and the originator of falsehood.

Key Points:

1. Spiritual Lineage: Jesus asserts a stark contrast between those who follow Him and those who oppose Him. He implies that

the opponents' actions align with the desires of their spiritual father, the devil.

2. The Devil as a Murderer and Liar: Jesus describes the devil as a murderer from the beginning, pointing to the spiritual death caused by sin. Additionally, he emphasizes the devil's inherent dishonesty, labeling him as the father of lies.

3. Origin of Lies: Jesus explains that when the devil speaks lies, he speaks from his own nature, reinforcing the idea that deception is fundamental to the devil's character.

References:
- The concept of spiritual lineage and the choice between God and the devil is found elsewhere in the Bible (Matthew 12:30, 1 John 3:10).
- The devil's deceptive nature is a consistent theme throughout the Bible (Genesis 3:1, Revelation 12:9).

Key Takeaway:
This verse underscores the spiritual battle between truth and falsehood, righteousness and sin. Jesus challenges the spiritual identity of his opponents, attributing their actions to a malevolent spiritual influence and highlighting the destructive and deceptive nature of the devil.

John 8:45 (King James Bible): "And because I tell you the truth, ye believe me not."

Interpretation and Commentary:

In this verse, Jesus expresses the irony that despite speaking the truth, his opponents refuse to believe in him. This reflects a broader theme in the Gospel of John, highlighting the resistance of some individuals to accept the truth of Jesus' teachings.

Key Points:

1. Truth Rejected: Jesus, as the embodiment of truth, encounters skepticism and rejection. This emphasizes the human tendency to resist accepting truths that may challenge preconceived notions or beliefs.

2. Irony of Unbelief: The irony lies in the fact that Jesus, who is the Truth (John 14:6), faces disbelief from those to whom he speaks. This theme echoes throughout the Gospel, illustrating the spiritual blindness and hardness of heart that can hinder people from recognizing divine truth.

References:
- Jesus identifies himself as the Truth in John 14:6, emphasizing the exclusive nature of his teachings.

Key Takeaway:
This verse highlights the challenging reality that even when confronted with divine truth in the person of Jesus, some individuals may choose unbelief. It prompts reflection on the role of receptivity and openness to truth in spiritual understanding.

John 8:46 (King James Bible): "Which of you convinceth me of sin? And if I say the truth, why do ye not believe me?"

Interpretation and Commentary:

In this verse, Jesus challenges his accusers to point out any sin in him. He asserts his moral purity and questions why they refuse to believe him despite his truthful words.

Key Points:

1. Jesus' Sinlessness: By asking, "Which of you convinceth me of sin?" Jesus emphasizes his sinless nature. This aligns with the broader biblical understanding of Jesus as the spotless Lamb of God (1 Peter 1:19) and the One without sin (Hebrews 4:15).

2. Challenge to Accusers: The challenge is rhetorical, as Jesus, being sinless, knows that none can legitimately accuse him of wrongdoing. This challenges the credibility of his accusers and underscores their unwillingness to accept the truth.

3. Emphasis on Truth: Jesus reiterates the theme of truth, questioning why, in the face of his truthful teachings and actions, his opponents persist in unbelief. This reinforces the central importance of accepting and believing in the truth.

References:
- Jesus' sinlessness is affirmed in various biblical passages, such as Hebrews 4:15 and 1 Peter 1:19.

Key Takeaway:
This verse underscores the moral integrity of Jesus and invites reflection on the importance of recognizing and believing in the truth, even when it challenges preconceived notions.

John 8:47 (King James Bible): "He that is of God heareth God's words: ye therefore hear them not, because ye are not of God."

Interpretation and Commentary:

In this verse, Jesus addresses those who oppose him, stating that those who belong to God will recognize and understand God's words, while his opponents do not comprehend because they are not of God.

Key Points:

1. Discerning God's Words: Jesus implies that a person's spiritual affiliation influences their ability to understand and accept divine truths. Those aligned with God are receptive to His words, indicating a connection and responsiveness to divine teachings.

2. Identification of Opposition: The statement indirectly identifies Jesus' opponents as not being of God, suggesting a

misalignment with divine principles. This emphasizes the contrast between those who accept Jesus' teachings as coming from God and those who reject them.

3. Spiritual Connection: The verse underscores the spiritual dimension of comprehension and belief. It implies that a person's spiritual condition shapes their ability to recognize divine truths, emphasizing the need for a relationship with God.

References:
- Similar sentiments are expressed in other passages, such as John 10:27, where Jesus speaks of His followers hearing His voice.

Key Takeaway:
This verse highlights the spiritual discernment required to understand God's words and implies that alignment with God influences one's ability to grasp divine truths. It prompts reflection on the spiritual aspect of comprehension and belief.

John 8:48 (King James Bible): "Then answered the Jews, and said unto him, Say we not well that thou art a Samaritan, and hast a devil?"

Interpretation and Commentary:

In this verse, the Jews respond to Jesus, accusing him of being a Samaritan and having a devil. This exchange reflects the hostility and rejection Jesus faced from some religious leaders.

Key Points:

1. Accusation of Being a Samaritan: The term "Samaritan" was used derogatorily by some Jews to insult Jesus. It was a way of questioning his Jewish identity and religious authenticity.

2. Claiming Possession by a Devil: Accusing Jesus of having a devil reflects a serious charge, suggesting that some opponents believed his actions and teachings were influenced by evil forces.

3. Increasing Hostility: The confrontation intensifies as Jesus' opponents resort to personal attacks, attempting to discredit him based on identity and accusing him of being under demonic influence.

References:
- Similar accusations are made in other parts of the Gospels, illustrating the growing opposition Jesus faced from certain religious authorities.

Key Takeaway:
This verse illustrates the escalating tension between Jesus and some Jewish leaders. The accusations of being a Samaritan and having a devil reveal the depth of hostility and rejection Jesus encountered from those who opposed his teachings and actions.

John 8:49 (King James Bible): "Jesus answered, I have not a devil; but I honour my Father, and ye do dishonour me."

Interpretation and Commentary:

In response to the accusation that he has a devil, Jesus denies this claim and emphasizes his reverence for the Father. This verse highlights Jesus' commitment to honoring God despite the dishonor he receives from his opponents.

Key Points:

1. Denial of Having a Devil: Jesus firmly rejects the accusation of being possessed by a devil. This reinforces his assertion of moral integrity and divine alignment.

2. Honoring the Father: Jesus expresses his dedication to honoring God the Father. His actions and teachings are in accordance with God's will, emphasizing his divine mission.

3. Contrast with Dishonor: Jesus contrasts his commitment to honoring the Father with the dishonor he receives from those who

accuse him. This emphasizes the stark difference between his divine purpose and the misunderstandings of his opponents.

References:
- This theme of Jesus being aligned with the Father's will and facing dishonor is consistent throughout the Gospels.

Key Takeaway:
In this verse, Jesus defends his character against the accusation of having a devil, emphasizing his commitment to honoring the Father. This exchange highlights the profound contrast between Jesus' divine mission and the dishonor he endures from those who oppose him.

John 8:50 (King James Bible): "And I seek not mine own glory: there is one that seeketh and judgeth."

Interpretation and Commentary:

In this verse, Jesus declares that he does not seek his own glory but defers judgment to the One who seeks and judges. This statement reflects Jesus' humility and submission to God's divine plan.

Key Points:

1. Selfless Motivation: Jesus disclaims any self-centered pursuit of glory. His focus is not on personal acclaim but on fulfilling the will of the Father and carrying out the divine mission.

2. Divine Judgment: Jesus acknowledges that ultimate judgment belongs to God. This recognition emphasizes the divine authority and justice inherent in God's plan.

References:
- This aligns with Jesus' consistent teachings about humility, selflessness, and reliance on God's will throughout the Gospels.

Key Takeaway:

In proclaiming that he does not seek personal glory and leaving judgment to the divine, Jesus underscores his humility and submission to God's plan. This aligns with his overarching message of selfless service and obedience to the Father.

John 8:51 (King James Bible): "Verily, verily, I say unto you, If a man keep my saying, he shall never see death."

Interpretation and Commentary:

In this profound statement, Jesus uses the solemn affirmation "Verily, verily" to emphasize the importance of his words. He promises eternal life to those who keep and follow his teachings, assuring them that they will never experience spiritual death.

Key Points:

1. Eternal Life Through Obedience: Jesus links the concept of eternal life directly to obedience to his teachings. Those who heed his words and live according to his commands are promised a life that transcends physical death.

2. Spiritual Perspective: The promise of not seeing death goes beyond physical existence; it speaks to the spiritual dimension. Followers of Jesus are assured of a life that extends beyond earthly limitations.

References:
- This aligns with Jesus' consistent teaching on the centrality of faith, obedience, and eternal life throughout the Gospels.

Key Takeaway:
Jesus, with solemnity, declares the transformative power of his teachings, assuring believers of eternal life if they faithfully follow and keep his words. This promise reflects the core message of salvation and spiritual life through a relationship with Christ.

John 8:52 (King James Bible): "Then said the Jews unto him, Now we know that thou hast a devil. Abraham is dead, and the prophets, and thou sayest, If a man keep my saying, he shall never taste of death."

Interpretation and Commentary:

The response of the Jews reflects a misunderstanding of Jesus' spiritual message. They interpret his words literally, pointing out that Abraham and the prophets have died, questioning how Jesus could promise that those who follow him will never taste death.

Key Points:

1. Literal Misunderstanding: The Jews struggle with the spiritual nature of Jesus' statement. They interpret his words in a purely physical sense, not grasping the deeper spiritual truth he is conveying.

2. Accusation of Possession: Accusing Jesus of having a devil is an attempt to discredit him. They question the source of his teachings, suggesting a demonic influence.

References:
- This interaction highlights the ongoing tension and misunderstanding between Jesus and the religious leaders, who often struggled to comprehend the spiritual depth of his messages.

Key Takeaway:
The exchange underscores the challenge of conveying spiritual truths to those who are bound by literal interpretations. The Jews' response reveals their skepticism and resistance to Jesus' message, emphasizing the need for spiritual discernment when engaging with divine teachings.

John 8:53 (King James Bible): "Art thou greater than our father Abraham, which is dead? and the prophets are dead: whom makest thou thyself?"

Interpretation and Commentary:

The Jews, questioning Jesus, challenge his assertion about not tasting death. They appeal to the authority of their revered ancestor, Abraham, and the prophets, implying that Jesus cannot be greater than them. Their inquiry is a challenge to Jesus' claims and an attempt to establish his identity.

Key Points:

1. Appeal to Ancestry: The Jews emphasize the revered status of Abraham and the prophets, suggesting that Jesus' statements are in conflict with the esteemed figures of their religious heritage.

2. Identity Challenge: Implicit in their question is a challenge to Jesus' identity. They question how he can make himself greater than Abraham and the prophets, demanding clarification on his self-proclaimed significance.

References:
- This verse contributes to the ongoing tension between Jesus and the religious leaders, highlighting their struggle to accept his claims about his identity and mission.

Key Takeaway:
The Jews' question reveals their resistance to acknowledging Jesus' authority and challenges him to justify his claims in the context of their religious heritage. This encounter further illustrates the deep-seated skepticism and misunderstanding that often characterized the interactions between Jesus and the religious authorities of his time.

John 8:54 (King James Bible): "Jesus answered, If I honour myself, my honour is nothing: it is my Father that honoureth me; of whom ye say, that he is your God."

Interpretation and Commentary:

In response to the Jews' challenge about his greatness compared to Abraham and the prophets, Jesus emphasizes that he does not seek honor for himself. Instead, he asserts that his honor comes from the Father. By doing so, Jesus directs attention to the divine source of his authority and positions God as the ultimate source of validation.

Key Points:

1. Humility and Divine Honor: Jesus exhibits humility by disassociating himself from self-promotion. He redirects the focus to God, highlighting the divine honor bestowed upon him by the Father.

2. Recognition of God's Authority: Jesus subtly challenges the Jews to recognize and acknowledge the authority of the Father, whom they claim as their God.

References:
- This statement aligns with Jesus' consistent teaching about his dependence on the Father and his submission to God's will.

Key Takeaway:
Jesus emphasizes the divine source of his honor and redirects attention from himself to God the Father. This response underscores the humility and submission that characterize Jesus' relationship with the Father, inviting the Jews to recognize the authority of the God they claim to worship.

John 8:55 (King James Bible): "Yet ye have not known him; but I know him: and if I should say, I know him not, I shall be a liar like unto you: but I know him, and keep his saying."

Interpretation and Commentary:

Jesus contrasts the Jews' lack of knowledge of God with his own intimate knowledge of the Father. He asserts that denying knowledge of God, as the Jews often did in their rejection of Jesus, would be a lie. Jesus affirms his genuine knowledge of the Father, reinforcing his claim to a unique relationship with God.

Key Points:

1. Intimate Knowledge of God: Jesus claims a deep, personal knowledge of the Father, emphasizing a relationship beyond intellectual understanding—a knowledge rooted in connection and intimacy.

2. Truthfulness: Jesus highlights the inconsistency and falsehood in denying knowledge of God. By doing so, he challenges the Jews to recognize the authenticity of his claims.

References:
- This aligns with Jesus' broader teachings about his relationship with the Father and his role as the revealer of God.

Key Takeaway:
Jesus asserts his genuine, intimate knowledge of the Father, challenging the Jews to acknowledge the truth of his relationship with God. This statement underscores the authenticity of Jesus' claims and confronts the Jews with the inconsistency of their position.

John 8:56 (King James Bible): "Your father Abraham rejoiced to see my day: and he saw it, and was glad."

Interpretation and Commentary:

In this verse, Jesus speaks to the Jews about Abraham, claiming that Abraham looked forward to the coming of Jesus' day and rejoiced at the prospect. Jesus suggests a spiritual connection that goes beyond time, implying that Abraham, though living centuries earlier, somehow anticipated and was pleased by the realization of God's plan in Jesus.

Key Points:

1. Abraham's Rejoicing: Jesus asserts that Abraham, a revered figure in Judaism, anticipated and celebrated the fulfillment of God's plan in Jesus.

2. Transcending Time: Jesus implies a connection that surpasses temporal boundaries, suggesting a divine understanding and participation in the unfolding of God's redemptive plan.

References:
- This aligns with the broader biblical narrative of God's promise to bless all nations through Abraham's descendants.

Key Takeaway:
Jesus emphasizes a spiritual connection between himself and Abraham, suggesting that Abraham looked forward to the fulfillment of God's plan in Jesus and rejoiced at the prospect. This statement highlights Jesus as the culmination of God's redemptive purposes.

John 8:57 (King James Bible): "Then said the Jews unto him, Thou art not yet fifty years old, and hast thou seen Abraham?"

Interpretation and Commentary:

The Jews respond incredulously to Jesus' claim about Abraham, pointing out what they perceive as a contradiction. They question how Jesus, who appears to be less than fifty years old, could have possibly seen Abraham, who lived centuries earlier. This reflects their misunderstanding of Jesus' reference to Abraham's rejoicing.

Key Points:

1. Misunderstanding Jesus: The Jews misunderstand Jesus' statement about Abraham, taking it literally rather than recognizing the spiritual and transcendent nature of his reference.

2. Focus on Jesus' Age: The Jews highlight Jesus' apparent age, emphasizing their skepticism about his connection to Abraham.

References:
- The dialogue reflects the ongoing misunderstanding between Jesus and the Jewish leaders, who often interpret his teachings in a literal and earthly manner.

Key Takeaway:
The Jews, focused on the physical aspect of age, question how Jesus, who seems relatively young, could claim to have seen Abraham. This interaction underscores the challenge of conveying spiritual truths to those who are entrenched in literal interpretations.

John 8:58 (King James Bible): "Jesus said unto them, Verily, verily, I say unto you, Before Abraham was, I am."

Interpretation and Commentary:

This statement by Jesus is profound and holds deep theological significance. By declaring, "Before Abraham was, I am," Jesus not only claims pre-existence but also uses the divine title "I am," echoing God's self-revelation to Moses at the burning bush.

Key Points:

1. Divine Identity: Jesus' use of "I am" asserts his divine identity, aligning himself with God's eternal nature. This statement emphasizes his timeless existence.

2. Continuity of Being: "Before Abraham was" implies that Jesus' existence predates Abraham, reinforcing the idea of his eternal nature.

References:
- Exodus 3:14 (God's revelation to Moses): "And God said unto Moses, I AM THAT I AM." This echoes Jesus' use of "I am" and emphasizes his divine nature.

Key Takeaway:

In this powerful declaration, Jesus asserts not only his pre-existence but also his identity with the eternal God, using the divine title "I am" to emphasize his timeless and divine nature.

John 8:59 (King James Bible): "Then took they up stones to cast at him: but Jesus hid himself, and went out of the temple, going through the midst of them, and so passed by."

Interpretation and Commentary:

The reaction of the people, picking up stones to cast at Jesus, reflects their anger and rejection of his claims. Stoning was a form of punishment for blasphemy under Jewish law.

Key Points:

1. Hostility toward Jesus: The crowd's violent response indicates their refusal to accept Jesus' statements about his divine nature and pre-existence.

2. Divine Intervention: Jesus, by miraculously hiding himself, demonstrates divine intervention, indicating that his time had not yet come for confrontation or death.

References:
- Leviticus 24:16 (regarding blasphemy): "And he that blasphemeth the name of the Lord, he shall surely be put to death, and all the congregation shall certainly stone him." The crowd's reaction reflects the seriousness of the claims Jesus made.

Key Takeaway:
The people's violent response highlights the intensity of the conflict between Jesus and those who opposed his divine claims. His ability to evade harm shows divine control over the situation.

CHAPTER NINE

A Man Born Blind Receives Sight

John 9:1 (King James Bible): "And as Jesus passed by, he saw a man which was blind from his birth."

Interpretation and Commentary:

In this verse, Jesus encounters a man who has been blind since birth, setting the stage for a miraculous healing that will take place in the following verses.

Key Points:

1. Divine Awareness: Jesus, in his divine awareness, sees the man's condition. This emphasizes Jesus' compassionate nature, as he takes notice of those in need.

References:
- Exodus 4:11: "And the Lord said unto him, Who hath made man's mouth? or who maketh the dumb, or deaf, or the seeing, or the blind? have not I the Lord?" God's sovereign control over physical conditions.

Key Takeaway:
This verse introduces a significant miracle where Jesus demonstrates his power to heal and brings attention to his compassionate response to human suffering.

John 9:2 (King James Bible): "And his disciples asked him, saying, Master, who did sin, this man, or his parents, that he was born blind?"

Interpretation and Commentary:

The disciples, upon seeing the blind man, pose a question to Jesus that reflects a common belief in their cultural context. They inquire whether the man's blindness is a result of his own sin or the sin of his parents.

Key Points:

1. Cultural Belief: During this time, there was a prevalent belief that illness or disability could be a consequence of sin, either by the individual or their ancestors.

2. Disciples' Inquiry: The disciples seek to understand the cause of the man's condition, possibly to reconcile their understanding of God's justice with the man's blindness.

References:
- Exodus 20:5: "Thou shalt not bow down thyself to them, nor serve them: for I the Lord thy God am a jealous God, visiting the iniquity of the fathers upon the children unto the third and fourth generation of them that hate me." This verse addresses generational consequences of sin.

Key Takeaway:
The disciples' question reveals the common cultural belief of associating physical conditions with sin. Jesus' response challenges this belief and redirects the focus toward a higher purpose.

John 9:3 (King James Bible): "Jesus answered, Neither hath this man sinned, nor his parents: but that the works of God should be made manifest in him."

Interpretation and Commentary:

In response to the disciples' question about the cause of the man's blindness, Jesus challenges the common belief that the man's condition is a result of sin, either his own or his parents'. Instead, Jesus asserts a different perspective.

Key Points:

1. Rejection of Direct Cause: Jesus rejects the notion that the man's blindness is a direct result of sin, challenging the cause-and-effect assumption.

2. Manifestation of God's Works: Jesus provides a profound insight, stating that the man's blindness serves a purpose—to manifest the works of God. This suggests that challenges and hardships can become opportunities for divine intervention and revelation.

References:
- Exodus 4:11: "And the Lord said unto him, Who hath made man's mouth? or who maketh the dumb, or deaf, or the seeing, or the blind? have not I the Lord?" This verse emphasizes God's sovereignty over various conditions.

Key Takeaway:
Jesus redirects the focus from assigning blame to recognizing an opportunity for God to work and reveal His power through the man's condition. This challenges the disciples and readers to view challenges in life as potential avenues for divine manifestation.

John 9:4 (King James Bible): "I must work the works of him that sent me, while it is day: the night cometh, when no man can work."

Interpretation and Commentary:

Jesus speaks about the urgency of His mission and the limited time available to fulfill it. This verse reflects the sense of divine purpose and the importance of seizing the opportunity for active ministry.

Key Points:

1. Divine Mission: Jesus acknowledges that He has a specific mission given by the One who sent Him. This mission involves performing the works assigned to Him by God.

2. Temporal Urgency: The reference to day and night symbolizes the limited time during which Jesus can carry out His earthly ministry. "While it is day" suggests the time of active engagement and opportunity.

References:
- Psalm 143:8: "Cause me to hear thy lovingkindness in the morning; for in thee do I trust: cause me to know the way wherein I should walk; for I lift up my soul unto thee." This psalm reflects the idea of seeking divine guidance and purpose.

Key Takeaway:
This verse emphasizes the urgency of fulfilling one's divine purpose and mission within the allotted time. It encourages believers to actively engage in the work assigned by God while the opportunity is available.

John 9:5 (King James Bible): "As long as I am in the world, I am the light of the world."

Interpretation and Commentary:

In this verse, Jesus declares Himself as the light of the world, signifying His role in bringing spiritual illumination and understanding to humanity during His earthly presence.

Key Points:

1. Symbolic Light: Jesus uses the metaphor of light to represent spiritual enlightenment, guidance, and revelation. His teachings and presence dispel darkness and ignorance.

2. Temporal Reference: The phrase "As long as I am in the world" indicates that this role as the light of the world is tied to His earthly presence. It implies that, after His departure, others may carry on this role.

References:

- John 1:4-5: "In him was life; and the life was the light of men. And the light shineth in darkness, and the darkness comprehended it not." This echoes the theme of Jesus being the light that brings life and understanding.

Key Takeaway:
Jesus asserts His unique role as the spiritual light that brings clarity and understanding to the world. This metaphor emphasizes the transformative power of His teachings and presence in dispelling spiritual darkness.

John 9:6 (King James Bible): "When he had thus spoken, he spat on the ground, and made clay of the spittle, and he anointed the eyes of the blind man with the clay."

Interpretation and Commentary:

In this verse, Jesus performs a unique and unconventional act to bring about healing for a blind man. His use of spit and clay demonstrates the diverse ways in which divine power can work.

Key Points:

1. Symbolic Actions: Jesus often uses symbolic actions to convey deeper spiritual truths. Here, His use of spit and clay may symbolize the creative power of God, who formed humanity from the dust of the ground (Genesis 2:7).

2. Physical Interaction: Jesus' physical interaction with the blind man emphasizes the tangible and personal nature of His ministry. He engages directly with the man, demonstrating compassion and a willingness to meet people in their specific needs.

References:
- Genesis 2:7: "And the Lord God formed man of the dust of the ground, and breathed into his nostrils the breath of life; and man became a living soul." This reference highlights the connection between humanity's creation from dust and Jesus' use of clay.

62

Key Takeaway:
Jesus employs a unique method to bring about healing, emphasizing the personal and creative nature of His ministry. This act also challenges traditional expectations, highlighting the diverse ways in which divine power can manifest for the well-being of individuals.

John 9:7 (King James Bible): "And said unto him, Go, wash in the pool of Siloam, (which is by interpretation, Sent.) He went his way therefore, and washed, and came seeing."

Interpretation and Commentary:

In this verse, Jesus instructs the blind man to go and wash in the pool of Siloam, resulting in the restoration of his sight. This interaction holds symbolic and spiritual significance.

Key Points:

1. Symbolism of Siloam: The name "Siloam" means "Sent," emphasizing a connection to the mission and purpose of Jesus. The act of washing in Siloam becomes a symbol of obedience and faith.

2. Spiritual Cleansing: The washing in Siloam not only restores physical sight but also symbolizes a deeper spiritual cleansing. Water, in biblical imagery, often represents purification and renewal. This gesture may underscore the transformative power of faith and obedience to Christ's commands.

References:
- Isaiah 8:6: "Forasmuch as this people refuseth the waters of Shiloah that go softly, and rejoice in Rezin and Remaliah's son..." While this verse refers to Shiloah, the similarity in name provides context for the symbolic use of water.

Key Takeaway:
The blind man's obedience to Jesus' command to wash in the pool of Siloam not only restores his physical sight but also symbolizes

the spiritual cleansing and renewal that comes through faith and obedience to Christ. The encounter highlights the transformative power of Jesus' instructions.

John 9:8 (King James Bible): "The neighbours therefore, and they which before had seen him that he was blind, said, Is not this he that sat and begged?"

Interpretation and Commentary:

This verse depicts the reaction of the neighbors and those who had previously known the blind man when they see him after receiving his sight.

Key Points:

1. Recognition and Amazement: The neighbors and acquaintances are astonished at the transformation in the formerly blind man. They question whether he is indeed the same person who used to sit and beg. This reaction underscores the remarkable and visible change that has occurred.

2. Significance of Begging: The mention of the man sitting and begging adds context to his previous condition. Begging was a common occupation for blind individuals in ancient times, highlighting the man's dependence on others for his livelihood.

References:
- John 9:9: "Some said, This is he: others said, He is like him: but he said, I am he." This verse continues the narrative, showing different reactions and the man confirming his identity.

Key Takeaway:
The neighbors' recognition of the man and their questioning reflect the dramatic nature of the healing. The contrast between his former state of begging and his newfound ability to see emphasizes the profound change brought about by Jesus. This sets the stage for further inquiry into the details of his healing.

John 9:9 (King James Bible): "Some said, This is he: others said, He is like him: but he said, I am he."

Interpretation and Commentary:

This verse captures the diverse reactions and opinions of people who knew the formerly blind man upon seeing him after he received his sight.

Key Points:

1. Diverse Reactions: There is a range of responses from those who encounter the healed man. Some confidently identify him, stating, "This is he," while others express uncertainty, saying, "He is like him." This diversity of opinions adds a human and realistic element to the narrative, illustrating how people perceive and react differently to extraordinary events.

2. Assertive Confirmation: In contrast to the varying opinions, the man himself confirms his identity with a straightforward statement: "I am he." His assertive response adds credibility to the fact that he is indeed the one who was blind, emphasizing the reality of his healing.

References:
- John 9:10: "Therefore said they unto him, How were thine eyes opened?" This verse marks the continuation of the narrative, as the people inquire about the details of the healing.

Key Takeaway:
The diversity in reactions highlights the human tendency to interpret and respond differently to miraculous events. The healed man's confident affirmation reinforces the authenticity of his healing, setting the stage for further exploration of the miraculous event.

John 9:10 (King James Bible): "Therefore said they unto him, How were thine eyes opened?"

Interpretation and Commentary:

This verse captures the immediate response of the people to the healed man's assertion that he is indeed the one who was blind.

Key Points:

1. Inquisitive Inquiry: The people respond to the healed man's affirmation with a natural and inquisitive question: "How were thine eyes opened?" This question reflects the human curiosity to understand the details of a miraculous event. The healing of the blind man is perceived as extraordinary, prompting a desire for an explanation.

References:
- John 9:11: "He answered and said, A man that is called Jesus made clay, and anointed mine eyes, and said unto me, Go to the pool of Siloam, and wash: and I went and washed, and I received sight." The healed man proceeds to provide details about the process of his healing, attributing it to Jesus.

Key Takeaway:
The question posed by the people sets the stage for the healed man to share the specific details of how his sight was restored, leading to a deeper exploration of the miraculous intervention by Jesus.

John 9:11 (King James Bible): "He answered and said, A man that is called Jesus made clay, and anointed mine eyes, and said unto me, Go to the pool of Siloam, and wash: and I went and washed, and I received sight."

Interpretation and Commentary:

This verse contains the response of the man who was healed, providing specific details about the process through which Jesus restored his sight.

Key Points:

1. Identification of Jesus: The healed man refers to Jesus as "a man that is called Jesus." This acknowledgment indicates that, at this point, he may not fully comprehend the identity and significance of Jesus.

2. Healing Process: The man describes the steps Jesus took to heal him. Jesus made clay, anointed the man's eyes with it, and instructed him to go to the pool of Siloam to wash. The use of clay and the act of washing in the pool symbolize a ritualistic or symbolic aspect of the healing process.

3. Obedience and Restoration: The man emphasizes his obedience to Jesus' instructions. He went, washed, and as a result, received his sight. This highlights the importance of faith and obedience in experiencing the transformative power of Jesus.

References:
- John 9:6-7: "When he had thus spoken, he spat on the ground, and made clay of the spittle, and he anointed the eyes of the blind man with the clay. And said unto him, Go, wash in the pool of Siloam (which is by interpretation, Sent). He went his way therefore, and washed, and came seeing." This provides additional context about the actions of Jesus in the healing process.

Key Takeaway:
The detailed account of the healing process underscores the role of faith, obedience, and the symbolic use of elements in Jesus' miraculous acts.

John 9:12 (King James Bible): "Then said they unto him, Where is he? He said, I know not."

Interpretation and Commentary:

In this verse, the people who knew the man inquire about the whereabouts of Jesus after his sight was restored.

Key Points:

1. Inquiry about Jesus: The people are curious and inquire about the location of Jesus. Their question indicates a desire to find Jesus, possibly to understand more about the healing or to witness other miracles.

2. Lack of Information: The man who was healed responds by saying, "I know not." This suggests that he might not have paid much attention to where Jesus went after the healing. It could also indicate that he didn't have prior knowledge of Jesus' whereabouts.

References:
- John 9:11: "He answered and said, A man that is called Jesus made clay, and anointed mine eyes, and said unto me, Go to the pool of Siloam, and wash: and I went and washed, and I received sight." This verse provides context about the healing that sparked the people's inquiry.

Key Takeaway:
The people's inquiry reflects a growing interest in Jesus' actions and miracles. The man's response, indicating a lack of knowledge about Jesus' whereabouts, adds an element of mystery and anticipation to the unfolding narrative.

John 9:13 (King James Bible): "They brought to the Pharisees him that aforetime was blind."

Interpretation and Commentary:

In this verse, the people bring the man who was once blind to the Pharisees, likely to report the miraculous healing and to seek their opinion on the matter.

Key Points:

1. Pharisees' Authority: The Pharisees were a religious sect known for their strict adherence to Jewish law. Bringing the healed man to them suggests a recognition of their authority and a desire for a religious interpretation of the healing.

2. Investigation Begins: This action marks the beginning of an investigation by the religious authorities into the circumstances surrounding the healing. It sets the stage for a more detailed examination of the events.

References:
- John 9:12: "Then said they unto him, Where is he? He said, I know not." This verse directly precedes the current one and establishes the context of the people inquiring about Jesus.

Key Takeaway:
The decision to bring the formerly blind man to the Pharisees indicates the significance of the healing event and the people's interest in understanding its religious implications. It also sets the stage for a deeper exploration of the relationship between Jesus and the religious authorities.

John 9:14 (King James Bible): "And it was the sabbath day when Jesus made the clay, and opened his eyes."

Interpretation and Commentary:

This verse refers to the fact that the miraculous healing performed by Jesus, where he made clay and opened the eyes of the blind man, occurred on the Sabbath day.

Key Points:

1. Sabbath Controversy: The mention of the Sabbath day is significant because it adds a layer of controversy to the healing. According to Jewish law, doing work, including healing, on the Sabbath was generally considered a violation.

2. Jesus' Actions: Jesus not only healed the blind man but did so in a way that involved making clay. This act of creating a substance (clay) might have been interpreted as work, raising questions among the religious leaders.

3. Sabbath Significance: The Sabbath was a holy day of rest, and activities considered work were typically prohibited. Jesus' choice to heal on this day would have provoked the attention of the religious authorities.

References:
- John 9:6-7: "When he had thus spoken, he spat on the ground, and made clay of the spittle, and he anointed the eyes of the blind man with the clay. And said unto him, Go, wash in the pool of Siloam (which is by interpretation, Sent). He went his way therefore, and washed, and came seeing." These verses provide the details of Jesus' healing method.

Key Takeaway:
The Sabbath setting adds a layer of complexity to the healing incident, setting the stage for further scrutiny and questioning by the religious authorities regarding Jesus' actions on this sacred day.

John 9:15 (King James Bible): "Then again the Pharisees also asked him how he had received his sight. He said unto them, He put clay upon mine eyes, and I washed, and do see."

Interpretation and Commentary:

In this verse, the Pharisees continue their questioning of the man who was blind but now sees, seeking more details about the healing performed by Jesus.

Key Points:

1. Persistent Inquiry: The Pharisees, who were religious leaders and part of the Jewish sect known for strict adherence to the law, persist in questioning the man about the events surrounding his

healing. Their interest indicates both skepticism and a desire to find fault.

2. Simple Account: The healed man provides a straightforward account of the healing. He explains that Jesus put clay on his eyes, and after washing, he gained his sight. The simplicity of his response contrasts with the Pharisees' complex expectations.

3. Clarity in Testimony: The man's testimony is clear and direct. He attributes his healing to the actions of Jesus involving clay and washing.

References:
- John 9:6-7: "When he had thus spoken, he spat on the ground, and made clay of the spittle, and he anointed the eyes of the blind man with the clay. And said unto him, Go, wash in the pool of Siloam (which is by interpretation, Sent). He went his way therefore, and washed, and came seeing." These verses describe the details of Jesus' healing method, which the man conveys to the Pharisees.

Key Takeaway:
The Pharisees' persistent questioning and the man's clear and simple testimony contribute to the unfolding narrative of skepticism and inquiry surrounding Jesus' miraculous acts.

John 9:16 (King James Bible): "Therefore said some of the Pharisees, This man is not of God because he keepeth not the sabbath day. Others said, How can a man that is a sinner do such miracles? And there was a division among them."

Interpretation and Commentary:

In this verse, a division arises among the Pharisees regarding Jesus and his actions.

Key Points:

1. Sabbath Controversy: Some Pharisees express their skepticism about Jesus, asserting that he cannot be from God because, in their view, he does not observe the Sabbath according to their interpretation of the law. This reflects the Pharisees' strict adherence to Sabbath regulations and their judgment of others based on observance.

2. Miracles vs. Sin: On the other hand, another group of Pharisees raises a counterargument. They question how a person who is deemed a sinner (by not strictly adhering to their interpretation of the law) could perform such extraordinary miracles. This indicates a theological and moral debate among the Pharisees.

3. Internal Division: The differing opinions within the Pharisees create a division among them. This internal conflict foreshadows the growing tension and opposition Jesus faced from religious authorities.

References:
- Exodus 20:8 (Sabbath Commandment): "Remember the sabbath day, to keep it holy." The Sabbath was a central part of Jewish law, and its observance was highly significant to the Pharisees.
- John 5:16: "And therefore did the Jews persecute Jesus, and sought to slay him because he had done these things on the sabbath day." This verse provides a context for the Pharisees' concerns about Jesus' Sabbath observance.

Key Takeaway:
The division among the Pharisees reflects the complexity of attitudes toward Jesus within the religious community. Some focus on his perceived violation of Sabbath regulations, while others are intrigued by the miraculous signs he performs, leading to internal discord among the religious leaders.

John 9:17 (King James Bible): "They say unto the blind man again, What sayest thou of him, that he hath opened thine eyes? He said, He is a prophet."

Interpretation and Commentary:

In this verse, the Pharisees continue questioning the man who was once blind about Jesus and his miraculous healing.

Key Points:

1. Interrogation Continues: The Pharisees, not satisfied with the answers they've received, persist in questioning the man who was blind. They seek his opinion about Jesus, particularly in light of the miracle of restoring his sight.

2. Response - Jesus as a Prophet: The man who was blind responds by acknowledging Jesus as a prophet. This recognition indicates that, based on the miraculous healing, the man attributes a special and divine status to Jesus. In Jewish tradition, prophets were seen as individuals through whom God communicated messages and demonstrated divine power.

References:
- Deuteronomy 18:15 (Prophecy of a Prophet): "The Lord thy God will raise up unto thee a Prophet from the midst of thee, of thy brethren, like unto me; unto him ye shall hearken." This prophecy foretells the coming of a prophet like Moses, and the man who was once blind seems to identify Jesus as fulfilling this role.

Key Takeaway:
The recognition of Jesus as a prophet by the man who was healed highlights the evolving understanding of Jesus' identity. While the Pharisees are still grappling with their own opinions about Jesus, the man perceives him not merely as a healer but as someone with a divine connection, a prophet in the line of God's messengers in Jewish history.

John 9:18 (King James Bible): "But the Jews did not believe concerning him, that he had been blind, and received his sight, until they called the parents of him that had received his sight."

Interpretation and Commentary:

In this verse, the skepticism of the Jews regarding the miraculous healing of the blind man continues.

Key Points:

1. Unbelief of the Jews: Despite the testimony of the man who was once blind, the Jewish authorities remain skeptical about the authenticity of the healing. Their lack of belief in this extraordinary event reflects their hardened hearts and resistance to accepting Jesus' divine authority.

2. Decision to Call the Parents: The Jews decide to call in the parents of the man who received his sight. This action indicates their determination to verify the details of the healing and possibly to find any inconsistency that could challenge the credibility of the miracle.

References:
- John 9:24 (Later in the chapter): "Then again called they the man that was blind, and said unto him, Give God the praise: we know that this man is a sinner." The ongoing dialogue between the Jews and the man who was healed reveals their persistent disbelief and attempts to discredit Jesus.

Key Takeaway:
The continued unbelief of the Jewish authorities sets the stage for further investigation and confrontation. The episode illustrates the deep-seated resistance some had to acknowledging the divine nature of Jesus' actions, despite clear evidence to the contrary.

John 9:19 (King James Bible): "And they asked them, saying, Is this your son, who ye say was born blind? how then doth he now see?"

Interpretation and Commentary:

In this verse, the Jewish authorities inquire of the parents, seeking confirmation and details about the miraculous healing of their son.

Key Points:

1. Verification of Identity: The authorities want to confirm the identity of the healed man and establish if he is indeed the son of the parents. This reflects their determination to thoroughly investigate the situation and gather evidence.

2. Challenging the Blindness Claim: The question "who ye say was born blind?" implies doubt regarding the parents' assertion that their son was born blind. The authorities seem to question the very foundation of the miracle by challenging the initial state of the man's sight.

References:
- John 9:20 (Following verse): "His parents answered them and said, We know that this is our son, and that he was born blind." The parents affirm their son's identity and the fact that he was born blind, countering the authorities' skepticism.

Key Takeaway:
The authorities' inquiry intensifies as they seek to scrutinize the details of the healing. The parents' response becomes crucial in defending the authenticity of the miracle and confirming the identity of their son who was once blind.

John 9:20 (King James Bible): "His parents answered them and said, We know that this is our son, and that he was born blind."

Interpretation and Commentary:

In this verse, the parents of the man born blind respond to the authorities' inquiry, confirming the identity of their son and affirming that he was indeed born blind.

Key Points:

1. Certainty of Identity: The parents express confidence in recognizing their son. This certainty emphasizes the personal connection and familial acknowledgment of the healed man.

2. Affirmation of Blindness: The parents also assert that their son was born blind. This statement reinforces the miraculous nature of the healing, as it involves restoring sight to someone who had been blind since birth.

References:
- John 9:19 (Previous verse): "And they asked them, saying, Is this your son, who ye say was born blind? how then doth he now see?" The parents' response follows the authorities' questioning about the identity and healing of their son.

Key Takeaway:
The parents' confident affirmation serves to establish the authenticity of the healing and counters the authorities' doubt. The acknowledgment of the son's identity and his congenital blindness becomes crucial in the unfolding narrative.

John 9:21 (King James Bible): "But by what means he now seeth, we know not; or who hath opened his eyes, we know not: he is of age; ask him: he shall speak for himself."

Interpretation and Commentary:

In this verse, the parents, having confirmed their son's identity and his congenital blindness, express ignorance about the specifics of how his sight was restored. They defer to their son, emphasizing his maturity and autonomy to provide details about the miraculous healing.

Key Points:

1. Parents' Lack of Knowledge: The parents admit that they don't know the means by which their son regained his sight or who performed the healing. This could be a cautious response, possibly influenced by fear of the authorities who had questioned them earlier.

2. Emphasis on the Son's Autonomy: By stating that their son is of age, the parents signal that he is capable of speaking for himself. This underscores the son's independence and his ability to provide an account of the events surrounding his healing.

References:
- John 9:20 (Previous verse): "His parents answered them and said, We know that this is our son, and that he was born blind." The parents' response about their son's identity and congenital blindness precedes this verse.

Key Takeaway:
The parents, cautious in their response, direct the authorities to their son for details about the miraculous healing, highlighting his maturity and ability to speak for himself. This sets the stage for the son's testimony in the subsequent verses.

John 9:22 (King James Bible): "These words spake his parents, because they feared the Jews: for the Jews had agreed already, that if any man did confess that he was Christ, he should be put out of the synagogue."

Interpretation and Commentary:

This verse reveals the motive behind the parents' cautious response. They spoke with fear of the Jews, who had an established agreement that anyone confessing Jesus as the Christ would be expelled from the synagogue. The parents, being aware of this consequence, chose not to provide details about the healing to protect themselves from potential repercussions.

Key Points:

1. Fear of Repercussions: The parents' fear of the Jews and the established consequences for acknowledging Jesus as the Christ influenced their response. The threat of being expelled from the synagogue, a significant social and religious institution, weighed heavily on their decision.

2. Political and Religious Context: This verse provides insight into the tense political and religious climate of the time. Openly acknowledging Jesus as the Christ could lead to social exclusion and religious consequences.

References:
- John 9:21 (Previous verse): "But by what means he now seeth, we know not; or who hath opened his eyes, we know not: he is of age; ask him: he shall speak for himself." The parents' response expressing ignorance about the healing precedes this verse.

Key Takeaway:
The fear of social and religious consequences, specifically the threat of being expelled from the synagogue, shaped the parents' careful response about the healing of their son. This sets the stage for the continued investigation by the authorities.

John 9:23 (King James Bible): "Therefore said his parents, He is of age; ask him."

Interpretation and Commentary:

This verse continues the narrative of the parents responding cautiously due to fear of the consequences set by the Jewish authorities. The parents, recognizing their son is of age, redirect the questioning to him. This tactic serves to distance themselves from any potential backlash while emphasizing that their son is capable of speaking for himself.

Key Points:

1. Strategic Deflection: The parents, aware of the risks associated with openly acknowledging Jesus as the Christ, strategically deflect the inquiry by emphasizing their son's maturity and ability to speak for himself.

2. Avoidance of Confrontation: By redirecting the authorities to their son, the parents attempt to avoid direct involvement in the unfolding situation. This reflects the tension between personal beliefs and the societal and religious expectations of that time.

References:
- John 9:22 (Previous verse): "These words spake his parents, because they feared the Jews: for the Jews had agreed already, that if any man did confess that he was Christ, he should be put out of the synagogue." The fear of repercussions and expulsion from the synagogue prompted the parents' cautious response.

Key Takeaway:
The parents, mindful of the risks, strategically guide the authorities to their son, emphasizing his ability to provide information independently. This underscores the delicate balance individuals faced between personal beliefs and societal expectations in the context of religious and political tensions.

John 9:24 (King James Bible): "Then again called they the man that was blind, and said unto him, Give God the praise: we know that this man is a sinner."

Interpretation and Commentary:

In this verse, the authorities recall the formerly blind man, urging him to give glory to God instead of Jesus. Their statement reflects skepticism and disapproval toward Jesus, whom they perceive as a sinner. The authorities attempt to influence the man's testimony to align with their negative view of Jesus.

Key Points:

1. Pressure to Conform: The authorities employ a religious appeal, asking the man to "Give God the praise," suggesting that he should attribute his healing to God rather than Jesus. This is a tactic to influence his testimony and conform to their perspective.

2. Prejudiced View of Jesus: The authorities express a predetermined belief that Jesus is a sinner. This bias shapes their approach to the situation and their interaction with the healed man.

References:
- John 9:22 (Previous verse): "These words spake his parents, because they feared the Jews: for the Jews had agreed already, that if any man did confess that he was Christ, he should be put out of the synagogue." The fear of consequences for confessing Jesus as the Christ sets the context for the authorities' pressure on the healed man.

Key Takeaway:
The authorities, maintaining a negative view of Jesus, attempt to manipulate the healed man's testimony by urging him to give credit to God and casting doubt on Jesus' legitimacy. This reflects the broader religious and political tensions present in the narrative.

John 9:25 (King James Bible): "He answered and said, Whether he be a sinner or no, I know not: one thing I know, that, whereas I was blind, now I see."

Interpretation and Commentary:

In this verse, the healed man responds to the authorities' assertion that Jesus is a sinner. His reply reveals a simple yet powerful testimony of personal experience. The man doesn't engage in theological debates about Jesus' nature; instead, he emphasizes the undeniable transformation he has experienced – moving from blindness to sight.

Key Points:

1. Personal Testimony: The man focuses on his personal encounter with Jesus and the tangible change in his life. This approach is effective in cutting through theological arguments and emphasizing the transformative power of Jesus' actions.

2. Ignorance of Jesus' Sin Status: The man acknowledges his lack of knowledge regarding whether Jesus is a sinner or not. His testimony is rooted in his personal experience rather than theological speculation.

References:
- John 9:24 (Previous verse): "Then again called they the man that was blind, and said unto him, Give God the praise: we know that this man is a sinner." The authorities had asserted that Jesus was a sinner, prompting the man's response.

Key Takeaway:
The healed man's response exemplifies the simplicity and authenticity of a personal testimony. He doesn't get entangled in theological debates but confidently affirms the reality of his transformed life, leaving the question of Jesus' sin status unanswered. This emphasizes the power of personal encounters with Jesus over theoretical discussions.

John 9:26 (King James Bible): "Then said they to him again, What did he to thee? how opened he thine eyes?"

Interpretation and Commentary:

The authorities persist in questioning the man about the details of his healing. Their inquiry reflects a desire to understand how Jesus performed the miraculous act of restoring sight to the blind man.

Key Points:

1. Persistent Inquiry: The authorities are determined to gather information about the healing. Their repeated questioning indicates a

sense of urgency to understand the nature of the miracle and, perhaps, to find fault with Jesus.

2. Focus on the Miracle: The authorities direct their questions specifically to the method by which Jesus opened the man's eyes. This emphasizes their interest in the miraculous aspect of the healing rather than the broader implications of the event.

References:
- John 9:25 (Previous verse): "He answered and said, Whether he be a sinner or no, I know not: one thing I know, that, whereas I was blind, now I see." The man responds to the authorities' assertion about Jesus being a sinner.

Key Takeaway:
The authorities' persistent questioning reveals their intense scrutiny of Jesus' actions and a focus on the specific details of the healing. This further sets the stage for the unfolding dialogue between the healed man and the religious leaders.

John 9:27 (King James Bible): "He answered them, I have told you already, and ye did not hear: wherefore would ye hear it again? will ye also be his disciples?"

Interpretation and Commentary:

The healed man expresses frustration with the authorities' persistent questioning. His response suggests that he has already provided them with the information they seek, and he questions whether they are genuinely interested in understanding or if they are considering becoming disciples of Jesus.

Key Points:

1. Frustration with Inattentiveness: The man conveys frustration, stating that he has already shared the details of his healing, but the authorities did not heed his words. This reflects the authorities' unwillingness to acknowledge the truth.

2. Challenge to Their Intentions: By asking if they want to hear it again and if they would also become disciples of Jesus, the man challenges the sincerity of the authorities' inquiry. He questions whether they are genuinely seeking understanding or if their motives are different.

References:
- John 9:26 (Previous verse): "Then said they to him again, What did he to thee? how opened he thine eyes?" The authorities continue their questioning about the details of the healing.

Key Takeaway:
The healed man, frustrated by the authorities' persistent questioning, challenges their intentions and questions whether they are open to accepting the truth about Jesus. This sets the stage for a deeper confrontation between the man and the religious leaders.

John 9:28 (King James Bible): "Then they reviled him, and said, Thou art his disciple; but we are Moses' disciples."

Interpretation and Commentary:

In response to the healed man's challenging questions, the authorities resort to reviling him. They accuse him of being a disciple of Jesus and contrast themselves as followers of Moses.

Key Points:

1. Reviling Response: The authorities react with hostility, resorting to insults against the healed man. This reflects their growing frustration and refusal to accept the possibility that Jesus is a divine figure.

2. Identity as Moses' Disciples: The authorities assert their allegiance to Moses, a prominent figure in Judaism. This reveals their reluctance to embrace a new teaching or acknowledge Jesus as a legitimate authority.

References:
- John 9:27 (Previous verse): "He answered them, I have told you already, and ye did not hear: wherefore would ye hear it again? will ye also be his disciples?" The healed man questions the authorities' intentions.

Key Takeaway:
The authorities, unwilling to engage in a constructive dialogue, respond to the healed man's questions with insults. Their reference to Moses underscores their allegiance to traditional Jewish teachings and their rejection of Jesus as a significant figure.

John 9:29 (King James Bible): "We know that God spake unto Moses: as for this fellow, we know not from whence he is."

Interpretation and Commentary:

The religious authorities continue their response to the healed man, emphasizing their certainty in God's communication with Moses. However, they express ignorance regarding Jesus' origin, questioning his legitimacy.

Key Points:

1. Knowledge of God's Communication: The authorities assert their confidence in the divine communication with Moses, highlighting their adherence to traditional teachings.

2. Ignorance about Jesus: Despite their confidence in Moses' connection with God, the authorities admit ignorance about Jesus' origin. This reflects their skepticism and reluctance to acknowledge Jesus as a divine figure.

References:
- John 9:28 (Previous verse): "Then they reviled him, and said, Thou art his disciple; but we are Moses' disciples." The authorities

respond defensively to the healed man's questions, emphasizing their allegiance to Moses.

Key Takeaway:
The religious authorities affirm their belief in God's communication with Moses but express uncertainty about Jesus, revealing their skepticism and unwillingness to accept him as a legitimate figure.

John 9:30 (King James Bible): "The man answered and said unto them, Why herein is a marvellous thing, that ye know not from whence he is, and yet he hath opened mine eyes."

Interpretation and Commentary:

The healed man responds to the religious authorities, expressing amazement at their lack of knowledge about Jesus' origin despite the miraculous healing he has experienced.

Key Points:

1. Marvellous Ignorance: The man finds it remarkable that the religious authorities, who should have knowledge and insight, remain unaware of Jesus' origin despite the extraordinary miracle of restoring his sight.

2. Power of Healing: The man highlights the undeniable evidence of Jesus' power in his life. The fact that Jesus healed his blindness should have prompted the authorities to seek deeper understanding.

References:
- John 9:29 (Previous verse): "We know that God spake unto Moses: as for this fellow, we know not from whence he is." The authorities express their lack of knowledge about Jesus' origin.
- John 9:25 (Previous verse): "He answered and said, Whether he be a sinner or no, I know not: one thing I know, that, whereas I

was blind, now I see." The healed man testifies to the undeniable reality of his healing by Jesus.

Key Takeaway:
The healed man is astonished at the authorities' ignorance regarding Jesus' origin, emphasizing the transformative power of the miracle he experienced and questioning the leaders' understanding.

John 9:31 (King James Bible): "Now we know that God heareth not sinners: but if any man be a worshipper of God, and doeth his will, him he heareth."

Interpretation and Commentary:

The man, having faced interrogation, makes a profound statement about the relationship between God and those who follow His will. It reflects a deep understanding of divine principles.

Key Points:

1. God's Response to Sinners: The man asserts that God does not typically listen to sinners. This aligns with the concept that a righteous and obedient life is more likely to receive divine favor.

2. Worshippers of God: The man suggests that those who are true worshippers of God, actively doing His will, are the ones whom God hears. This emphasizes the importance of both faith and obedience.

References:
- Proverbs 15:29: "The Lord is far from the wicked: but he heareth the prayer of the righteous." This aligns with the idea that God is attentive to the righteous.
- Psalm 34:15: "The eyes of the Lord are upon the righteous, and his ears are open unto their cry." Similar to the idea expressed in John 9:31, this verse emphasizes God's attention to the righteous.

Key Takeaway:

The man's statement underscores the connection between righteousness, worship of God, and the divine response. It reflects a theological perspective on the conditions under which God is more likely to hear and respond to prayers.

John 9:32 (King James Bible): "Since the world began was it not heard that any man opened the eyes of one that was born blind."

Interpretation and Commentary:

The man born blind continues to express his awe and amazement at the miracle performed on him. He acknowledges the unprecedented nature of this event, emphasizing that such a miraculous healing has not been recorded since the beginning of the world.

Key Points:

1. Unprecedented Miracle: The man born blind highlights the uniqueness of his healing. This reinforces the extraordinary nature of the miracle performed by Jesus, adding weight to the significance of the event.

References:
- No direct reference in the King James Bible, but the statement echoes the man's conviction that this miraculous act is unparalleled in history.

Key Takeaway:
The man's declaration contributes to building the case for the extraordinary nature of Jesus' miraculous works, especially the healing of someone born blind. It emphasizes the unprecedented impact of Jesus' ministry on individuals and challenges conventional expectations.

John 9:33 (King James Bible): "If this man were not of God, he could do nothing."

Interpretation and Commentary:

The man born blind, having experienced the miraculous healing by Jesus, makes a profound statement affirming the divine origin of Jesus' actions. He asserts that Jesus, being capable of such extraordinary deeds, must be someone sent by God.

Key Points:

1. Divine Attribution: The man recognizes the connection between Jesus and God. His reasoning implies that the power demonstrated by Jesus in the healing is a sign of divine authority and approval.

References:
- While the statement aligns with the concept of divine authority, there is no direct reference in the King James Bible that echoes this specific affirmation.

Key Takeaway:
The man's declaration not only acknowledges Jesus as a miraculous healer but also attributes the source of Jesus' power to a divine origin. This perspective contributes to the growing recognition of Jesus as more than a mere man and points to a deeper understanding of his identity.

John 9:34 (King James Bible): "They answered and said unto him, Thou wast altogether born in sins, and dost thou teach us? And they cast him out."

Interpretation and Commentary:

In response to the man born blind's statement affirming Jesus' divine connection, the Pharisees react with arrogance and dismissiveness. They reject the man's perspective, asserting that he was born in sin, and they question his audacity to teach or instruct them. The consequence of their prideful response is the expulsion of the man from their presence.

Key Points:

1. Spiritual Arrogance: The Pharisees' response reveals their spiritual arrogance. They dismiss the man's testimony and refuse to acknowledge the possibility that Jesus might be divinely sent.

2. Excommunication: The Pharisees, in their pride, cast the man out. This signifies not only a rejection of his testimony but also a form of excommunication from the religious community.

References:
- This verse highlights the growing tension between Jesus' followers and the religious authorities, foreshadowing the conflicts that will escalate throughout the Gospel of John.

Key Takeaway:
The Pharisees' response reflects a hardening of their hearts against the possibility of recognizing Jesus' divine authority. Their rejection of the man and his testimony sets the stage for further confrontations between Jesus and the religious leaders.

John 9:35 (King James Bible): "Jesus heard that they had cast him out; and when he had found him, he said unto him, Dost thou believe on the Son of God?"

Interpretation and Commentary:

Upon learning that the man born blind had been cast out by the Pharisees, Jesus seeks him out. This demonstrates Jesus' compassion and concern for those who face rejection for their faith. Jesus then engages the man with a profound question, asking if he believes in the Son of God.

Key Points:

1. Seeking the Outcast: Jesus actively seeks the one who has faced rejection. This underscores his caring nature and willingness to reach out to those who are marginalized or cast aside.

2. Identifying the Son of God: Jesus poses a crucial question about belief in the Son of God. This sets the stage for the man's confession of faith and a deeper revelation of Jesus' identity.

References:
- This episode emphasizes Jesus' role as the Good Shepherd who seeks out and cares for each lost sheep (John 10:14-15).

Key Takeaway:
Even in the face of rejection by religious authorities, Jesus actively seeks those who are cast out, demonstrating his compassion and inviting them into a deeper understanding of faith.

John 9:36 (King James Bible): "He answered and said, Who is he, Lord, that I might believe on him?"

Interpretation and Commentary:

The man born blind responds to Jesus' question with a sincere inquiry. He addresses Jesus as "Lord," indicating a growing recognition of Jesus' authority. His willingness to believe is evident in his question, showing an openness to faith.

Key Points:

1. Recognition of Authority: The man's address as "Lord" reveals a developing acknowledgment of Jesus' authority. This recognition is a crucial step in the journey toward faith.

2. Desire to Believe: The man expresses a genuine desire to believe, seeking more information about the one he should put his faith in. This demonstrates an openness and readiness to accept the truth.

References:
- This mirrors the pattern seen in other encounters where individuals acknowledge Jesus' authority and express a desire to believe (e.g., John 4:10, 4:15, 4:19).

Key Takeaway:
The man's sincere inquiry reflects a growing awareness of Jesus' authority and a genuine willingness to believe. This sets the stage for a deeper revelation of Jesus' identity and the man's confession of faith.

John 9:37 (King James Bible): "And Jesus said unto him, Thou hast both seen him, and it is he that talketh with thee."

Interpretation and Commentary:

In this verse, Jesus responds to the man born blind who expressed a desire to believe. Jesus affirms that the man has not only seen him physically but that he is the one speaking to him. This revelation is a powerful moment, as Jesus discloses his identity to someone who was once blind but now sees both physically and spiritually.

Key Points:

1. Direct Revelation: Jesus directly reveals his identity to the man, confirming that the one he sees and converses with is indeed the Son of God.

2. Spiritual Insight: The man's physical healing is accompanied by a deeper spiritual insight as he comes to recognize Jesus as the one who has transformed his life.

References:
- This encounter echoes the spiritual blindness theme discussed earlier in the chapter (John 9:39-41), emphasizing the profound transformation that comes with recognizing Jesus.

Key Takeaway:
Jesus, in revealing himself to the man born blind, emphasizes the connection between physical and spiritual sight. The man not only gains his physical eyesight but also perceives the true identity of Jesus, experiencing a profound spiritual transformation.

John 9:38 (King James Bible): "And he said, Lord, I believe. And he worshipped him."

Interpretation and Commentary:

In this verse, the man born blind responds to Jesus' revelation of his identity with a profound acknowledgment of faith. He not only declares his belief but also takes the significant step of worshiping Jesus.

Key Points:

1. Confession of Faith: The man's words, "Lord, I believe," express a deep conviction in Jesus as Lord and Messiah. This confession is a pivotal moment in his spiritual journey.

2. Act of Worship: The act of worship is a natural response to recognizing Jesus as Lord. It signifies the man's reverence and submission to Jesus' divine authority.

References:
- This declaration of faith and worship aligns with the Gospel's broader theme of individuals recognizing and responding to Jesus as the Son of God.

Key Takeaway:
The healed man's confession of faith and worship underscores the transformative power of encountering Jesus. His acknowledgment goes beyond physical healing, revealing a profound spiritual awakening and acceptance of Jesus' divine nature.

John 9:39 (King James Bible): "And Jesus said, For judgment I am come into this world, that they which see not might see, and that they which see might be made blind."

Interpretation and Commentary:

In this verse, Jesus reflects on the purpose of His coming into the world. He uses the metaphors of sight and blindness to convey spiritual truths about understanding and judgment.

Key Points:

1. Purpose of Jesus' Coming: Jesus states that His coming into the world has a dual effect. On one hand, it brings sight to those who were spiritually blind, offering understanding, knowledge, and salvation. On the other hand, it results in a kind of blindness for those who claim to see but reject the truth.

2. Symbolism of Sight and Blindness: The metaphor of sight represents spiritual insight and understanding, while blindness symbolizes spiritual ignorance or rejection of the truth.

References:
- This statement aligns with the broader theme in the Gospel of John, emphasizing Jesus as the Light of the world and the revealer of truth.

Key Takeaway:
Jesus' words highlight the transformative impact of His presence. Those who recognize their spiritual need and turn to Him gain insight and understanding, while those who reject Him remain in spiritual darkness. The verse underscores the importance of humility and openness to receive the truth that Jesus brings.

John 9:40 (King James Bible): "And some of the Pharisees which were with him heard these words and said unto him, Are we blind also?"

Interpretation and Commentary:

This verse captures the response of some Pharisees who overheard Jesus' statement about sight and blindness. Their question reveals a mix of curiosity, skepticism, and perhaps a hint of defensiveness.

Key Points:

1. Pharisees' Reaction: The Pharisees, known for their religious authority and adherence to traditions, react to Jesus' words with a question. Their inquiry, "Are we blind also?" indicates a potential discomfort with the idea that they might lack spiritual insight.

2. Spiritual Blindness: Jesus' previous statement about blindness and sight prompts self-reflection among the Pharisees. It challenges their assumption of spiritual superiority and authority.

3. Irony in the Question: There is a touch of irony in the Pharisees' question. While they physically see, Jesus suggests that spiritual insight is not guaranteed by mere religious adherence.

References:
- This episode aligns with the broader narrative in the Gospels, where religious leaders often grapple with Jesus' teachings and question His authority.

Key Takeaway:
The Pharisees' question reflects a moment of tension and self-examination. It serves as an opportunity for them to recognize the potential spiritual blindness that could result from rigid adherence to legalistic traditions rather than embracing the transformative message of Jesus.

John 9:41 (King James Bible): "Jesus said unto them, If ye were blind, ye should have no sin: but now ye say, We see; therefore, your sin remaineth."

Interpretation and Commentary:

In this verse, Jesus responds to the Pharisees' question about blindness. His words carry a profound message about spiritual insight, acknowledgment of sin, and the consequences of claiming to have understanding.

Key Points:

1. Conditional Statement: Jesus begins with a conditional statement, "If ye were blind," suggesting that if they were truly unaware or ignorant, there would be no guilt in their sin. This underscores the principle of accountability based on knowledge and understanding.

2. Claim of Sight: However, the Pharisees, asserting their spiritual insight and understanding, say, "We see." This claim indicates a self-righteous confidence in their religious knowledge and authority.

3. Consequence of False Assurance: Jesus asserts that because they claim to see, their sin remains. This highlights the severity of claiming spiritual understanding without genuine humility and openness to God's truth.

References:
- This passage reflects Jesus' recurring theme of challenging religious pride and emphasizing the importance of humility and acknowledgment of one's spiritual condition.

Key Takeaway:
The verse underscores the significance of genuine self-awareness and humility in acknowledging one's spiritual state. Claiming to see without true understanding and recognition of one's need for God's guidance can lead to spiritual blindness and the persistence of sin.

CHAPTER TEN

Jesus the True Shepherd

John 10:1 (King James Bible): "Verily, verily, I say unto you, He that entereth not by the door into the sheepfold, but climbeth up some other way, the same is a thief and a robber."

Interpretation and Commentary:

In this verse, Jesus uses a metaphor of a sheepfold to convey essential truths about Himself as the true Shepherd, and the consequences for those who do not approach Him with the right intent.

Key Points:

1. Authority of Jesus: Jesus begins with the solemn declaration, "Verily, verily" (truly, truly), emphasizing the importance of what He is about to say. This signals a significant teaching.

2. The Sheepfold as a Metaphor: The sheepfold represents a place of safety and care for the sheep, symbolizing God's people. Jesus asserts that the legitimate way to enter this fold is through the door.

3. Thieves and Robbers: Anyone who doesn't enter through the door but tries to climb in some other way is labeled as a thief and a robber. This metaphor likely points to false teachers or leaders who try to gain access to God's people through illegitimate means.

References:
This imagery of Jesus as the Shepherd and His followers as the sheep is a recurring theme in the Bible, emphasizing the relationship between Christ and His followers.

Key Takeaway:
The verse highlights the exclusive and legitimate means of access to God's people, emphasizing Jesus as the true Shepherd. Those who attempt to lead or influence without aligning with the proper channels are likened to thieves and robbers, stressing the importance of recognizing Christ's authority in matters of faith and spiritual guidance.

John 10:2 (King James Bible): "But he that entereth in by the door is the shepherd of the sheep."

Interpretation and Commentary:

Continuing from the previous verse, Jesus elaborates on the metaphor of the sheepfold and the door. Here, He introduces the concept of the true shepherd who enters through the door, contrasting with the thieves and robbers mentioned earlier.

Key Points:

1. The Legitimate Shepherd: In contrast to the unauthorized entry of thieves and robbers, the legitimate shepherd is the one who enters through the door. This reinforces the idea that there is an authorized and proper way to approach God's people.

2. Christ as the True Shepherd: This statement by Jesus aligns with the recurring biblical theme of Christ as the Shepherd. He is the legitimate and appointed leader of God's people.

References:
- This imagery draws on various Old Testament passages that depict God as the Shepherd of Israel and anticipates Jesus' claim to be the Good Shepherd later in this chapter.

Key Takeaway:
The verse emphasizes the importance of legitimacy and authorization in spiritual leadership. Jesus identifies Himself as the true Shepherd who enters through the proper means. This reinforces the exclusivity of His role in guiding and caring for God's people.

John 10:3 (King James Bible): "To him the porter openeth, and the sheep hear his voice: and he calleth his own sheep by name, and leadeth them out."

Interpretation and Commentary:

In this verse, Jesus continues the analogy of the shepherd and the sheep, introducing the role of the porter and highlighting the intimate relationship between the shepherd and his flock.

Key Points:

1. The Role of the Porter: The porter, or gatekeeper, plays a crucial role in allowing access. This signifies that there is an orderly and authorized way for the shepherd to enter the sheepfold.

2. Recognition and Intimacy: The shepherd's relationship with the sheep is deeply personal. He knows each sheep by name, emphasizing the intimate connection between the shepherd and the flock. This mirrors the personal relationship Jesus has with His followers.

3. Leading the Sheep Out: The shepherd not only calls the sheep by name but also leads them out. This implies guidance, protection, and a purposeful direction provided by the shepherd.

References:
- The Old Testament imagery of God knowing His people by name and leading them is reflected in this metaphor. Also, it echoes the concept of God as a personal and caring Shepherd found in Psalms.

Key Takeaway:
The verse underscores the personal and intimate relationship believers have with Jesus, the Shepherd. He is not a distant or indifferent leader; instead, He knows each follower individually and guides them purposefully. The portrayal of Jesus as the one who leads His people emphasizes His role as the ultimate guide and protector.

John 10:4 (King James Bible): "And when he putteth forth his own sheep, he goeth before them, and the sheep follow him: for they know his voice."

Interpretation and Commentary:

In this verse, Jesus continues to elaborate on the relationship between the shepherd and the sheep, emphasizing the dynamic between them as the shepherd leads and the sheep follow.

Key Points:

1. Leadership and Initiative: The shepherd takes the initiative in leading his sheep. He "goeth before them," indicating that he leads the way. This highlights the active and guiding role of Jesus as the Shepherd of believers.

2. Recognition of the Shepherd's Voice: The sheep follow the shepherd because they "know his voice." This speaks to the familiarity and trust the sheep have in the shepherd. It also implies a level of discernment among the sheep to distinguish the shepherd's voice from others.

References:
- The imagery of Jesus as the Shepherd leading His followers is consistent with the Old Testament portrayal of God guiding His people. The concept of recognizing God's voice is present in various Old Testament passages.

Key Takeaway:
This verse underscores the active and leading role of Jesus in the lives of believers. As the Good Shepherd, He takes the initiative to guide His followers. The emphasis on the sheep knowing His voice emphasizes the importance of familiarity, trust, and discernment in the relationship between Jesus and His followers.

John 10:5 (King James Bible): "And a stranger will they not follow, but will flee from him: for they know not the voice of strangers."

Interpretation and Commentary:

Continuing the analogy of the shepherd and his sheep, Jesus emphasizes the discernment of His followers. In this verse, the idea is that the sheep will not follow a stranger; instead, they will flee from someone whose voice they do not recognize.

Key Points:

1. Discernment: The sheep, symbolizing believers, possess a discerning nature. They have the ability to distinguish the voice of their true shepherd from that of a stranger. This discernment is crucial for their safety and well-being.

2. Rejection of Strangers: The refusal to follow a stranger reflects the loyalty and trust the sheep place in their shepherd. The unfamiliar voice represents false teachings or influences that believers are wise to avoid.

References:
 - This concept aligns with various teachings in the New Testament that caution believers against false prophets and teachings. (Matthew 7:15; 1 John 4:1)

Key Takeaway:
This verse underscores the importance of spiritual discernment among believers. They are encouraged to know and follow the voice of their true Shepherd, Jesus, while rejecting the influence of strangers or false teachings. The emphasis is on the loyalty and trust that believers place in Jesus as their guide and protector.

John 10:6 (King James Bible): "This parable spake Jesus unto them: but they understood not what things they were which he spake unto them."

Interpretation and Commentary:

Jesus, after presenting the analogy of the shepherd and his sheep, notes that the people to whom He spoke did not fully comprehend the meaning of His words. This acknowledgment by

Jesus highlights the spiritual blindness and lack of understanding among some of His listeners.

Key Points:

1. Parabolic Teaching: Jesus frequently used parables to convey spiritual truths. These stories were often metaphorical and required a deeper understanding to grasp their intended meaning.

2. Limited Understanding: Despite Jesus' efforts to communicate profound truths through parables, some of His audience struggled to comprehend the spiritual significance behind His words. This points to the spiritual blindness that can hinder people from grasping deeper truths.

References:
- Similar instances of Jesus using parables can be found throughout the Gospels, emphasizing the importance of spiritual insight and receptivity to understand His teachings.

Key Takeaway:
This verse underscores the challenges in conveying spiritual truths to individuals whose hearts and minds are not open to understanding. It emphasizes the need for spiritual receptivity and an openness to deeper insights to grasp the profound teachings of Jesus.

John 10:7 (King James Bible): "Then said Jesus unto them again, Verily, verily, I say unto you, I am the door of the sheep."

Interpretation and Commentary:

In this verse, Jesus makes a profound statement, declaring Himself as "the door of the sheep." This metaphorical language emphasizes His role as the exclusive means of access to salvation and a relationship with God. The imagery of a door suggests that through Jesus, individuals can enter into a secure and transformative connection with God.

Key Points:

1. Exclusive Access: Jesus uses the metaphor of a door to convey that He is the only way to enter into a relationship with God. This aligns with His earlier statement in John 14:6, where He declares, "I am the way, the truth, and the life: no man cometh unto the Father, but by me."

2. Security and Protection: The concept of Jesus as the door also implies a sense of security and protection. The shepherd's role is to safeguard the sheep, and by identifying Himself as the door, Jesus emphasizes His role in providing spiritual security and protection for believers.

References:
- John 14:6 - "Jesus saith unto him, I am the way, the truth, and the life: no man cometh unto the Father, but by me."

Key Takeaway:
This verse highlights the exclusivity of the relationship with God through Jesus Christ. He is not merely a way but the door—the sole means by which individuals can access the blessings of salvation, security, and a transformative connection with God.

John 10:8 (King James Bible): "All that ever came before me are thieves and robbers: but the sheep did not hear them."

Interpretation and Commentary:

In this verse, Jesus contrasts Himself as the true shepherd with those who came before Him, referring to false leaders as "thieves and robbers." This statement emphasizes the exclusive and legitimate nature of Jesus' leadership. The sheep, representing believers, recognize His voice and do not heed the false teachings of those who claim illegitimate authority.

Key Points:

1. Exclusive Legitimacy: Jesus asserts that anyone who came before Him, claiming to lead or guide God's people, without a genuine connection to God, is a "thief" or a "robber." This underscores the exclusive legitimacy of Jesus as the true shepherd and leader.

2. Discernment of the Sheep: The sheep, symbolizing believers, possess the ability to discern the true shepherd's voice. This reflects the importance of spiritual discernment among followers of Jesus, as they are guided by His teachings and are not deceived by false leaders.

References:
- Matthew 7:15 - "Beware of false prophets, which come to you in sheep's clothing, but inwardly they are ravening wolves."

Key Takeaway:
Jesus asserts His exclusive legitimacy as the true shepherd, warning against false leaders who deceive. The importance of discernment among believers is highlighted, emphasizing the need to recognize and follow the authentic voice of the true shepherd, Jesus Christ.

John 10:9 (King James Bible): "I am the door: by me if any man enter in, he shall be saved, and shall go in and out, and find pasture."

Interpretation and Commentary:

In this verse, Jesus declares Himself as the door, emphasizing that through Him, anyone who enters will be saved. The imagery of a door implies access, salvation, and security. Those who enter through Christ will experience spiritual freedom, finding nourishment and fulfillment.

Key Points:

1. Exclusive Access to Salvation: Jesus presents Himself as the exclusive means of salvation. He is the door through which individuals

must enter to be saved, reinforcing the uniqueness of Christ in the redemptive process.

2. Security and Freedom: The notion of going in and out signifies a sense of security and freedom. Through Christ, believers experience a liberated and abundant life, finding spiritual nourishment and fulfillment.

References:
- John 14:6 - "Jesus saith unto him, I am the way, the truth, and the life: no man cometh unto the Father, but by me."
- Acts 4:12 - "Neither is there salvation in any other: for there is none other name under heaven given among men, whereby we must be saved."

Key Takeaway:
Jesus asserts Himself as the exclusive door to salvation, highlighting the necessity of entering through Him. Those who do so experience not only salvation but also spiritual security, freedom, and fulfillment in the abundant life He provides.

John 10:10 (King James Bible): "The thief cometh not, but for to steal, and to kill, and to destroy: I am come that they might have life, and that they might have it more abundantly."

Interpretation and Commentary:

In this verse, Jesus contrasts His purpose with that of the thief. The thief symbolizes forces opposing God, seeking to steal, kill, and destroy. In contrast, Jesus declares His mission to bring abundant life to those who follow Him.

Key Points:

1. Thief vs. Shepherd: The thief represents evil, with destructive intentions. Jesus, as the Good Shepherd, stands in opposition, bringing life and protection to His followers.

2. Abundant Life: Jesus promises more than just existence; He offers abundant life. This life transcends the mere physical and extends to spiritual and eternal dimensions, characterized by fulfillment and purpose.

References:
- John 14:6 - "Jesus saith unto him, I am the way, the truth, and the life: no man cometh unto the Father, but by me."
- 1 Peter 5:8 - "Be sober, be vigilant; because your adversary the devil, as a roaring lion, walketh about, seeking whom he may devour."

Key Takeaway:
Jesus exposes the destructive intentions of opposing forces and affirms His mission to bring abundant life. Believers can find security, purpose, and fulfillment by following the Good Shepherd who protects them from the thief's harmful designs.

John 10:11 (King James Bible): "I am the good shepherd: the good shepherd giveth his life for the sheep."

Interpretation and Commentary:

In this verse, Jesus identifies Himself as the Good Shepherd, emphasizing the sacrificial nature of His role. A good shepherd cares for and protects the sheep, even to the extent of laying down his life for them.

Key Points:

1. Good Shepherd Analogy: Jesus employs the metaphor of a shepherd to illustrate His relationship with believers. The shepherd-sheep dynamic signifies guidance, care, and protection.

2. Sacrificial Love: Jesus goes beyond the expected role of a shepherd by stating that He will give His life for the sheep. This foreshadows His ultimate sacrifice on the cross for the salvation of humanity.

References:

- Isaiah 40:11 - "He shall feed his flock like a shepherd: he shall gather the lambs with his arm, and carry them in his bosom, and shall gently lead those that are with young."

- 1 Peter 2:25 - "For ye were as sheep going astray; but are now returned unto the Shepherd and Bishop of your souls."

- John 15:13 - "Greater love hath no man than this, that a man lay down his life for his friends."

Key Takeaway:

Jesus, as the Good Shepherd, embodies sacrificial love by giving His life for the well-being of His followers. This highlights the depth of His commitment and care, offering a profound example of selflessness and love.

John 10:12 (King James Bible): "But he that is an hireling, and not the shepherd, whose own the sheep are not, seeth the wolf coming, and leaveth the sheep, and fleeth: and the wolf catcheth them, and scattereth the sheep."

Interpretation and Commentary:

In this verse, Jesus contrasts the Good Shepherd with a hireling, illustrating the difference in their commitment to the well-being of the sheep.

Key Points:

1. Hireling vs. Good Shepherd: The hireling, being a hired worker and not the owner of the sheep, lacks the same level of care and responsibility. When danger approaches, such as the threat of a wolf, the hireling abandons the sheep to save himself.

2. Abandonment and Scattering: The hireling's response to danger results in the scattering of the sheep, leaving them vulnerable to harm. This emphasizes the importance of a shepherd's steadfast commitment to protecting and caring for the flock.

References:

- Ezekiel 34:2-5 - "Woe be to the shepherds of Israel that do feed themselves! should not the shepherds feed the flocks? Ye eat the fat, and ye clothe you with the wool, ye kill them that are fed: but ye feed not the flock. The diseased have ye not strengthened, neither have ye healed that which was sick, neither have ye bound up that which was broken, neither have ye brought again that which was driven away, neither have ye sought that which was lost..."

- Zechariah 11:16-17 - "For, lo, I will raise up a shepherd in the land, which shall not visit those that be cut off, neither shall seek the young one, nor heal that that is broken, nor feed that that standeth still: but he shall eat the flesh of the fat, and tear their claws in pieces."

Key Takeaway:

Jesus underscores the depth of His commitment as the Good Shepherd, contrasting it with the potential neglect and abandonment of a hireling. This reinforces the importance of genuine care and sacrifice in shepherding God's people.

John 10:13 (King James Bible): "The hireling fleeth, because he is an hireling, and careth not for the sheep."

Interpretation and Commentary:

This verse further emphasizes the contrast between the hireling and the Good Shepherd.

Key Points:

1. Motivation of the Hireling: The hireling's primary motivation is financial gain, as indicated by the term "hireling." His commitment to the sheep is superficial, and when faced with danger, he flees to protect himself, showing that his care for the sheep is conditional.

References:

- Ezekiel 34:8 - "As I live, saith the Lord God, surely because my flock became a prey, and my flock became meat to every beast of the field, because there was no shepherd, neither did my shepherds search for my flock, but the shepherds fed themselves, and fed not my flock."

Key Takeaway:
The hireling's lack of genuine care and sacrificial commitment highlights the importance of true shepherds who prioritize the well-being of the flock over personal interests. This echoes the broader theme of Jesus as the Good Shepherd who selflessly cares for His people.

John 10:14 (King James Bible): "I am the good shepherd, and know my sheep, and am known of mine."

Interpretation and Commentary:

In this verse, Jesus explicitly identifies Himself as the Good Shepherd, emphasizing an intimate and reciprocal relationship with His sheep.

Key Points:

1. The Good Shepherd: Jesus declares His role as the Good Shepherd, drawing from the rich Old Testament imagery of God as the Shepherd of His people.

2. Intimate Knowledge: The Good Shepherd knows His sheep intimately. This knowledge goes beyond mere recognition; it implies a deep, personal understanding of each individual within the flock.

3. Reciprocal Relationship: Not only does the Good Shepherd know His sheep, but His sheep also know Him. This points to a mutual relationship of trust, familiarity, and recognition between Jesus and His followers.

References:

- Psalm 23:1 - "The Lord is my shepherd; I shall not want."
- Jeremiah 31:33 - "But this shall be the covenant that I will make with the house of Israel; After those days, saith the Lord, I will put my law in their inward parts, and write it in their hearts; and will be their God, and they shall be my people."

Key Takeaway:
Jesus, as the Good Shepherd, establishes a profound and personal connection with His followers. This relationship is marked by His intimate knowledge of them and their reciprocal knowledge of Him, highlighting the depth of connection in the shepherd-sheep metaphor.

John 10:15 (King James Bible): "As the Father knoweth me, even so know I the Father: and I lay down my life for the sheep."

Interpretation and Commentary:

In this verse, Jesus deepens the understanding of His relationship with the Father and emphasizes His sacrificial love for His followers.

Key Points:

1. Intimate Knowledge between Jesus and the Father: Jesus draws a parallel between the way the Father knows Him and His knowledge of the Father. This highlights the profound and intimate relationship within the Trinity.

2. Sacrificial Love: Jesus declares His willingness to lay down His life for the sheep. This foreshadows the ultimate act of love and sacrifice, referring to His upcoming crucifixion for the redemption of humanity.

References:
- John 17:25-26 - "O righteous Father, the world hath not known thee: but I have known thee, and these have known that thou hast sent me. And I have declared unto them thy name, and will

declare it: that the love wherewith thou hast loved me may be in them, and I in them."

Key Takeaway:
Jesus affirms the depth of His knowledge of the Father and expresses His sacrificial love by stating His willingness to lay down His life for the sheep. This lays the foundation for understanding the profound nature of Christ's redemptive work on the cross.

John 10:16 (King James Bible): "And other sheep I have, which are not of this fold: them also I must bring, and they shall hear my voice; and there shall be one fold, and one shepherd."

Interpretation and Commentary:

In this verse, Jesus speaks about a broader scope of His mission, indicating the inclusion of Gentiles in addition to the Jewish believers.

Key Points:

1. Inclusivity of the Flock: Jesus refers to "other sheep" who are not part of the current fold, signifying the extension of God's salvation to the Gentiles. This emphasizes the universal nature of Jesus' redemptive work.

2. Unity in Christ: The ultimate goal is to bring all these sheep together to form one flock under one shepherd, emphasizing unity in Christ. This unity transcends cultural, ethnic, and geographical boundaries.

3. Hearing the Voice of Jesus: A common characteristic of the sheep is their ability to hear the voice of the shepherd. This signifies the spiritual receptiveness of believers, regardless of their background.

References:
- Ephesians 2:13-14 - "But now in Christ Jesus ye who sometimes were far off are made nigh by the blood of Christ. For he

is our peace, who hath made both one, and hath broken down the middle wall of partition between us."

Key Takeaway:
Jesus reveals the expansive reach of His redemptive mission, encompassing people beyond the Jewish community. The unity in Christ brings diverse believers together as one flock, illustrating the universality of God's love and salvation.

John 10:17 (King James Bible): "Therefore doth my Father love me, because I lay down my life, that I might take it again."

Interpretation and Commentary:

In this verse, Jesus explains the profound relationship between Him and the Father, highlighting the sacrificial nature of His mission and the authority He has over His own life.

Key Points:

1. Father's Love for the Son: Jesus asserts that the Father loves Him because of His willingness to lay down His life. This emphasizes the Father's approval and affirmation of Jesus' sacrificial mission.

2. Voluntary Sacrifice: Jesus speaks of laying down His life voluntarily. This underscores the selflessness of His sacrifice, emphasizing that no one takes His life from Him; He willingly gives it.

3. Resurrection Authority: The purpose of laying down His life is to take it up again. This points to Jesus' authority over death and His ability to conquer it through resurrection.

References:
- Philippians 2:8 - "And being found in fashion as a man, he humbled himself, and became obedient unto death, even the death of the cross."

- John 10:18 - "No man taketh it from me, but I lay it down of myself. I have power to lay it down, and I have power to take it again. This commandment have I received of my Father."

Key Takeaway:
Jesus highlights the unique relationship between Him and the Father, emphasizing the voluntary nature of His sacrificial death and His authority over life and death. This lays the foundation for the resurrection, a central aspect of Christian faith.

John 10:18 (King James Bible): "No man taketh it from me, but I lay it down of myself. I have power to lay it down, and I have power to take it again. This commandment have I received of my Father."

Interpretation and Commentary:

In this verse, Jesus emphasizes His divine authority over His own life and death, highlighting the voluntary nature of His sacrifice and the obedience to the Father's command.

Key Points:

1. Voluntary Sacrifice: Jesus reiterates that no one can forcibly take His life from Him. His death is not a result of external circumstances or human intervention but is a voluntary act on His part.

2. Divine Authority: Jesus declares that He has the power both to lay down His life and to take it up again. This statement underscores His divine authority over life and death, demonstrating His unique position as the Son of God.

3. Obedience to the Father: Jesus acknowledges that this authority to sacrifice and resurrect is in accordance with the commandment He received from the Father. This highlights the unity of purpose between the Father and the Son in the redemptive plan.

References:
- Philippians 2:8 - "And being found in fashion as a man, he humbled himself, and became obedient unto death, even the death of the cross."
- John 5:19 - "Then answered Jesus and said unto them, Verily, verily, I say unto you, The Son can do nothing of himself, but what he seeth the Father do: for what things soever he doeth, these also doeth the Son likewise."

Key Takeaway:
This verse underscores the divine authority of Jesus over His own life and death, emphasizing the voluntary nature of His sacrifice and His obedience to the Father's command in the redemptive plan. It reinforces the theological significance of Christ's sacrificial death and resurrection.

John 10:19 (King James Bible): "There was a division therefore again among the Jews for these sayings."

Interpretation and Commentary:

This verse highlights the divisive nature of Jesus' teachings among the Jews. The statements made by Jesus, especially regarding His authority over life and death, stirred controversy and led to a division among the people.

Key Points:

1. Impactful Statements: Jesus' declarations about His divine authority and the voluntary nature of His sacrifice had a profound impact, causing a split in opinions among the Jewish audience.

2. Response to Controversy: Throughout the Gospel of John, we see that Jesus' words often sparked debates and differing reactions. His claims challenged traditional beliefs and provoked strong responses from those who heard Him.

3. Foreshadowing Opposition: The division among the Jews foreshadows the increasing opposition and hostility that Jesus would face as His ministry progressed, ultimately leading to His crucifixion.

References:

- John 7:43 - "So there was a division among the people because of him."

- John 9:16 - "Therefore said some of the Pharisees, This man is not of God, because he keepeth not the sabbath day. Others said, How can a man that is a sinner do such miracles? And there was a division among them."

Key Takeaway:

This verse illustrates the controversial impact of Jesus' statements, leading to a division among the Jews. It sets the stage for the increasing opposition that Jesus would face, highlighting the profound and challenging nature of His teachings.

John 10:20 (King James Bible): "And many of them said, He hath a devil, and is mad; why hear ye him?"

Interpretation and Commentary:

In this verse, a segment of the audience responds to Jesus by accusing Him of having a devil and being mad or insane. They question why others would listen to someone they perceive as being influenced by a demonic force and mentally unstable.

Key Points:

1. Accusations of Possession and Madness: The people's response reflects a harsh rejection of Jesus. They not only attribute His actions and words to demonic influence but also go further to suggest that He is mentally deranged or insane.

2. Resistance to Acceptance: The rejection of Jesus by some is intense, demonstrating a deep resistance to accepting His teachings

and claims. The accusations of possession and madness aim to discredit His authority and message.

3. Challenges to Authority: This verse highlights the challenges Jesus faced in convincing certain individuals of His divine authority. The accusations of demonic influence and madness reveal the extent of opposition and disbelief.

References:
- Mark 3:21 - "And when his friends heard of it, they went out to lay hold on him: for they said, He is beside himself."
- Luke 8:49 - "While he yet spake, there cometh one from the ruler of the synagogue's house, saying to him, Thy daughter is dead; trouble not the Master."

Key Takeaway:
The accusations of having a devil and being mad illustrate the strong opposition Jesus faced from some individuals. This opposition goes beyond questioning His teachings and challenges His mental stability, emphasizing the deep resistance to accepting Him as a legitimate authority.

John 10:21 (King James Bible): "Others said, These are not the words of him that hath a devil. Can a devil open the eyes of the blind?"

Interpretation and Commentary:

In this verse, some people are expressing a different perspective regarding Jesus. They reject the idea that His words are the result of demonic influence and present a rhetorical question, emphasizing that the ability to open the eyes of the blind is inconsistent with demonic actions.

Key Points:

1. Divergent Opinions: The people are divided in their interpretations of Jesus' words and actions. While some accuse Him

of having a devil, others challenge this view, pointing to the benevolent miracles He performs, such as restoring sight to the blind.

2. Miracles as Evidence: The rhetorical question posed suggests that the ability to perform miracles, especially one as significant as restoring sight to the blind, contradicts the notion that Jesus is influenced by evil forces.

3. Critical Evaluation: This verse reflects the ongoing debate and critical evaluation of Jesus' identity among the people. His words and deeds prompt various reactions, and individuals grapple with understanding the source and nature of His authority.

References:
- Matthew 12:22 - "Then was brought unto him one possessed with a devil, blind, and dumb: and he healed him, insomuch that the blind and dumb both spake and saw."
- Luke 11:14 - "And he was casting out a devil, and it was dumb. And it came to pass, when the devil was gone out, the dumb spake; and the people wondered."

Key Takeaway:
This verse captures the diversity of opinions about Jesus, with some rejecting the idea that He is demon-possessed by highlighting His miraculous ability to heal, specifically citing the restoration of sight to the blind as evidence against such accusations.

John 10:22 (King James Bible): "And it was at Jerusalem the feast of the dedication, and it was winter."

Interpretation and Commentary:

In this verse, the setting is described as Jerusalem during the feast of the dedication, which is also known as Hanukkah. This festival is not one of the original Mosaic feasts but commemorates the rededication of the Second Temple after the Maccabean Revolt.

Key Points:

1. Feast of the Dedication (Hanukkah): The feast of the dedication was an annual celebration commemorating the rededication of the Second Temple in Jerusalem after it was desecrated by Antiochus IV Epiphanes. It is a festival of lights and is not part of the original set of feasts prescribed in the Mosaic Law.

2. Winter Setting: The mention of winter may serve both as a historical detail and a reminder of the cold season. It emphasizes the temporal context of the events described during this feast.

References:
- Hanukkah is historically documented in the Books of Maccabees, particularly 1 Maccabees 4:36-59.

Key Takeaway:
The verse sets the stage for the narrative by providing the context of the feast of the dedication in Jerusalem during winter. It hints at the historical and cultural backdrop of the events that follow, providing readers with a sense of the timing and setting.

John 10:23 (King James Bible): "And Jesus walked in the temple in Solomon's porch."

Interpretation and Commentary:

This verse describes Jesus walking in the temple, specifically in Solomon's porch. The setting is important as it places Jesus in a significant area of the temple complex.

Key Points:

1. Temple Setting: The temple was a central place for Jewish worship in Jerusalem. Jesus' presence in the temple signifies his engagement with the religious and spiritual life of the people.

2. Solomon's Porch: Solomon's porch was a covered colonnade or portico on the eastern side of the temple. It was a place where people gathered, and it held cultural and religious significance.

References:
- Solomon's porch is mentioned in other parts of the New Testament, such as Acts 3:11 and Acts 5:12.

Key Takeaway:
The verse illustrates Jesus' connection to the temple and his public presence in an area that held cultural and religious importance. It sets the stage for potential interactions and teachings within the temple complex.

John 10:24 (King James Bible): "Then came the Jews round about him, and said unto him, How long dost thou make us to doubt? If thou be the Christ, tell us plainly."

Interpretation and Commentary:

In this verse, the Jews confront Jesus with a direct question, expressing their frustration and desire for clarity regarding his identity.

Key Points:

1. Jews' Inquiry: The term "Jews" here likely refers to the religious leaders or a group of people who were questioning Jesus. They approached him, seeking a straightforward answer regarding his identity.

2. Seeking Clarity on Messiahship: The Jews ask Jesus to openly declare whether he is the Christ (Messiah). They express impatience and perhaps skepticism, wanting a clear and unambiguous response.

References:

- This interaction reflects the ongoing tension and questioning that Jesus faced from the religious authorities throughout the Gospel of John.

Key Takeaway:
The Jews' direct question highlights the central theme of Jesus' identity as the Messiah. Their request for a clear declaration reveals the anticipation and skepticism surrounding Jesus' claim to be the Christ.

John 10:25 (King James Bible): "Jesus answered them, I told you, and ye believed not: the works that I do in my Father's name, they bear witness of me."

Interpretation and Commentary:

In this verse, Jesus responds to the Jews' question about his identity, emphasizing the evidence of his works as a testimony to his divine nature.

Key Points:

1. Jesus' Previous Declarations: Jesus begins his response by stating that he has already told them about his identity, but they did not believe. This likely refers to his previous teachings and claims regarding his divine nature, including the use of titles such as the Son of God.

2. Works as Testimony: Jesus points to the works that he performs in his Father's name as evidence of his divine authority. Throughout the Gospel of John, Jesus performs miracles and acts of compassion, and these actions serve as a witness to his true identity.

References:
- Throughout the Gospel of John, Jesus emphasizes the importance of belief based on his teachings and miraculous works.

Key Takeaway:

Jesus asserts that his works, performed in alignment with the Father's name, serve as a compelling testimony to his divine nature. The emphasis is on the evidence provided through his actions, challenging the Jews to recognize the truth in what he has revealed.

John 10:26 (King James Bible): "But ye believe not, because ye are not of my sheep, as I said unto you."

Interpretation and Commentary:

Jesus continues to address the lack of belief among the Jews, attributing it to their not being among his sheep.

Key Points:

1. Unbelief Rooted in Identity: Jesus attributes the Jews' lack of belief to their identity, stating that they are not part of his sheep. This aligns with the metaphorical language used throughout the chapter, where Jesus is portrayed as the Good Shepherd and believers as his sheep.

2. Sheep as Symbol of Believers: In biblical imagery, sheep often symbolize believers or followers of God. Jesus, as the Good Shepherd, cares for and protects his sheep. The statement reinforces the idea that belief in Jesus is intricately linked to being part of his chosen followers.

References:
- Earlier in John 10, Jesus refers to himself as the Good Shepherd who knows his sheep, and they know him (John 10:14). This sets the context for the metaphorical language used in this verse.

Key Takeaway:
Jesus explains the root cause of the Jews' unbelief, tying it to their not being part of his chosen followers or "sheep." This reinforces the metaphor of Jesus as the caring and protective Shepherd, underscoring the intimate relationship between the Shepherd and his sheep, who recognize and follow his voice.

John 10:27 (King James Bible): "My sheep hear my voice, and I know them, and they follow me."

Interpretation and Commentary:

In this verse, Jesus emphasizes the unique relationship between himself and his followers, symbolized by the metaphor of sheep and a shepherd.

Key Points:

1. Sheep Hearing the Shepherd's Voice: The metaphorical language portrays believers as Jesus' sheep who have the ability to hear and recognize his voice. This signifies an intimate, personal connection between Jesus and his followers.

2. Mutual Knowledge: Jesus declares that he knows his sheep. This mutual knowledge suggests a deep and personal relationship, reinforcing the idea of a caring and attentive Shepherd who intimately knows each of his followers.

3. Following the Shepherd: The culmination of this relationship is seen in the sheep's response—they follow Jesus. This emphasizes the act of obedience and discipleship, where believers respond to the Shepherd's voice by following him.

References:
- The shepherd-sheep metaphor is consistent with Jesus' earlier statements in John 10, where he identifies himself as the Good Shepherd (John 10:11) who lays down his life for the sheep.

Key Takeaway:
This verse encapsulates the essence of the relationship between Jesus and his followers. Believers are portrayed as attentive sheep who recognize and respond to the voice of their Shepherd. The mutual knowledge and the act of following highlight the intimacy and obedience within this relationship.

John 10:28 (King James Bible): "And I give unto them eternal life, and they shall never perish, neither shall any man pluck them out of my hand."

Interpretation and Commentary:

In this verse, Jesus offers a profound assurance of security and eternal life to his followers.

Key Points:

1. Eternal Life as a Gift: Jesus declares that he gives his followers eternal life. This underscores the idea that salvation and the promise of life beyond this earthly existence are not earned but are graciously given by Jesus.

2. Unshakable Security: The statement "they shall never perish" emphasizes the unshakable nature of the eternal life provided by Jesus. This assurance counters the fear of losing one's salvation.

3. Unyielding Protection: Jesus employs the powerful imagery of holding his followers in his hand. This symbolizes the unyielding protection and care that believers receive from him. The phrase "neither shall any man pluck them out of my hand" reinforces the security and permanence of this protection.

References:
- This verse echoes themes of security and eternal life found elsewhere in the New Testament, emphasizing the unbreakable bond between believers and Christ.

Key Takeaway:
John 10:28 offers believers profound comfort by assuring them of the gift of eternal life, the security of their salvation, and the unyielding protection provided by Jesus. This verse encapsulates the unwavering nature of the relationship between Christ and his followers.

John 10:29 (King James Bible): "My Father, which gave them me, is greater than all; and no man is able to pluck them out of my Father's hand."

Interpretation and Commentary:

In this verse, Jesus emphasizes the secure foundation of the believers' eternal life by highlighting the greatness and protective power of God the Father.

Key Points:

1. Divine Endowment: Jesus affirms that the Father gave the believers to Him. This emphasizes the divine initiative in salvation, highlighting that it is God's gracious act that establishes and maintains the relationship between the believers and Jesus.

2. God's Sovereignty: The declaration "My Father, which gave them me, is greater than all" underscores the sovereignty and supremacy of God. No force or entity surpasses the authority and power of God, ensuring the safety of those entrusted to Jesus.

3. Unassailable Security: The phrase "no man is able to pluck them out of my Father's hand" reinforces the secure position of believers. It emphasizes the impossibility of any external force or influence separating believers from the protective and preserving hand of God.

References:
- Similar themes of divine sovereignty and security are echoed in various passages throughout the Bible, reinforcing the idea of God's unwavering protection over His people.

Key Takeaway:
John 10:29 provides a profound assurance of the unassailable security of believers. It emphasizes God's sovereignty, His role in initiating salvation, and the impenetrable protection that His hand

provides. This verse underscores the idea that once believers are in God's hands, nothing can snatch them away.

John 10:30 (King James Bible): "I and my Father are one."

Interpretation and Commentary:

This powerful statement by Jesus, "I and my Father are one," encapsulates the profound unity and oneness between Jesus and God the Father.

Key Points:

1. Divine Unity: Jesus asserts a oneness with the Father, highlighting the divine unity within the Godhead. This goes beyond a mere agreement or cooperation; it signifies a complete and intrinsic unity of essence and purpose.

2. Theological Implication: This statement has significant theological implications, affirming the concept of the Trinity—the Father, the Son (Jesus), and the Holy Spirit as one God in three persons. It underscores the mystery of the Godhead.

3. Equality with God: Jesus' declaration implies equality with God. The phrase "are one" indicates not only a shared purpose but an essential equality in divinity. It affirms that Jesus is not a created being but is co-equal with the Father.

References:
- The concept of the Trinity is reinforced in other parts of the Bible, such as Matthew 28:19 and 2 Corinthians 13:14.
- In John 14:9, Jesus says, "He that hath seen me hath seen the Father," further emphasizing the unity and equality between Himself and the Father.

Key Takeaway:
John 10:30 is a pivotal verse highlighting the inseparable unity between Jesus and the Father. It provides a glimpse into the divine

nature of Christ and affirms the foundational doctrine of the Trinity, illustrating the profound mystery of God's triune nature. This verse serves as a cornerstone for understanding Jesus' deity and equality with the Father.

John 10:31 (King James Bible): "Then the Jews took up stones again to stone him."

Interpretation and Commentary:

This verse marks a critical moment in the life of Jesus, illustrating the escalating tension between Him and the religious leaders.

Key Points:

1. Hostility of the Jews: The reaction of the Jews, taking up stones to stone Jesus, reflects their increasing hostility towards Him. Stoning was a punishment prescribed by Jewish law for blasphemy, and the Jews perceived Jesus' claim of oneness with the Father as blasphemous.

2. Rejection of Jesus' Claims: The Jews' response indicates their rejection of Jesus' divine claims. They considered His statements about His relationship with God to be offensive and contrary to their understanding of monotheism.

3. Fulfillment of Prophecy: Jesus' encounter with opposition, including threats of stoning, aligns with the broader narrative of His rejection and the fulfillment of prophetic scriptures (e.g., Psalm 118:22, Isaiah 53:3).

References:
- The threat of stoning for blasphemy is rooted in the Mosaic Law (Leviticus 24:16).
- Psalm 118:22 is quoted by Jesus in Matthew 21:42, foreshadowing His rejection.

- Isaiah 53:3 prophesies about the Messiah being despised and rejected.

Key Takeaway:
John 10:31 underscores the growing opposition to Jesus, culminating in a serious threat to His life. This event sets the stage for further conflict between Jesus and the religious authorities, ultimately leading to His crucifixion. It also emphasizes the fulfillment of prophecies regarding the rejection and suffering of the Messiah.

John 10:32 (King James Bible): "Jesus answered them, Many good works have I shewed you from my Father; for which of those works do ye stone me?"

Interpretation and Commentary:

In response to the Jews' threat to stone Him, Jesus confronts them with a question that challenges the basis of their hostility.

Key Points:

1. Appeal to Good Works: Jesus draws attention to the many good works He has performed, attributing them to His Father. These miracles and acts of compassion were visible demonstrations of divine power and love, illustrating the benevolence of God.

2. Implicit Rebuke: Jesus' question implicitly rebukes the Jews for their readiness to stone Him despite the evidence of His good works. He challenges them to consider the inconsistency of their actions in light of the compassionate and miraculous deeds He has carried out.

3. Invitation to Reflect: By asking, "For which of those works do ye stone me?" Jesus invites the Jews to reflect on the nature of His ministry and the undeniable goodness manifested in His actions. This challenges them to reconsider their hostile stance.

References:

- Jesus often performed miracles that demonstrated divine power and compassion (John 5:36; 9:1-7).

- The question echoes the theme of Jesus appealing to His works as a testimony to His identity and mission (John 5:36; 10:25, 38).

Key Takeaway:
John 10:32 highlights Jesus' defense against the threat of stoning by pointing to His benevolent and miraculous works. This challenges the Jews to confront the inconsistency of their intent to stone someone who has consistently demonstrated God's goodness. It reinforces the theme of Jesus' works as a powerful testimony to His divine nature and mission.

John 10:33 (King James Bible): "The Jews answered him, saying, For a good work we stone thee not; but for blasphemy; and because that thou, being a man, makest thyself God."

Interpretation and Commentary:

The Jews respond to Jesus, explaining the reason behind their threat to stone Him. Their objection is twofold, focusing on blasphemy and the claim of divinity.

Key Points:

1. Charge of Blasphemy: The Jews accuse Jesus of blasphemy, claiming that His statements and actions are disrespectful and offensive to God. Blasphemy, according to Jewish law, was a serious offense punishable by death.

2. Claim of Divinity: The second part of their objection addresses Jesus' assertion of divinity. They accuse Him of making Himself equal to God by identifying as the Son of God. The Jews, steeped in monotheistic beliefs, find this claim provocative and incompatible with their understanding of God's oneness.

3. Theological Tension: The confrontation highlights a deep theological tension. Jesus, by claiming a unique relationship with God, challenges the traditional Jewish understanding of God's nature. The Jews' reaction reveals their struggle to accept Jesus as more than a mere man.

References:
- The charge of blasphemy reflects the seriousness with which Jews treated offenses against God (Leviticus 24:16).
- Jesus' claim to be the Son of God and one with the Father is a recurring theme in the Gospel of John (John 5:18; 8:58; 14:9).

Key Takeaway:
John 10:33 unveils the core reasons behind the Jews' objection to Jesus, centering on charges of blasphemy and the perceived assertion of divinity. This encounter underscores the profound theological implications of Jesus' claims and the challenges they posed to the existing religious framework.

John 10:34 (King James Bible): "Jesus answered them, Is it not written in your law, I said, Ye are gods?"

Interpretation and Commentary:

In response to the Jews' accusation of blasphemy, Jesus refers to a scriptural passage, challenging them to reconsider their understanding.

Key Points:

1. Scriptural Reference: Jesus alludes to a passage from the Psalms, specifically Psalm 82:6. In this psalm, God addresses judges or rulers, calling them "gods" (elohim). Jesus uses this reference to argue that the term "gods" was applied to humans in the Scripture.

2. Context of Psalm 82: In Psalm 82, God stands in the divine assembly and rebukes the unjust judges, addressing them as "gods." Jesus draws attention to this use of the term, suggesting that if the

Scripture can refer to human judges as "gods," His claim to be the Son of God should not be considered blasphemy.

3. Argument for His Identity: Jesus, by invoking this scripture, makes a nuanced argument. If human judges could be called "gods" in a metaphorical sense, then His claim to be the Son of God should be understood in a higher, non-blasphemous sense, emphasizing His unique relationship with the Father.

References:
- Psalm 82:6 is a poetic passage where God addresses judges as "gods" (elohim).
- Jesus' reference underscores the importance of interpreting scripture in context and with sensitivity to metaphorical language.

Key Takeaway:
John 10:34 reveals Jesus' skillful use of scripture to engage in a theological discussion with the Jews. By referencing Psalm 82, He challenges them to reconsider the application of the term "gods" to humans in the Scriptures, thereby providing a foundation for His claims without compromising the reverence for God's oneness.

John 10:35 (King James Bible): "If he called them gods, unto whom the word of God came, and the scripture cannot be broken;"

Interpretation and Commentary:

In this verse, Jesus continues to elaborate on the concept of being called "gods," emphasizing the authority of the scripture and the unbreakable nature of God's Word.

Key Points:

1. Authority of the Word of God: Jesus acknowledges that the term "gods" was applied to those to whom the Word of God came. This suggests that individuals, such as the judges in Psalm 82, received a certain authority or divine commission.

2. Scripture Cannot be Broken: Jesus asserts the absolute reliability and authority of the scripture. The phrase "the scripture cannot be broken" emphasizes the enduring and unalterable nature of God's Word. It stands as a foundational principle in the discourse.

3. Logical Inference: By acknowledging the application of the term "gods" to those to whom the Word of God came, Jesus logically extends the argument. If the scripture itself refers to humans as "gods" in a certain context, then His claim to be the Son of God should be understood within a valid and scriptural framework.

References:
- Jesus builds on the reference to Psalm 82:6, where judges are called "gods" (elohim).
- The phrase "the scripture cannot be broken" emphasizes the enduring and authoritative nature of God's Word.

Key Takeaway:
John 10:35 reinforces Jesus' skillful use of scripture, pointing to the authority of the Word of God and asserting the unbreakable nature of the scripture. This serves as a foundation for His argument that if the scripture itself refers to humans as "gods" in certain contexts, then His claim to be the Son of God aligns with the revealed Word of God.

John 10:36 (King James Bible): "Say ye of him, whom the Father hath sanctified, and sent into the world, Thou blasphemest; because I said, I am the Son of God?"

Interpretation and Commentary:

In this verse, Jesus confronts the Jews who accuse Him of blasphemy for claiming to be the Son of God. He challenges them to consider the deeper significance of His statement, emphasizing His unique relationship with the Father.

Key Points:

1. Sanctified and Sent by the Father: Jesus asserts that He is the one "whom the Father hath sanctified, and sent into the world." This sanctification refers to being set apart or consecrated for a divine purpose. Jesus presents Himself as the one chosen and sent by the Father on a mission.

2. Accusation of Blasphemy: The Jews accuse Jesus of blasphemy for claiming to be the Son of God. Blasphemy, in their understanding, is the act of speaking sacrilegiously about God. Jesus challenges them to reconsider this accusation in light of the divine mission He claims to fulfill.

3. Understanding the Son of God: Jesus prompts a deeper reflection on the meaning of being the Son of God. He is not merely making a blasphemous claim but is highlighting a unique relationship with the Father that involves a divine mission and purpose.

References:
- The concept of being "sent" echoes the mission and purpose of Jesus in various passages.
- The accusation of blasphemy reflects the tension between Jesus and religious authorities.

Key Takeaway:
John 10:36 underscores Jesus' divine mission and challenges the accusations of blasphemy. He invites a deeper understanding of His claim to be the Son of God, emphasizing the sanctification by the Father and the purpose for which He was sent into the world. This sets the stage for a profound exploration of Jesus' unique identity and mission.

John 10:37 (King James Bible): "If I do not the works of my Father, believe me not."

Interpretation and Commentary:

In this verse, Jesus appeals to the evidence of His actions as a basis for belief. He asserts that if He does not perform the works consistent with the Father's nature, then skepticism is warranted.

Key Points:

1. Works as Evidence: Jesus places great significance on His actions, referring to them as the "works of my Father." Throughout the Gospel of John, Jesus performs miracles and acts of compassion that reveal the character and power of God.

2. Conditional Belief: Jesus introduces a conditional statement, stating that if His works do not align with the Father's, then there is no obligation to believe in Him. This underscores the connection between His deeds and His divine identity.

References:
- Throughout the Gospel of John, Jesus performs various miracles, such as healing the sick and feeding the multitude, as signs of His divine authority.

Key Takeaway:
John 10:37 emphasizes the evidential aspect of Jesus' works. He invites people to evaluate His actions, framing belief as contingent on the alignment of His deeds with the character and nature of the Father. This underscores the importance of the miraculous works as a testimony to His divine identity.

John 10:38 (King James Bible): "But if I do, though ye believe not me, believe the works: that ye may know, and believe, that the Father is in me, and I in him."

Interpretation and Commentary:

In this verse, Jesus continues to emphasize the relationship between His works and His divine identity. He acknowledges that even if the people struggle to believe His words, they should believe in the evidence of His miraculous works. The ultimate purpose is for them to recognize and believe in the profound unity between the Father and Himself.

Key Points:

1. Belief Through Works: Jesus acknowledges that belief can be anchored in the tangible evidence of His miraculous works. Even if people find His words challenging, the transformative nature of His deeds should serve as a compelling reason to believe.

2. Unity with the Father: The verse conveys a deep theological truth about the unity between Jesus and the Father. Jesus asserts that through belief in His works, people can come to understand and acknowledge the profound union between Himself and the Father.

References:
- Throughout the Gospel of John, Jesus performs miracles, such as healing the sick, giving sight to the blind, and raising the dead, demonstrating His divine authority and power.

Key Takeaway:
John 10:38 emphasizes the persuasive power of Jesus' miraculous works as a basis for belief. Jesus invites people to look beyond His words to the transformative impact of His deeds, ultimately leading to a recognition of the intimate connection between Him and the Father.

John 10:39 (King James Bible): "Therefore they sought again to take him: but he escaped out of their hand."

Interpretation and Commentary:

This verse narrates the reaction of the people to Jesus' statement in the previous verse. In response to His assertion about the unity with the Father, the people sought once again to apprehend Him. Despite their attempts, Jesus managed to elude their grasp, highlighting His authority over the situation and the timing of His eventual sacrifice.

Key Points:

1. Resistance to Jesus' Claims: The people's reaction reflects their continued resistance to Jesus' claims of divinity. His statements challenged their understanding, leading to a hostile response and an attempt to seize Him.

2. Divine Authority: Jesus' ability to escape from their hands underscores His divine authority and control over the unfolding events. It emphasizes that His arrest and sacrifice would occur according to God's plan and timing.

References:
 - This verse is part of the ongoing narrative in which Jesus engages with the religious leaders and the people, revealing His identity and purpose.

Key Takeaway:
John 10:39 captures the tension between Jesus and those who opposed His claims. Despite their attempts to apprehend Him, Jesus eludes them, illustrating His divine authority and the fulfillment of God's plan in His redemptive mission.

John 10:40 (King James Bible): "And went away again beyond Jordan into the place where John at first baptized; and there he abode."

Interpretation and Commentary:

Following the unsuccessful attempt to seize Jesus, this verse reveals that He withdrew to an area beyond the Jordan River, returning to the place where John the Baptist initially baptized. By choosing this location, Jesus might have sought a quieter and less confrontational setting. His decision to stay there suggests a deliberate choice to continue His ministry in a region associated with John's earlier activities.

Key Points:

1. Strategic Withdrawal: Jesus' move beyond the Jordan reflects a strategic withdrawal from the heightened opposition in Jerusalem. It allows Him to continue His mission in a different context, demonstrating prudence in His ministry approach.

2. Connection to John the Baptist: Returning to the place of John's baptisms may signify a connection to John's earlier ministry and a continuation of the message of repentance and the Kingdom of God.

3. Teaching and Ministry: Despite the challenges, Jesus remains engaged in teaching and ministering to those who would seek Him in this new location.

References:
- This verse contributes to the narrative of Jesus' movements and interactions, highlighting His strategic decisions in response to opposition.

Key Takeaway:
John 10:40 depicts Jesus' strategic withdrawal from Jerusalem to an area beyond the Jordan. This move allows Him to continue His ministry in a different setting, possibly emphasizing the continuity with John the Baptist's message and avoiding immediate confrontation with those who sought to apprehend Him.

John 10:41 (King James Bible): "And many resorted unto him, and said, John did no miracle: but all things that John spake of this man were true."

Interpretation and Commentary:

This verse highlights the response of the people who gathered around Jesus. Many of them acknowledged that John the Baptist had not performed miracles, but everything he had spoken about Jesus was true. The focus shifts from miraculous signs to the fulfillment of John's words, emphasizing the credibility of John's testimony.

Key Points:

1. John's Authenticity: The people recognize John's authenticity as a prophet. They acknowledge that he didn't perform miracles like Jesus, but his words about Jesus were accurate.

2. Fulfillment of Prophecy: This verse underscores the fulfillment of John's prophetic statements about Jesus. It strengthens the connection between John's ministry and the person of Jesus.

3. Significance of Truth: The emphasis on truth in John's words points to the reliability of the message. Even without miraculous signs, John's testimony holds weight because it aligns with the reality of who Jesus is.

References:
- This verse reinforces the authenticity of John the Baptist's testimony and underscores the reliability of his words regarding Jesus.

Key Takeaway:
John 10:41 emphasizes the people's recognition of John the Baptist's authenticity as a prophet. Although John did not perform miracles, his truthful statements about Jesus were being validated as the people witnessed the unfolding of events in Jesus' ministry. This reinforces the credibility and accuracy of John's prophetic role in preparing the way for the Messiah.

John 10:42 (King James Bible): "And many believed on him there."

Interpretation and Commentary:

The concluding verse of John 10 summarizes the impact of Jesus' presence in that place. Many individuals came to believe in Him.

This verse encapsulates the transformative power of encountering Jesus – a theme that resonates throughout the Gospel of John.

Key Points:

1. Conversion and Faith: The phrase "many believed on him" signifies a significant response to Jesus' teachings and presence. It reflects a transformative shift in the hearts and minds of those who encountered Him.

2. Location's Significance: The mention of "there" highlights the specific place where this belief took root. The location serves as a backdrop for the spiritual transformation and conversion of the people.

3. Continuation of Themes: The belief mentioned here aligns with the overarching theme of belief and faith found throughout the Gospel of John. It reinforces the idea that encountering Jesus leads to a profound change in one's spiritual disposition.

References:
- This verse echoes the ongoing theme of belief in the Gospel of John, emphasizing the transformative power of encountering Jesus.

Key Takeaway:
John 10:42 succinctly captures the transformative impact of Jesus' presence in a specific location. The belief that many individuals placed in Him signifies a shift in their understanding and acceptance of His teachings. This verse serves as a culmination of the themes of belief and faith that are central to the Gospel of John, reinforcing the idea that encountering Jesus brings about a profound spiritual transformation.

CHAPTER ELEVEN
The Death of Lazarus
I Am the Resurrection and the Life

John 11:1 (KJV)

"Now a certain man was sick, named Lazarus, of Bethany, the town of Mary and her sister Martha."

Exposition:

In this opening verse, we are introduced to Lazarus, a man who is unwell. The mention of Bethany, the hometown of Mary and Martha, sets the stage for the significant events that will unfold. It's worth noting that these three individuals are close friends of Jesus, and their relationship adds depth to the upcoming narrative.

Commentary:

The use of the term "sick" emphasizes Lazarus's condition, indicating a serious illness. This sets the scene for the miraculous event that will follow, highlighting the power of Jesus over sickness and death. The choice of Bethany as the setting is significant; it was a place where Jesus found friendship and solace.

As we delve into this chapter, we'll witness not only the unfolding of a miraculous resurrection but also the deep emotions, faith, and profound teachings that characterize the interactions between Jesus and those around Him. The unfolding narrative in John 11 will reveal layers of meaning, emphasizing themes of faith, life, death, and the glory of God.

John 11:2 (KJV)

"(It was that Mary which anointed the Lord with ointment, and wiped his feet with her hair, whose brother Lazarus was sick.)"

Exposition:

This verse provides additional information about Mary, referencing a past event where she anointed Jesus with costly ointment and wiped His feet with her hair. The connection is made clear that Mary, the sister of Lazarus, is the one facing the current trial of her brother's illness.

Commentary:

The mention of Mary's act of anointing Jesus with expensive ointment and wiping His feet with her hair refers to an incident recorded in Luke 7:36-50 and Matthew 26:6-13. This act symbolizes deep reverence, love, and humility towards Jesus. The use of this reference serves to highlight the close relationship between Jesus and the family of Lazarus, emphasizing their devotion and intimacy with the Lord.

As we move forward in this chapter, the background information about Mary's previous interaction with Jesus adds emotional weight to the impending situation. The connection between Mary, the anointing, and Lazarus's illness sets the stage for a powerful display of Jesus's compassion and authority over life and death. The narrative invites readers to reflect on the intertwining themes of faith, love, and the divine purpose that will unfold in the subsequent verses.

John 11:3 (KJV)
"Therefore his sisters sent unto him, saying, Lord, behold, he whom thou lovest is sick."

Exposition:
Lazarus's sisters, Mary and Martha, send a message to Jesus informing Him of their brother's sickness. Their message underscores the close relationship they share with Jesus and the implicit request for His intervention.

Commentary:
The sisters' message is a poignant expression of both urgency and faith. Their appeal begins with a humble acknowledgment of Jesus as "Lord," recognizing His authority and sovereignty. The phrase "he whom thou lovest is sick" reflects not only the gravity of Lazarus's condition but also the sisters' confidence in Jesus's love and healing power.

This verse lays the groundwork for Jesus's response, revealing the intricate dynamics of love, faith, and divine timing. The sisters' approach exemplifies a model of bringing concerns to the Lord, recognizing His love and authority even in the face of challenging circumstances.

As readers, we are prompted to consider our own approach to God in times of distress, acknowledging His love and authority while trusting in His perfect timing and wisdom. This verse sets the stage for the unfolding drama of resurrection, reinforcing themes of trust, faith, and the profound love Jesus has for those who believe in Him.

John 11:4 (KJV)
"When Jesus heard that, he said, This sickness is not unto death, but for the glory of God, that the Son of God might be glorified thereby."

Exposition:
Upon receiving the message about Lazarus's sickness, Jesus responds with a proclamation regarding the purpose of this illness. He declares that it is not unto death but for the glory of God, ultimately leading to the glorification of the Son of God.

Commentary:
Jesus's statement carries profound significance. By asserting that Lazarus's sickness is "not unto death," Jesus is foreshadowing the miraculous event to come—Lazarus's resurrection. This highlights Jesus's foreknowledge and control over the situation. The purpose assigned to the sickness is pivotal: it is for the glory of God.

The divine purpose behind Lazarus's illness points to a deeper reality—God's redemptive plan through Christ. The forthcoming miracle will not only showcase Jesus's power over death but also reveal the glory of God through the resurrection. The ultimate aim is to bring honor and praise to the Son of God.

This verse invites readers to reflect on the broader context of suffering, recognizing that even in challenging circumstances, God's glory can be manifested. Jesus's words pave the way for a profound demonstration of His authority over life and death, reinforcing themes of divine purpose, faith, and the glorification of the Son of God.

John 11:5 (KJV)
"Now Jesus loved Martha, and her sister, and Lazarus."

Exposition:
This verse explicitly states Jesus's love for Martha, her sister Mary, and Lazarus. The emphasis on love reinforces the deep, personal connection between Jesus and this family.

Commentary:
The brevity of this verse carries profound meaning. In the midst of impending events, it serves as a reminder of Jesus's genuine and affectionate relationship with those around Him. The explicit mention of His love for Martha, Mary, and Lazarus foreshadows the compassion and empathy He will demonstrate in the face of Lazarus's death.

The knowledge of Jesus's love provides comfort and assurance, especially in times of trial. It sets the tone for the forthcoming miraculous intervention, highlighting the intertwining themes of love, faith, and divine purpose. The narrative unfolding in John 11 showcases not only the power of Christ but also His tender care for individuals who hold a special place in His heart.

As readers, we are invited to contemplate the depth of Jesus's love in our own lives, recognizing that His affection extends to each of us individually. This verse serves as a poignant reminder of the personal nature of our relationship with Christ, reinforcing the central theme of love that permeates the Gospel narrative.

John 11:6 (KJV)
"When he had heard therefore that he was sick, he abode two days still in the same place where he was."

Exposition:
Upon receiving the news of Lazarus's illness, Jesus makes a deliberate decision to stay in the same place for two additional days.

This action may seem puzzling at first, but it sets the stage for a miraculous demonstration of His power.

Commentary:
Jesus's choice to remain in the same location for two days raises questions about His apparent delay in responding to the urgent situation. However, this delay serves a purpose in the divine plan. Jesus, in His wisdom, allows Lazarus's condition to progress to a point where human intervention is futile. This intentional delay is a key element in the unfolding narrative, showcasing Jesus's authority over life and death.

The delay also reinforces the overarching theme of divine timing. By waiting, Jesus magnifies the significance of the impending miracle. It underscores that what follows is not a mere healing but a resurrection, an act that transcends human limitations.

As readers, we are prompted to reflect on our own experiences of waiting on God's timing and trusting in His sovereign plan. This verse challenges us to recognize that, even in apparent delays, God's purposes are at work, leading to outcomes that ultimately bring glory to Him. The deliberate pause before the miracle in John 11 serves as a powerful lesson in trusting God's timing and acknowledging His higher ways.

John 11:7 (KJV)
"Then after that saith he to his disciples, Let us go into Judaea again."

Exposition:
Following the two-day delay, Jesus speaks to His disciples, expressing the intention to return to Judaea. This decision signifies a significant shift in the narrative, as Judaea is the region where Bethany, the home of Lazarus, Mary, and Martha, is located.

Commentary:
Jesus's announcement to go to Judaea raises awareness among the disciples about the gravity of the situation. Judaea is not only the

place where Jesus had recently faced opposition and danger (see John 10:31-39) but also where the news of Lazarus's sickness had reached Him.

This decision to return to Judaea is a courageous and purposeful move. It demonstrates Jesus's commitment to fulfilling the divine plan despite potential risks. The disciples' reaction and subsequent events in Judaea will further unfold the themes of faith, trust, and the inevitability of divine purpose.

As readers, we are invited to consider the significance of Jesus's deliberate actions and decisions. His journey into Judaea reflects a determination to confront challenges head-on and fulfill His mission, ultimately leading to the manifestation of God's glory. This verse prompts reflection on our own willingness to follow Jesus into uncertain or challenging situations, trusting in His guidance and purpose.

John 11:8 (KJV)
"His disciples say unto him, Master, the Jews of late sought to stone thee, and goest thou thither again?"

Exposition:
The disciples express concern and caution to Jesus, reminding Him of the recent threat on His life in Judaea. They question the wisdom of returning to a place where hostility and danger awaited Him.

Commentary:
The disciples' response reflects their human perspective and concern for Jesus's safety. The mention of the Jews seeking to stone Him refers to the previous hostility in Judaea (see John 10:31). The disciples, in their limited understanding, are troubled by the idea of Jesus willingly going back to a potentially perilous situation.

This interaction unveils the tension between human reasoning and divine purpose. While the disciples focus on the immediate threat, Jesus sees beyond the dangers, guided by a higher plan. It sets the stage for Jesus to impart deeper truths about spiritual vision, faith, and the importance of walking in the light of God's appointed time.

As readers, we are reminded of the challenges that may arise when following Jesus. This verse prompts reflection on our own responses to uncertainty and potential difficulties, encouraging us to trust in the wisdom of God's plan even when it surpasses our understanding. The dialogue between Jesus and His disciples serves as a lesson in faith and the necessity of aligning our perspectives with God's purpose.

John 11:9 (KJV)
"Jesus answered, Are there not twelve hours in the day? If any man walk in the day, he stumbleth not, because he seeth the light of this world."

Exposition:
Jesus responds to the disciples' concerns by using metaphorical language related to the concept of daylight. He emphasizes that those who walk in the day, guided by the light, do not stumble.

Commentary:
Jesus employs the metaphor of daylight to convey spiritual truths. The twelve hours in the day symbolize the time allotted for His earthly ministry, emphasizing the importance of walking in alignment with God's plan within the designated timeframe. The metaphorical use of "day" suggests a period of opportunity and divine purpose.

The statement, "he seeth the light of this world," signifies those who follow Christ and adhere to God's guidance. It implies spiritual insight and understanding that comes from walking in the light of Christ's teachings.

This response serves to reassure the disciples and, by extension, all believers, that when they align themselves with God's plan and follow Jesus, they will not stumble in the darkness of worldly concerns or fears. It underscores the idea that there is a divine order and purpose even in the face of potential challenges.

As readers, we are encouraged to consider our own walk with Christ, recognizing the importance of spiritual insight and alignment with God's timing. The metaphor of daylight prompts reflection on our dependence on the light of Christ to navigate life's journey without stumbling in the darkness of doubt or fear.

John 11:10 (KJV)
"But if a man walk in the night, he stumbleth, because there is no light in him."

Exposition:
Continuing with the metaphor of walking, Jesus contrasts walking in the day with walking in the night. He highlights that stumbling occurs when one walks in the night due to the absence of light.

Commentary:
In this metaphorical language, Jesus draws a clear distinction between those who align with the light of God's purpose and those who walk in spiritual darkness. The night symbolizes a state of spiritual ignorance, separation from God's guidance, and a lack of understanding.

The statement "he stumbleth because there is no light in him" underscores the consequences of navigating life without the divine illumination provided by Christ. Stumbling represents the pitfalls, errors, and challenges that arise when individuals operate without the spiritual insight that comes from a relationship with God.

This verse serves as a call to embrace the light of Christ, emphasizing the importance of spiritual understanding in navigating life's journey. It echoes the broader theme found in the Gospel of John, where Jesus is portrayed as the light that dispels darkness and guides believers on the path of righteousness.

As readers, we are prompted to examine our own spiritual walk and consider the significance of aligning with the light of Christ. The metaphor invites reflection on the consequences of spiritual darkness and the assurance that walking in the light brings clarity, direction, and protection from stumbling in life's challenges.

John 11:11 (KJV)
"These things said he: and after that he saith unto them, Our friend Lazarus sleepeth; but I go, that I may awake him out of sleep."

Exposition:
Following the metaphorical discussion about walking in the day and night, Jesus addresses the disciples directly, stating that Lazarus is asleep. However, He clarifies that He intends to go to awaken Lazarus from his sleep.

Commentary:
The use of the term "sleepeth" is a metaphor employed by Jesus to describe Lazarus's death. This metaphor is significant because it reflects the temporary nature of death for believers. Sleep, in this context, conveys the idea of rest and a future awakening rather than a permanent state.

Jesus's statement about waking Lazarus emphasizes His authority over death. He frames the upcoming events not as a tragic ending but as a temporary rest from which Lazarus will be awakened. This sets the stage for one of the most remarkable miracles in the Gospels—the resurrection of Lazarus.

The use of the term "Our friend" adds a personal touch to the narrative, highlighting the emotional connection Jesus has with Lazarus. The unfolding events will not only showcase Jesus's divine power but also His compassion and personal investment in the lives of those He loves.

As readers, we are invited to reflect on the profound truth of resurrection and the hope that Jesus brings even in the face of death. The term "sleep" challenges our understanding of mortality and points to the eternal perspective that Christ offers. This verse sets the tone for the climactic moment when Jesus will demonstrate His authority over death, affirming His role as the Resurrection and the Life (John 11:25).

John 11:12 (KJV)
"Then said his disciples, Lord, if he sleep, he shall do well."

Exposition:
The disciples, misunderstanding Jesus's metaphor, interpret Lazarus's sleep as beneficial, thinking that rest would contribute to his recovery.

Commentary:
The disciples' response reflects a common human interpretation of Jesus's figurative language. They assume that Lazarus's physical rest is a positive sign for his health, not realizing that Jesus was speaking of death in symbolic terms.

This interaction highlights the challenge of grasping spiritual truths using earthly perspectives. The disciples, like many throughout history, struggle to understand the deeper spiritual meanings Jesus often conveys. Their well-intentioned response reveals their limited comprehension of the imminent miraculous event.

This moment serves as a reminder that spiritual discernment requires openness to the symbolic language used by Jesus. It also sets the stage for Jesus to clarify and reveal the true nature of Lazarus's condition, leading to a profound revelation of His power over death.

As readers, we are encouraged to approach the teachings of Jesus with humility and a willingness to seek deeper understanding. The disciples' initial misunderstanding prompts us to reflect on our own perceptions of spiritual matters and underscores the importance of allowing Jesus to illuminate the true meanings behind His words.

John 11:13 (KJV)

"Howbeit Jesus spake of his death: but they thought that he had spoken of taking of rest in sleep."

Exposition:
This verse explicitly clarifies the misunderstanding between Jesus and the disciples. Jesus had been referring to Lazarus's death, but the disciples, in their limited understanding, interpreted it as a reference to physical rest during sleep.

Commentary:
The verse highlights the communication gap between Jesus and His disciples. Jesus, using metaphorical language, was addressing the spiritual reality of Lazarus's death, emphasizing the temporary nature of it. However, the disciples, grounded in their earthly perspectives, took His words literally, thinking of ordinary sleep.

This misinterpretation sets the stage for Jesus to provide further clarification and reveal the miraculous event that is about to unfold. The disciples' struggle to grasp the deeper spiritual meaning of Jesus's words is a common theme throughout the Gospels, showcasing the ongoing process of their spiritual growth and understanding.

This moment invites readers to consider the challenges of bridging the gap between divine truths and human comprehension. It emphasizes the need for spiritual insight and the guidance of the Holy Spirit to discern the profound teachings of Jesus. As the narrative unfolds, the disciples will witness not only the clarification of Jesus's metaphor but also the manifestation of His power over death, reinforcing the transformative nature of their journey with Him.

John 11:14 (KJV)
"Then said Jesus unto them plainly, Lazarus is dead."

Exposition:
In response to the disciples' misunderstanding, Jesus dispels any ambiguity and speaks directly, declaring the plain reality: Lazarus has died.

Commentary:
Jesus's straightforward statement serves as a pivotal moment in the narrative. He moves from metaphorical language to a clear declaration of Lazarus's death, eliminating any room for further misunderstanding. This moment marks a shift in the discourse, emphasizing the gravity of the situation and preparing the disciples for the extraordinary miracle that will follow.

The directness of Jesus's words underscores His transparency with the disciples. It reflects His desire for them to fully comprehend the magnitude of what is about to happen. This revelation of Lazarus's death sets the stage for Jesus to demonstrate His authority over death and solidifies the context for the upcoming miracle.

As readers, we are reminded of the necessity of clarity in understanding spiritual truths. Jesus's plain declaration prompts us to confront the harsh reality of death while simultaneously anticipating the miraculous intervention that will follow. The verse invites reflection on the straightforward nature of Christ's teachings and the transformative power that comes when we face truth with faith in His ability to bring life even in the face of death.

John 11:15 (KJV)
"And I am glad for your sakes that I was not there, to the intent ye may believe; nevertheless let us go unto him."

Exposition:
Jesus, after declaring Lazarus's death, expresses a unique perspective—He is glad that He was not present when Lazarus fell ill. He explains that this circumstance is for the disciples' benefit, intending to strengthen their faith.

Commentary:
Jesus's statement might seem paradoxical at first. Why would He be glad about not being there for Lazarus? The answer lies in His desire to cultivate a deeper faith in His disciples. By allowing Lazarus

to die and then raising him from the dead, Jesus provides a tangible and undeniable demonstration of His power over death.

The phrase "to the intent ye may believe" underscores the purpose behind this specific sequence of events. Jesus is orchestrating a situation that will profoundly impact the disciples' faith. Their belief will not be based solely on what they've seen before, such as healings, but on a resurrection—a miraculous act that transcends their previous experiences.

"Nevertheless let us go unto him" shows Jesus's resolve to go to Bethany despite the challenges and potential dangers. It emphasizes His commitment to fulfilling the Father's will and reinforces the narrative's overarching theme of divine timing and purpose.

As readers, we are encouraged to reflect on the role of faith in our own journeys with Christ. Jesus's intentional actions challenge us to trust in His wisdom, even when circumstances seem perplexing, and to recognize that challenges can be opportunities for our faith to deepen and mature.

John 11:16 (KJV)
"Then said Thomas, which is called Didymus, unto his fellow disciples, Let us also go, that we may die with him."

Exposition:
Thomas, often remembered as "Doubting Thomas," responds to Jesus's decision to go to Bethany by urging the other disciples to accompany Jesus, expressing a willingness to face potential danger, even death.

Commentary:
Thomas's statement reflects a mixture of loyalty, courage, and perhaps a sense of resignation. His nickname "Didymus" means "twin," and this episode provides a glimpse into his character. While he is often remembered for doubting the resurrection (John 20:24-29), here he displays a readiness to face potential threats alongside Jesus.

Thomas's words convey a sense of loyalty and commitment. Despite the danger they perceive in returning to Judaea, he is determined to stand by Jesus. His willingness to go and potentially die with Jesus reveals a level of devotion and solidarity with the Master, even in the face of uncertainty.

This verse highlights the diversity of responses among the disciples. While Thomas expresses a courageous commitment, others might have been more apprehensive. The disciples' varied reactions mirror the complexities of human responses to challenges and uncertainties, illustrating the ongoing process of their spiritual growth.

As readers, we can find resonance with Thomas's mix of loyalty and realism. It prompts us to consider our own responses to challenges and uncertainties in our walk with Christ. The episode sets the stage for the unfolding drama in Bethany, where the disciples will witness not only the power of resurrection but also a deepening understanding of Jesus's mission and identity.

John 11:17 (KJV)
"Then when Jesus came, he found that he had lain in the grave four days already."

Exposition:
Upon arriving in Bethany, Jesus discovers that Lazarus has been in the tomb for four days, emphasizing the significance of the situation.

Commentary:
The mention of four days is crucial in understanding the unfolding miracle. In Jewish tradition, it was believed that the soul lingered near the body for three days after death, and then decomposition would begin. By waiting four days, Jesus intentionally allows for a situation where the miracle would be beyond any doubt, emphasizing the complete and irreversible nature of death.

This deliberate delay further accentuates the miraculous nature of what is about to happen. The decay process would have started, and any hope of a natural recovery would be eliminated. The circumstances surrounding Lazarus's death become a canvas upon which Jesus will paint a powerful picture of resurrection and life.

This verse invites readers to ponder the significance of divine timing. Jesus's actions are purposeful, and the waiting period amplifies the magnitude of the upcoming miracle. The narrative encourages us to trust in God's timing even when circumstances seem bleak, knowing that His plan encompasses a broader perspective that goes beyond immediate understanding.

John 11:18 (KJV)
"Now Bethany was nigh unto Jerusalem, about fifteen furlongs off."

Exposition:
This verse provides geographical context, indicating that Bethany is close to Jerusalem, approximately fifteen furlongs (about two miles) away.

Commentary:
The proximity of Bethany to Jerusalem is significant for several reasons. Firstly, it underscores the potential danger and opposition Jesus might face, as Jerusalem was a place where religious leaders had sought to stone Him (John 10:31). Secondly, it highlights the accessibility of Bethany to people from Jerusalem, setting the stage for the large crowd that will gather to witness the miraculous event.

The mention of the distance in furlongs serves to emphasize the close connection between Bethany and the religious center of Jerusalem. This geographical detail contributes to the unfolding tension in the narrative, foreshadowing the heightened scrutiny and challenges that Jesus will face.

As readers, we are prompted to consider the strategic nature of Jesus's actions. His decision to approach Bethany, near Jerusalem, further amplifies the significance of the upcoming miracle, taking place in a location where both supporters and skeptics could witness the power of God. The verse invites reflection on the broader context and implications of Jesus's ministry as He moves toward Jerusalem, a journey that will lead to His own ultimate confrontation with death and victory over it.

John 11:19 (KJV)
"And many of the Jews came to Martha and Mary, to comfort them concerning their brother."

Exposition:
A multitude of Jewish people come to offer comfort to Martha and Mary following the death of their brother Lazarus.

Commentary:
This verse sets the scene for the communal response to Lazarus's death. The presence of many Jews reflects the support system and cultural practices of mourning during that time. It was customary for people to gather and offer condolences to the bereaved family.

The fact that people came to comfort Martha and Mary highlights the community's awareness of their close relationship with Jesus and the significance of Lazarus's death. The mourning process in this context is communal, emphasizing shared grief and the importance of community support during times of loss.

As the narrative progresses, the presence of this gathering becomes instrumental in the unfolding miracle. The people who are there to mourn Lazarus will witness firsthand the extraordinary power of Jesus over death, contributing to the broader impact and understanding of His divine authority.

This verse prompts reflection on the communal aspects of grief and support in times of loss. It also foreshadows the public nature of the miracle that is about to take place, underlining the broader implications of Jesus's actions beyond the immediate circle of Martha and Mary.

John 11:20 (KJV)
"Then Martha, as soon as she heard that Jesus was coming, went and met him: but Mary sat still in the house."

Exposition:
Upon hearing that Jesus was approaching, Martha is proactive and goes out to meet Him, while Mary remains at home.

Commentary:
Martha's swift response reflects her proactive and assertive personality, as seen in Luke 10:38-42 where she is busy serving while Mary sits at Jesus's feet. In this context, her decision to meet Jesus suggests a mix of grief, urgency, and perhaps a desire to seek comfort or understanding from Him.

On the other hand, Mary's decision to remain in the house may indicate a deeper emotional struggle or a different approach to coping with grief. It sets the stage for a poignant encounter between Mary and Jesus later in the chapter, revealing the unique dynamics of the sisters' relationship with Jesus.

This verse invites readers to consider the diverse ways people respond to grief and seek solace. Martha's proactive approach contrasts with Mary's initial hesitation. Both responses are valid expressions of grief, and the narrative will unfold to showcase Jesus's understanding and compassion toward each sister in their distinct emotional states.

As the story progresses, Martha's encounter with Jesus will lead to a profound theological discussion, highlighting her faith, while Mary's later interaction with Jesus will reveal deep emotions and the compassionate response of Christ to individual needs. This verse sets the stage for the nuanced exploration of grief, faith, and personal encounters with Jesus in the following verses.

John 11:21 (KJV)
"Then said Martha unto Jesus, Lord, if thou hadst been here, my brother had not died."

Exposition:
Martha, upon meeting Jesus, expresses a mix of faith and lamentation, acknowledging her belief in Jesus's ability to prevent Lazarus's death had He been present.

Commentary:
Martha's statement reflects a complex blend of faith and sorrow. While expressing confidence in Jesus's power to heal, she also reveals a sense of disappointment or questioning regarding His absence during Lazarus's illness and subsequent death.

Her words echo a sentiment shared by Mary when she later meets Jesus (John 11:32). Both sisters convey a profound trust in Jesus's healing abilities, yet their grief is intertwined with a degree of confusion about the timing of His arrival.

Martha's statement becomes a pivotal moment in the narrative, setting the stage for Jesus to reveal His identity as the Resurrection and the Life (John 11:25). Her faith, though tinged with sorrow and questioning, creates a space for Jesus to demonstrate His power in a way that transcends immediate expectations.

As readers, we can empathize with Martha's complex emotions. Her honesty and vulnerability pave the way for a deeper revelation of Christ's nature and purpose. This verse prompts reflection on our own responses to God's timing, acknowledging that even in moments of confusion or grief, Jesus invites us to trust in His ability to bring life out of death.

John 11:22 (KJV)
"But I know, that even now, whatsoever thou wilt ask of God, God will give it thee."

Exposition:
Martha, despite her expression of grief and questioning, acknowledges her faith in Jesus's relationship with God. She believes that God will grant whatever Jesus asks.

Commentary:
Martha's statement reveals a deep conviction in Jesus's connection with God and His divine authority. While grappling with the reality of Lazarus's death, she holds on to the belief that Jesus has a unique and direct channel to God. Her words express a resilient faith, recognizing Jesus's ability to intercede with God on behalf of her brother.

This declaration by Martha sets the stage for Jesus to affirm His role as the Resurrection and the Life. It demonstrates her understanding that Jesus possesses the authority not only to heal but also to bring about a transformation that goes beyond conventional expectations.

Martha's faith, though tested by grief and the apparent delay in Jesus's arrival, becomes a catalyst for a significant revelation. Jesus will use this moment to deepen her understanding of His identity and mission.

As readers, we are prompted to consider the nature of our own faith in times of challenge and sorrow. Martha's acknowledgment of Jesus's relationship with God encourages us to trust in the intercessory power of Christ, recognizing that He holds the authority to bring about transformative outcomes even in situations that seem beyond hope.

John 11:23 (KJV)
"Jesus saith unto her, Thy brother shall rise again."

Exposition:
In response to Martha's expression of faith, Jesus provides a direct and comforting assurance that her brother, Lazarus, will experience resurrection.

Commentary:
Jesus's statement is a pivotal moment in the narrative, as it lays the foundation for a profound revelation about His identity and

authority over death. By declaring, "Thy brother shall rise again," Jesus addresses Martha's faith and grief simultaneously. His words offer immediate comfort while pointing to a deeper reality that transcends the present circumstances.

This initial statement sets the stage for a more extended conversation about resurrection, leading to one of the most significant declarations in the Gospel of John—Jesus's proclamation, "I am the resurrection and the life" (John 11:25). Jesus uses this moment not only to assure Martha of Lazarus's resurrection but also to reveal His divine nature and role in the broader scheme of salvation.

As readers, we are invited to reflect on the assurance of resurrection that Jesus extends to believers. His words challenge us to embrace a perspective beyond the immediate challenges and losses we face, trusting in the promise of eternal life. The unfolding dialogue between Jesus and Martha will further illuminate the transformative power of faith and the profound truths that Jesus imparts to those who believe in Him.

John 11:24 (KJV)
"Martha saith unto him, I know that he shall rise again in the resurrection at the last day."

Exposition:
Martha responds to Jesus's assurance by expressing her belief in a general resurrection that she anticipates at the end of time.

Commentary:
Martha's response reveals a common understanding among Jews of her time regarding the resurrection. The belief in a future resurrection at the last day was part of Jewish eschatology, as seen in various Old Testament passages (e.g., Daniel 12:2). Martha's faith aligns with this broader theological expectation.

However, her statement also indicates a temporal limitation in her understanding. She envisions resurrection as a future event rather than an immediate possibility. Jesus, recognizing the depth of her faith and the opportunity to expand her understanding, will use this moment to impart a profound truth about Himself.

Martha's confession sets the stage for Jesus to make a revolutionary declaration about His identity and the nature of resurrection, emphasizing that the power of resurrection is not merely a future event but is embodied in Jesus Himself.

As readers, we are prompted to consider the richness and depth of our own understanding of resurrection. Martha's faith, while anchored in the general hope of future resurrection, will soon be elevated as Jesus unveils a more immediate and personal dimension of resurrection that extends beyond the last day. This interaction invites us to explore the transformative power of Christ's presence in our lives, bringing resurrection and life in the here and now.

John 11:25 (KJV)
"Jesus said unto her, I am the resurrection, and the life: he that believeth in me, though he were dead, yet shall he live."

Exposition:
In response to Martha's anticipation of a future resurrection, Jesus delivers a profound revelation about His identity. He declares Himself as "the resurrection and the life," emphasizing that belief in Him transcends death, leading to eternal life.

Commentary:
Jesus's declaration is a cornerstone of Christian theology, encapsulating the essence of His mission and the transformative power of faith. By proclaiming, "I am the resurrection, and the life," Jesus asserts His divine authority over life and death. The present tense of "I am" underscores the immediacy and eternality of His role in granting life beyond physical death.

The statement also introduces a powerful concept of spiritual resurrection. Belief in Jesus not only assures future resurrection but brings spiritual life here and now. This truth challenges the conventional understanding of resurrection as a distant event, expanding the horizon of faith to encompass the present reality of life in Christ.

Jesus's words foreshadow His imminent demonstration of resurrection power in raising Lazarus from the dead. The narrative unfolds to reveal not only the depth of Jesus's compassion for Martha and Mary but also the unparalleled authority He holds as the Son of God.

As readers, we are invited to contemplate the profound implications of Jesus's self-declaration. It prompts reflection on the transformative nature of faith in Christ, the assurance of eternal life, and the recognition that through Him, believers experience a spiritual resurrection that transcends the limitations of physical death.

John 11:26 (KJV)
"And whosoever liveth and believeth in me shall never die. Believest thou this?"

Exposition:
Jesus extends the profound revelation by stating that anyone who is alive and believes in Him will never experience spiritual death. He then challenges Martha with a direct question about her belief in this truth.

Commentary:
In this verse, Jesus deepens the understanding of eternal life, asserting that those who are spiritually alive through faith in Him will never face the ultimate separation from God—spiritual death. This is a radical and transformative concept, emphasizing the enduring and unbroken connection between believers and God.

The question, "Believest thou this?" is not merely a rhetorical query but an invitation for Martha to affirm her faith in the unprecedented truth Jesus has just revealed. It prompts her to grapple with the implications of a faith that transcends physical death and to consider whether she truly embraces this revolutionary concept.

This moment highlights the interactive nature of faith. Jesus, in asking for Martha's affirmation, engages her in a personal and intentional conversation about the nature of belief and the transformative power of trust in Him.

As readers, we are invited to consider the same question Jesus poses to Martha. Do we believe in the profound truth that through faith in Christ, we experience spiritual life that transcends death? The verse challenges us to reflect on the depth and authenticity of our own belief in the transformative power of Christ's promise of eternal life.

John 11:27 (KJV)
"She saith unto him, Yea, Lord: I believe that thou art the Christ, the Son of God, which should come into the world."

Exposition:
Martha responds to Jesus's question by affirming her belief in Him as the Messiah, the Son of God, foretold to come into the world.

Commentary:
Martha's response is a powerful declaration of faith and recognition of Jesus's divine identity. Her acknowledgment that Jesus is "the Christ, the Son of God" reflects a deep understanding of the Messianic prophecies in the Old Testament. In her confession, she attributes to Jesus the long-awaited role of the promised Messiah.

This confession by Martha stands as a climactic moment in the narrative. It marks a significant turning point in the understanding of Jesus's identity, moving beyond recognizing Him as a miracle worker or teacher to acknowledging Him as the long-awaited Redeemer with divine authority over life and death.

Martha's faith-filled declaration is not only a personal affirmation but also a theological milestone in the Gospel of John. It aligns with the overarching theme of recognizing Jesus's unique identity and purpose. Her acknowledgment sets the stage for Jesus's subsequent demonstration of His power over death in the raising of Lazarus.

162

As readers, we are invited to echo Martha's confession, recognizing Jesus as the Christ, the Son of God, and embracing the profound implications of this truth for our own lives. Her faith challenges us to move beyond a superficial understanding of Jesus and to fully acknowledge Him as the source of eternal life and the fulfillment of divine promises.

John 11:28 (KJV)
"And when she had so said, she went her way, and called Mary her sister secretly, saying, The Master is come, and calleth for thee."

Exposition:
Martha, after affirming her faith in Jesus, discreetly informs her sister Mary that Jesus has arrived and is asking for her.

Commentary:
Martha's discreet message to Mary reveals a practical and considerate approach. The use of the term "Master" highlights the respect and recognition of Jesus's authority. By conveying that Jesus is calling for Mary, Martha initiates a private and personal interaction between Mary and Jesus, recognizing the unique bond each sister shares with Him.

This verse contributes to the unfolding drama, building anticipation for Mary's encounter with Jesus. The discreet nature of Martha's message suggests an understanding of the emotional state of both sisters and the need for a personal connection with Jesus in the midst of their grief.

As the narrative progresses, Mary's response to Jesus's call will lead to a poignant and transformative encounter, adding another layer to the rich tapestry of faith, grief, and divine intervention in the story of Lazarus.

As readers, we are drawn into the narrative, anticipating the personal and intimate moments between Jesus and Mary. Martha's role in facilitating this encounter reflects a sensitivity to the unique dynamics of each sister's relationship with Jesus and sets the stage for a profound revelation of Christ's compassion and power.

John 11:29 (KJV)
"As soon as she heard that, she arose quickly, and came unto him."

Exposition:
Upon hearing Martha's message that Jesus is calling for her, Mary responds promptly, rising quickly to go to Him.

Commentary:
Mary's swift response to the news reflects her eagerness to be in the presence of Jesus. The immediacy of her reaction underscores the depth of her relationship with Him and the significance of His call for her. Her rapid movement suggests a mix of anticipation, urgency, and perhaps a longing for comfort in the midst of grief.

This verse highlights the personal and emotional dynamics of Mary's connection with Jesus. In contrast to Martha's more proactive and assertive personality, Mary's response is characterized by a sense of immediacy and emotional intensity. The narrative portrays the diverse ways individuals express their faith and respond to the presence of Jesus.

Mary's journey to meet Jesus sets the stage for a poignant encounter that will unfold in the subsequent verses. Her actions contribute to the narrative's exploration of grief, faith, and the transformative power of Christ's presence in the lives of those who seek Him.

As readers, we are invited to reflect on the nature of our own responses to Jesus's call. Mary's quick and eager movement prompts us to consider the level of anticipation and eagerness we bring to our encounters with Christ, recognizing the profound impact His presence can have on our lives, especially in moments of grief and longing.

John 11:30 (KJV)
"Now Jesus was not yet come into the town, but was in that place where Martha met him."

Exposition:
The verse clarifies that Jesus had not yet entered the village but remained in the location where Martha initially met Him.

Commentary:
This detail sets the geographical context and helps to visualize the unfolding events. While Mary has responded quickly to the call, Jesus has not yet reached the village. The narrative builds tension, creating a sense of anticipation as Mary approaches the location where Jesus awaits.

The specific mention of the place where Martha met Him underscores the continuity of the narrative and the significance of that initial encounter. It serves as a reminder of Martha's confession of faith and the subsequent private message she sent to Mary, which has initiated this series of events.

As readers, we are prompted to consider the timing and sequence of events, recognizing the deliberate pacing in the narrative. The emphasis on location contributes to the anticipation of Mary's encounter with Jesus, suggesting that the meeting will be more than a casual interaction but a moment of profound significance in the unfolding story of Lazarus's resurrection.

This verse invites us to engage with the narrative's spatial and temporal dimensions, heightening our anticipation for the transformative encounter that will follow as Mary approaches Jesus in the place where Martha had met Him.

John 11:31 (KJV)
"The Jews then which were with her in the house, and comforted her, when they saw Mary, that she rose up hastily and went out, followed her, saying, She goeth unto the grave to weep there."

Exposition:
The Jews who were providing comfort to Mary in her home notice her sudden departure and follow her, assuming she is going to the tomb to grieve.

Commentary:
This verse provides a glimpse into the cultural and communal aspects of mourning during that time. The presence of Jews in Mary's house, offering comfort, highlights the communal support extended to grieving individuals. The observation of Mary's abrupt departure prompts them to assume she is heading to the tomb for mourning, a customary practice during times of loss.

The cultural context adds depth to the narrative, emphasizing the shared experience of grief and the communal response to someone in mourning. The Jews' assumption reflects a cultural understanding of grief as a process that often involves visiting the tomb or burial site.

As the narrative unfolds, the assumption about Mary's destination will lead to a pivotal moment at the tomb of Lazarus. The cultural practices surrounding death and mourning become a backdrop against which Jesus will reveal His power over death in a profoundly transformative way.

As readers, we are invited to appreciate the cultural nuances in the narrative and recognize the communal nature of grief. This verse sets the stage for the broader impact of Jesus's impending miracle, extending beyond the immediate circle of Martha and Mary to the wider community present during this significant moment.

John 11:32 (KJV)
"Then when Mary was come where Jesus was, and saw him, she fell down at his feet, saying unto him, Lord, if thou hadst been here, my brother had not died."

Exposition:

Upon reaching Jesus, Mary falls at His feet, expressing grief and faith in her words, similar to Martha's earlier statement.

Commentary:
Mary's posture of falling at Jesus's feet is a poignant expression of her emotional state and reverence for Him. Her words echo Martha's previous lament, underscoring the shared sentiment of believing that Jesus could have prevented Lazarus's death.

This verse adds depth to the emotional and spiritual dynamics between Jesus, Mary, and Martha. While Martha had a more assertive approach, Mary's response is characterized by a deep emotional intensity. Her act of falling at Jesus's feet is an acknowledgment of His authority and a plea for understanding in the face of grief.

The repetition of the sisters' words emphasizes the genuine and raw emotions they are experiencing. Their expressions of faith and lamentation pave the way for Jesus to reveal His compassion and the extraordinary demonstration of His power over death.

As readers, we are invited to empathize with Mary's emotional response and consider our own posture before Jesus in times of grief and struggle. Mary's vulnerability and sincerity create a profound backdrop for the miraculous events that will follow, reinforcing the themes of faith, compassion, and the transformative power of Christ's presence in the midst of human sorrow.

John 11:33 (KJV)
"When Jesus therefore saw her weeping, and the Jews also weeping which came with her, he groaned in the spirit, and was troubled."

Exposition:
Observing Mary's grief and the mourning Jews accompanying her, Jesus is deeply moved in His spirit, experiencing a profound emotional response.

Commentary:

This verse provides a glimpse into the compassionate nature of Jesus as He encounters the sorrow of Mary and the gathered Jews. The phrase "He groaned in the spirit, and was troubled" captures the depth of His emotional response. It reveals a combination of empathy, sorrow, and a sense of disturbance in the face of human suffering and grief.

The collective weeping of Mary and the Jews underscores the shared experience of mourning, emphasizing the communal aspect of grief. Jesus's reaction goes beyond a detached observation; it reflects His humanity and His profound connection with the human experience, including its sorrows and pains.

The phrase "groaned in the spirit" suggests an inward sigh or deep emotional response that transcends mere sympathy. Jesus's troubled spirit signals a profound engagement with the brokenness and pain present in the moment. His reaction sets the stage for the subsequent display of His miraculous power over death, highlighting the compassionate heart of the Savior.

As readers, we are invited to reflect on the compassionate response of Jesus to human suffering. This verse prompts us to recognize that in our times of grief and anguish, Jesus intimately engages with our pain, offering not only empathy but also the promise of transformative and redemptive intervention in the midst of our deepest sorrows.

John 11:34 (KJV)
"And said, Where have ye laid him? They said unto him, Lord, come and see."

Exposition:
Jesus, after expressing deep emotion, asks about the location of Lazarus's tomb. The response from those present is an invitation for Him to come and witness the situation.

Commentary:

In this verse, Jesus transitions from a deep emotional response to practical inquiry. His question about the location of Lazarus's tomb reflects a tangible and immediate engagement with the situation. Despite His divine knowledge, Jesus invites those present to guide Him to the place of burial.

The response, "Lord, come and see," while seemingly straightforward, carries significant weight. It reflects a recognition of Jesus's authority and a willingness to involve Him in the reality of death. The invitation to "come and see" goes beyond a mere geographical indication; it symbolizes an invitation for Jesus to personally experience the grief and loss surrounding Lazarus's death.

This interaction sets the stage for one of the most iconic moments in the Gospels—the raising of Lazarus. Jesus's willingness to engage with the reality of death, coupled with His forthcoming miracle, underscores His compassion, authority over life and death, and the transformative power He brings to the most challenging circumstances.

As readers, we are invited to consider the profound nature of Jesus's involvement in our lives. The verse prompts reflection on our willingness to invite Him into the depths of our struggles and losses, trusting that His presence brings hope and transformation even in the face of seemingly insurmountable challenges.

John 11:35 (KJV)
"Jesus wept."

Exposition:
This concise verse records the shortest verse in the Bible, highlighting the humanity and compassion of Jesus as He sheds tears in response to the sorrow around Him.

Commentary:
"Jesus wept" is a profound and poignant expression of Jesus's humanity. Though fully divine, He also shared in the human experience, including the emotions of grief and sorrow. This verse

encapsulates the depth of Jesus's compassion and His ability to empathize with the pain and loss experienced by those around Him.

The tears of Jesus are not merely a response to the death of Lazarus but reflect a broader understanding of the brokenness of the world and the impact of sin, which brought death and suffering. In this moment, Jesus stands as the compassionate High Priest who can sympathize with our weaknesses (Hebrews 4:15).

The brevity of this verse doesn't diminish its significance. It resonates with the universal experience of grief and underscores the truth that our Savior is not distant or indifferent to our pain. Jesus's tears convey a powerful message about the depth of God's love and His identification with the human condition.

As readers, we are invited to reflect on the humanity of Jesus and His empathetic response to our sorrows. "Jesus wept" serves as a profound reminder that in our moments of deepest grief, we have a Savior who understands, cares, and ultimately brings comfort and hope through His redemptive work.

John 11:36 (KJV)
"Then said the Jews, Behold how he loved him!"

Exposition:
Witnessing Jesus's tears, the onlookers respond with the observation that Jesus deeply loved Lazarus.

Commentary:
The reaction of the Jews underscores the impact of Jesus's display of emotion. In their observation, "Behold how he loved him!" they recognize the sincerity and depth of Jesus's affection for Lazarus. The tears of Jesus are not just tears of sympathy but a tangible expression of love for His friend.

This response from the crowd also reflects a cultural understanding that genuine love involves a deep emotional connection. The tears of Jesus become a visible demonstration of the profound bond He shares with Lazarus and the depth of His care for those whom He loves.

This verse provides a poignant moment in the narrative where the love of Jesus is visibly demonstrated. It prepares the ground for the subsequent miracle of Lazarus's resurrection, emphasizing that the actions of Jesus are not detached or mechanical but rooted in genuine and deep compassion.

As readers, we are invited to contemplate the nature of Jesus's love for us. The verse prompts us to recognize that His love is not abstract but is expressed in tangible ways, including a willingness to enter into our pain and sorrows. The observation of the Jews challenges us to behold and appreciate the profound love of Christ that goes beyond words, manifesting in His sacrificial actions on our behalf.

John 11:37 (KJV)
"And some of them said, Could not this man, which opened the eyes of the blind, have caused that even this man should not have died?"

Exposition:
A portion of the crowd questions why Jesus, who performed miraculous healings like restoring sight to the blind, did not prevent Lazarus's death.

Commentary:
This verse captures a moment of skepticism and questioning among the onlookers. Having witnessed or heard of Jesus's miraculous healing abilities, some express confusion and doubt about why He did not intervene in Lazarus's illness to prevent his death.

The reference to Jesus opening the eyes of the blind recalls previous miracles, such as the healing of the man born blind in John 9. The implication is that if Jesus could perform such remarkable healings, preventing Lazarus's death should have been within His capabilities.

This reaction reveals the human tendency to assess situations based on past experiences and expectations. The crowd struggles to reconcile their understanding of Jesus's healing power with the present reality of Lazarus's death. It sets the stage for Jesus's impending miracle, which will transcend their preconceived notions and demonstrate His authority over death itself.

As readers, we can empathize with the crowd's perspective, acknowledging the challenges of reconciling our expectations with the mysterious and sovereign ways of God. This verse invites us to consider how we respond when God's actions seemingly deviate from our understanding, encouraging us to trust in His wisdom and recognize that His plans extend beyond our immediate comprehension.

John 11:38 (KJV)
"Jesus therefore again groaning in himself cometh to the grave. It was a cave, and a stone lay upon it."

Exposition:
Jesus, continuing to experience deep emotion, arrives at the tomb. The description of the tomb being a cave and sealed with a stone sets the scene for the upcoming miracle.

Commentary:
The repetition of Jesus's groaning emphasizes the ongoing emotional engagement He has with the situation. His groaning is not a fleeting reaction but a sustained expression of the emotional weight He carries. As He approaches the tomb, the physical details—being a cave with a stone sealing it—highlight the finality of death.

The use of a cave for a tomb was a common practice in that historical and cultural context. The mention of the stone further accentuates the permanence of death, serving as a barrier that seals the tomb and conceals its contents.

This verse serves as a transition to the climactic moment of Lazarus's resurrection. The cave and stone symbolize the sealed fate of the dead, and Jesus's arrival at this location anticipates the extraordinary intervention about to take place.

As readers, we are drawn into the scene, recognizing the tension between the finality of death and the imminent demonstration of Jesus's power over it. The details of the tomb's structure emphasize the reality of the situation, setting the stage for the miraculous revelation of Jesus as the Resurrection and the Life.

John 11:39 (KJV)
"Jesus said, Take ye away the stone. Martha, the sister of him that was dead, saith unto him, Lord, by this time he stinketh: for he hath been dead four days."

Exposition:
Jesus instructs those present to remove the stone from the tomb. Martha, expressing concern about the decay after four days, voices her practical considerations.

Commentary:
Jesus's command to remove the stone is a pivotal moment in the narrative, setting the stage for the miraculous resurrection of Lazarus. The removal of the stone is a tangible step toward confronting the finality of death and unveiling the power of Christ.

Martha's response, while practical, also reflects the harsh reality of decay associated with death. Her statement, "he stinketh," underscores the advanced state of decomposition after four days. Martha, in her human perspective, points to the natural order of death and decay, highlighting the seeming impossibility of any intervention at this point.

This interaction reveals a tension between human understanding and divine power. While Martha sees the physical and temporal limitations, Jesus is about to reveal His authority over the natural course of death. The removal of the stone becomes a metaphor for breaking through the barriers of death and unveiling the transformative power of Christ.

As readers, we are prompted to reflect on our own perceptions of limitations and impossibilities. Martha's initial response serves as a reminder that divine intervention often challenges our understanding of what is possible. The imminent miracle will demonstrate that Jesus is not bound by the natural order of decay but possesses the authority to bring life even in the face of death's finality.

John 11:40 (KJV)
"Jesus saith unto her, Said I not unto thee, that, if thou wouldest believe, thou shouldest see the glory of God?"

Exposition:
In response to Martha's concerns, Jesus reaffirms the importance of faith and reminds her of His earlier promise regarding the manifestation of God's glory through belief.

Commentary:
Jesus's statement underscores the critical role of faith in experiencing the transformative power of God. By reminding Martha of His previous words, He encourages her to shift her focus from the limitations of the natural order to the realm of divine possibilities. The connection between belief and witnessing the glory of God is a recurring theme in the Gospel of John.

The promise of seeing the glory of God is not merely a future hope but an immediate and tangible reality. Jesus invites Martha to embrace a perspective that transcends the visible and temporal, urging her to trust in His authority over life and death. The upcoming miracle of Lazarus's resurrection will be a demonstration of this glory and a fulfillment of Jesus's words.

This verse carries a broader theological significance, emphasizing the dynamic relationship between faith and divine manifestation. It challenges believers to move beyond a surface-level understanding of faith and recognize its transformative power in unveiling the glory of God in various aspects of life.

As readers, we are invited to consider the correlation between our faith and the manifestation of God's glory. Jesus's words to Martha encourage us to approach challenges and uncertainties with a steadfast belief in His promises, trusting that through faith, we too can witness the glory of God in our lives.

John 11:40 (KJV)
"Jesus saith unto her, Said I not unto thee, that, if thou wouldest believe, thou shouldest see the glory of God?"

Exposition:
Jesus reminds Martha of the correlation between faith and the manifestation of the glory of God, emphasizing that belief is a prerequisite for witnessing divine intervention.

Commentary:
This verse echoes a consistent theme in the Gospel of John— the transformative power of faith. Jesus's interaction with Martha emphasizes that belief is not just a passive acknowledgment but an active catalyst for experiencing the miraculous works of God.

The phrase "thou shouldest see the glory of God" encapsulates the promise that through faith, believers have the privilege of witnessing God's power and presence in extraordinary ways. The upcoming resurrection of Lazarus will be a tangible expression of this divine glory, affirming the connection between faith and miraculous revelation.

Jesus's reminder to Martha underscores the intimate relationship between trust in Him and the unfolding of God's purposes. It challenges Martha to move beyond her immediate concerns and embrace a perspective rooted in faith and expectancy.

As readers, we are invited to reflect on the role of belief in our own lives. The verse encourages us to approach challenges, uncertainties, and the apparent limitations of human understanding with unwavering faith, trusting that in our belief, we, too, can witness the glory of God in various aspects of our journey.

John 11:41 (KJV)
"Then they took away the stone from the place where the dead was laid. And Jesus lifted up his eyes, and said, Father, I thank thee that thou hast heard me."

Exposition:
Following Jesus's instruction, the stone is removed from the entrance of Lazarus's tomb. Jesus, before the impending miracle, expresses gratitude to the Father for hearing Him.

Commentary:
The removal of the stone marks a significant step toward the unfolding miracle. It symbolizes the breaking of barriers and the revelation of what lies beyond the realm of human understanding and expectation. The act of taking away the stone becomes a visual representation of faith in action.

Jesus's posture of lifting up His eyes and expressing gratitude to the Father adds a layer of spiritual depth to the narrative. The prayerful acknowledgment of the Father's response suggests a relational and collaborative aspect of the miracle. It reflects Jesus's submission to the Father's will and highlights the unity within the Trinity.

The expression "Father, I thank thee that thou hast heard me" conveys assurance and confidence in the divine partnership. Jesus, in His humanity, maintains a posture of gratitude, recognizing that the Father's response is both timely and certain.

As readers, we are drawn into the sacred moment of prayer and gratitude. This verse encourages us to embrace a spirit of thankfulness in our own prayers, recognizing the responsiveness of a loving God. It also prompts reflection on the nature of our faith—

whether we approach challenges with a spirit of expectancy, trusting that God hears and responds according to His perfect will.

John 11:42 (KJV)
"And I knew that thou hearest me always: but because of the people which stand by I said it, that they may believe that thou hast sent me."

Exposition:
Continuing His prayer, Jesus affirms His continuous connection with the Father and explains that His spoken words are for the benefit of those present, aiming to strengthen their belief in His divine mission.

Commentary:
In this verse, Jesus unveils the ongoing communion He shares with the Father. His statement, "I knew that thou hearest me always," underscores the unbroken and perpetual nature of His relationship with God. This intimate connection forms the foundation for His confidence in the forthcoming miracle.

However, Jesus makes it clear that His verbal acknowledgment is not for His own assurance but for the benefit of the onlookers. The phrase "because of the people which stand by I said it" reveals a strategic purpose behind Jesus's words. His goal is to use this moment as a teaching opportunity, inviting those present to recognize the divine authority behind His actions.

By openly expressing His communion with the Father, Jesus reinforces the concept of divine mission and delegation. The intention is to deepen the understanding and faith of the witnesses, paving the way for a more profound revelation of His identity and purpose.

As readers, we are invited to reflect on the interplay between Jesus's divinity and humanity. This verse challenges us to consider how our words and actions can be intentional expressions of our faith, aimed at drawing others closer to the knowledge of God and the recognition of His divine purposes in our lives.

John 11:43 (KJV)
"And when he thus had spoken, he cried with a loud voice, Lazarus, come forth."

Exposition:
Following His prayer, Jesus issues a powerful command, calling Lazarus by name and instructing him to come forth.

Commentary:
This verse captures the climactic moment of the narrative—the resurrection of Lazarus. Jesus's command, spoken with a loud voice, echoes with divine authority and power. The specificity of addressing Lazarus by name emphasizes the personal and intentional nature of the miracle.

The words "Lazarus, come forth" are a manifestation of Jesus's dominion over death. The command is not a desperate plea but a confident proclamation, demonstrating that the very Author of life possesses the authority to reverse its cessation. The loudness of Jesus's voice underscores the magnitude of the miracle and serves as a public declaration of His sovereignty.

The resurrection of Lazarus is a prelude to Jesus's own victory over death, foreshadowing the Easter event. It stands as a remarkable sign of Jesus's identity as the Resurrection and the Life, affirming His divine authority over life and death.

As readers, we are invited to witness the awe-inspiring moment of Lazarus's resurrection. This verse prompts us to contemplate the boundless power of Christ in our own lives, recognizing that He has the authority to bring forth life in situations that seem irreversibly dead. The resurrection of Lazarus also challenges us to deepen our understanding of Jesus's identity and to respond to His call to new life with faith and gratitude.

John 11:44 (KJV)

"And he that was dead came forth, bound hand and foot with graveclothes: and his face was bound about with a napkin. Jesus saith unto them, Loose him, and let him go."

Exposition:
Lazarus, responding to Jesus's command, emerges from the tomb. However, he is still bound in burial garments. Jesus instructs those present to free him.

Commentary:
The description of Lazarus coming forth from the tomb, still bound in graveclothes, adds a layer of realism to the miraculous event. While his resurrection is complete, the remnants of his burial attire serve as a visual reminder of the recent state of death.

Jesus's command to "loose him, and let him go" involves the community in the process of restoration. The physical act of unwrapping Lazarus becomes a symbolic representation of the liberation from the trappings of death. It highlights the collaborative nature of God's redemptive work, involving both divine power and human participation.

This scene also foreshadows the Easter narrative, where Jesus's own burial garments will be left behind in the empty tomb. The imagery of shedding burial clothes signifies not only the reversal of death but the ushering in of new life and freedom.

As readers, we are invited to contemplate the profound symbolism in this verse. It prompts us to recognize that Jesus's resurrection power not only brings us out of spiritual death but also involves an ongoing process of liberation from the vestiges of the past. The community's involvement in unwrapping Lazarus invites us to consider our role in supporting one another in the journey of spiritual renewal and freedom in Christ.

John 11:45 (KJV)
"Then many of the Jews which came to Mary, and had seen the things which Jesus did, believed on him."

Exposition:
Witnessing the resurrection of Lazarus, many Jews who had come to console Mary are profoundly impacted, leading to belief in Jesus.

Commentary:
This verse marks a significant response to the miraculous event. The resurrection of Lazarus becomes a catalyst for belief among those who were present. The impact of the miracle extends beyond the immediate witnesses, influencing a broader group of people who had come to offer comfort to Mary.

The phrase "believed on him" signifies a transformative shift in their perception of Jesus. The resurrection of Lazarus serves as a powerful confirmation of Jesus's identity as the Messiah, reinforcing the themes of life, resurrection, and divine authority that He had been teaching throughout His ministry.

This verse emphasizes the diverse ways in which individuals come to faith. For some, it takes witnessing extraordinary miracles to believe in Jesus. The resurrection of Lazarus becomes a decisive moment, breaking through skepticism and doubt.

As readers, we are invited to consider our own journeys of faith. The verse prompts reflection on the various factors that contribute to belief—whether through witnessing miraculous interventions, hearing the teachings of Jesus, or experiencing His transformative power in our lives. The resurrection of Lazarus serves as a compelling testimony to the profound impact of encountering the living Christ.

John 11:46 (KJV)
"But some of them went their ways to the Pharisees, and told them what things Jesus had done."

Exposition:

Instead of believing, some witnesses of Lazarus's resurrection choose to report the miraculous event to the Pharisees, the religious leaders.

Commentary:
This verse introduces a contrasting response to the resurrection miracle. While many who witnessed Lazarus's revival believed in Jesus, a faction chooses a different course of action. Instead of embracing the miraculous sign, they go to the Pharisees and report the events surrounding Lazarus.

The decision to inform the Pharisees reflects a deepening division and opposition to Jesus. It reveals a group that, despite witnessing an undeniable display of divine power, remains committed to opposing Jesus and maintaining the status quo. The motives behind their actions may include fear of losing influence, political concerns, or a hardened resistance to acknowledging Jesus as the Messiah.

This verse foreshadows the escalating tension that will lead to the decision to arrest and ultimately crucify Jesus. The contrasting responses highlight the diverse reactions to Jesus's ministry and the growing polarization within the religious community.

As readers, we are prompted to reflect on the complexity of human responses to divine revelation. The verse challenges us to examine our own hearts and consider how we respond to the signs and revelations of God in our lives. It serves as a sobering reminder that even in the presence of undeniable miracles, some hearts may remain resistant to the transformative power of Christ.

John 11:47 (KJV)
"Then gathered the chief priests and the Pharisees a council, and said, What do we? for this man doeth many miracles."

Exposition:
Reacting to the news of Lazarus's resurrection, the chief priests and Pharisees convene a council to deliberate on how to deal with Jesus, recognizing His ongoing display of miraculous power.

Commentary:
The gathering of the chief priests and Pharisees signals a heightened level of concern and urgency among the religious authorities. The phrase "What do we?" reflects a sense of perplexity and insecurity in the face of Jesus's growing influence and the undeniable nature of His miracles.

The acknowledgment that "this man doeth many miracles" underscores the central challenge posed by Jesus's ministry. His signs and wonders are impossible to dismiss, forcing the religious leaders to confront the reality of His extraordinary authority and divine power.

This verse sets the stage for the unfolding conflict between Jesus and the religious establishment, foreshadowing the plot to arrest and silence Him. The leaders' response to the resurrection of Lazarus becomes a catalyst for their determination to take decisive action against Jesus.

As readers, we are invited to recognize the tension building around Jesus's ministry. The verse prompts reflection on how individuals and institutions respond when faced with undeniable evidence of God's work. It also serves as a warning against allowing preconceived notions, fear, or personal agendas to hinder an open and receptive response to the transformative power of Christ.

John 11:48 (KJV)
"If we let him thus alone, all men will believe on him: and the Romans shall come and take away both our place and nation."

Exposition:
Concerned about Jesus's growing influence, the religious leaders express fear that if left unchecked, He will gain widespread support, leading to Roman intervention and potential loss of their positions and nation.

Commentary:

The statement by the religious leaders reveals a combination of fear, political calculation, and self-interest. Their primary concern is not the authenticity of Jesus's message or the welfare of the people but the potential threat to their own power and status.

The phrase "all men will believe on him" reflects a distorted perspective, portraying the growing faith in Jesus as a threat rather than an opportunity for spiritual renewal. The fear of Roman intervention further exposes the leaders' worldly priorities, suggesting a willingness to compromise moral and spiritual principles to maintain their position.

This verse highlights the ongoing tension between the spiritual kingdom that Jesus proclaimed and the earthly concerns of power and authority held by the religious leaders. It sets the stage for the intensifying conflict between Jesus and the religious establishment, ultimately leading to His arrest and crucifixion.

As readers, we are prompted to examine our own priorities and allegiances. The verse serves as a cautionary reminder of the dangers of prioritizing worldly power and status over the transformative message of Christ. It challenges us to align our hearts with God's kingdom and to resist the temptations of self-interest that can hinder our response to the genuine work of God.

John 11:49 (KJV)
"And one of them, named Caiaphas, being the high priest that same year, said unto them, Ye know nothing at all."

Exposition:
Caiaphas, the high priest, responds to the concerns of the religious leaders, dismissing their anxieties and asserting his authority.

Commentary:
Caiaphas, as the high priest, holds a position of significant influence and authority within the Jewish religious hierarchy. His response reveals a dismissive attitude toward the fears expressed by his colleagues. The phrase "Ye know nothing at all" conveys a sense

of superiority and implies that he alone possesses the understanding and insight needed to address the situation.

Caiaphas's statement sets the tone for his subsequent counsel and reveals a pragmatic approach to the perceived threat posed by Jesus. His response is not driven by a concern for truth or righteousness but by a desire to maintain control and stability within the existing religious and political order.

This verse foreshadows Caiaphas's role in the unfolding events, particularly his infamous counsel recorded in the following verses, where he suggests that it is expedient for one man to die for the people. This strategic perspective sets the stage for the conspiracy against Jesus, leading to His arrest and crucifixion.

As readers, we are invited to critically examine the motivations of those in positions of authority. The verse prompts reflection on the potential dangers of leaders prioritizing political expediency over ethical considerations and the genuine pursuit of God's truth. It also serves as a reminder to seek leaders who prioritize righteousness and justice in their decision-making.

John 11:50 (KJV)
"Nor consider that it is expedient for us, that one man should die for the people, and that the whole nation perish not."

Exposition:
Caiaphas, the high priest, suggests a utilitarian perspective, proposing that it is advantageous for one person (Jesus) to die for the greater good of preserving the nation.

Commentary:
Caiaphas's statement reveals a Machiavellian mindset, prioritizing political expediency over moral and ethical considerations. The phrase "it is expedient for us" underscores his pragmatic approach, suggesting that sacrificing one individual (Jesus) would serve the broader interest of preserving the nation and avoiding potential Roman intervention.

The utilitarian argument presented by Caiaphas is morally complex. While it appears to prioritize the welfare of the nation, it involves a willingness to compromise justice and truth for the sake of maintaining power and control. This perspective sets the stage for the conspiratorial actions against Jesus, leading to His arrest and crucifixion.

This verse highlights the ethical tension between the perceived needs of the state and the principles of justice and righteousness. It foreshadows the greater sacrifice of Jesus, who, according to Christian belief, willingly laid down His life for the salvation of humanity.

As readers, we are challenged to examine the ethical implications of decisions made in the name of political expediency. The verse prompts reflection on the importance of leaders who prioritize justice, truth, and moral principles, even in the face of challenging circumstances.

John 11:51 (KJV)
"And this spake he not of himself: but being high priest that year, he prophesied that Jesus should die for that nation."

Exposition:
The narrative clarifies that Caiaphas's utilitarian suggestion was not a conscious prophecy but, as the high priest, he unintentionally spoke a prophetic truth regarding Jesus's sacrificial death for the nation.

Commentary:
This verse offers a nuanced perspective on Caiaphas's words. While he may have spoken with a pragmatic political motive, the narrative interprets his words as unintentional prophecy. It underscores the idea that God can use even the words of those motivated by self-interest to fulfill His divine purposes.

Caiaphas, as the high priest, holds a symbolic role representing the people before God. In this unintended prophecy, he speaks of a truth beyond his immediate understanding—the redemptive significance of Jesus's death for the nation. The concept of one dying for the people aligns with Christian theology, emphasizing the sacrificial atonement provided by Jesus on the cross.

This verse introduces a layer of divine sovereignty, suggesting that God can work through human actions and words, even when they are not aligned with His intentions. It sets the stage for the unfolding events leading to the fulfillment of this unintended prophecy—the crucifixion of Jesus for the salvation of humanity.

As readers, we are invited to recognize the mysterious ways in which God works through human history. The verse prompts reflection on the providence of God, even in situations where human motives may be misguided. It underscores the ultimate purpose and redemptive power of Jesus's sacrificial death.

John 11:52 (KJV)
"And not for that nation only, but that also he should gather together in one the children of God that were scattered abroad."

Exposition:
Expanding on the unintended prophecy, the verse emphasizes that Jesus's sacrificial death extends beyond the nation of Israel. It has a universal scope, bringing together the scattered children of God.

Commentary:
This verse reveals a broader perspective on the redemptive purpose of Jesus's death. While Caiaphas's words initially referred to the nation of Israel, the narrative clarifies that the impact of Jesus's sacrifice transcends national boundaries. The phrase "gather together in one the children of God that were scattered abroad" emphasizes the inclusivity of God's plan of salvation.

The scattered children of God symbolize humanity, dispersed by sin and separated from God. Jesus's sacrificial death serves as the unifying force, bringing together people from every nation and background into a harmonious relationship with God.

This verse aligns with the universal theme present in the Gospel of John, emphasizing that the salvation brought by Jesus is not limited to a specific group but is offered to all who believe. It anticipates the Great Commission, where Jesus instructs His followers to make disciples of all nations.

As readers, we are invited to embrace the inclusive nature of God's redemptive plan. The verse prompts reflection on the universal impact of Jesus's sacrifice, encouraging us to recognize our identity as children of God and to participate in the mission of bringing others into the unifying love of Christ.

John 11:53 (KJV)
"Then from that day forth they took counsel together for to put him to death."

Exposition:
In response to Caiaphas's unintentional prophecy, the religious leaders intensify their resolve to plot against Jesus, now actively seeking to put Him to death.

Commentary:
The verse marks a significant turning point in the narrative. Caiaphas's prophecy, though unintended, becomes a catalyst for a more determined conspiracy against Jesus. The religious leaders transition from deliberation to decisive action, seeking to eliminate the perceived threat to their authority.

The phrase "they took counsel together" underscores the collaborative nature of the plot. The decision to "put him to death" reveals the escalating hostility and fear that Jesus's growing influence evokes among the religious establishment.

This verse sets the stage for the events leading to Jesus's arrest, trial, and eventual crucifixion. The opposition against Him becomes more overt and deliberate, fueled by a desire to suppress what they perceive as a challenge to their religious and political status quo.

As readers, we are prompted to consider the complex dynamics of power, fear, and resistance to divine revelation. The verse challenges us to reflect on the ways in which prejudice, self-interest, and the desire for control can hinder an open response to the transformative message of Christ. It also serves as a reminder of the ultimate sacrifice Jesus willingly embraced for the sake of redemption.

John 11:54 (KJV)
"Jesus therefore walked no more openly among the Jews; but went thence unto a country near to the wilderness, into a city called Ephraim, and there continued with his disciples."

Exposition:
In response to the escalating threat on His life, Jesus withdraws from public visibility, moving to a region near the wilderness, specifically to the city of Ephraim, where He continues His ministry with His disciples.

Commentary:
This verse reflects Jesus's strategic response to the intensifying opposition. The phrase "Jesus therefore walked no more openly among the Jews" indicates a shift in His public ministry. The growing hostility necessitates a more cautious approach to avoid premature confrontation.

The choice of Ephraim, a city near the wilderness, serves both practical and symbolic purposes. Geographically, it provides a less accessible and less populated area, offering a degree of seclusion and safety. Symbolically, the wilderness often represents a place of testing, preparation, and encounter with God in biblical narratives.

The verse highlights Jesus's awareness of the divine timing and the need for careful navigation of the unfolding events. His withdrawal does not indicate fear or defeat but a deliberate step to fulfill His mission in accordance with God's plan.

As readers, we are invited to discern the wisdom of Jesus's actions. The verse prompts reflection on the balance between bold proclamation and strategic navigation in the face of opposition. It also serves as a reminder that Jesus, in His earthly ministry, exemplifies a purposeful and intentional approach to fulfill the divine purposes leading to the ultimate sacrifice for humanity's redemption.

John 11:55 (KJV)
"And the Jews' passover was nigh at hand: and many went out of the country up to Jerusalem before the passover, to purify themselves."

Exposition:
The mention of the approaching Passover sets the stage for the continuation of the narrative, emphasizing the significance of this festival in the life of the Jewish people. Many traveled to Jerusalem to observe the Passover and undergo purification rituals.

Commentary:
The proximity of the Passover adds a layer of tension and anticipation to the narrative. This festival held deep religious and cultural significance for the Jewish people, commemorating the historical event of their liberation from slavery in Egypt.

The mention of people traveling to Jerusalem to purify themselves aligns with the ceremonial practices associated with the Passover. Purification rituals were essential for participation in the sacred events of the festival. The symbolism of purification also resonates with the broader themes of spiritual cleansing and renewal.

This verse serves as a narrative bridge, connecting the preceding events with the approaching climax of Jesus's ministry and the fulfillment of His mission. The convergence of the Passover and the unfolding plot against Jesus heightens the dramatic tension in the narrative.

As readers, we are invited to appreciate the intricate timing of events in the biblical narrative. The verse prompts reflection on the intersection of divine providence and cultural traditions, setting the stage for the pivotal moments in Jesus's final days on earth.

John 11:56 (KJV)
"Then sought they for Jesus, and spake among themselves, as they stood in the temple, What think ye, that he will not come to the feast?"

Exposition:
As people gather in the temple for the approaching Passover, there is speculation and discussion about whether Jesus will attend the feast.

Commentary:
The anticipation surrounding Jesus's presence at the Passover feast becomes a topic of discussion among those in the temple. The question "What think ye, that he will not come to the feast?" reflects a sense of uncertainty and curiosity. Some may have been expecting Jesus to make a public appearance during this significant religious event.

The temple, as the central place of worship, serves as a fitting setting for discussions about Jesus, especially in the context of a major festival like the Passover. The atmosphere is charged with expectation and speculation about the actions and intentions of Jesus.

This verse adds a layer of dramatic irony to the narrative. While some are questioning whether Jesus will attend the feast, the readers are aware of the unfolding events and the increasing threat on Jesus's life. The anticipation of Jesus's presence at the Passover sets the stage for the subsequent events in the Gospel.

As readers, we are invited to engage with the uncertainty and speculation surrounding Jesus's actions. The verse prompts reflection on the varied expectations people may have had regarding Jesus and the challenges of discerning divine purposes in the midst of cultural and religious traditions.

John 11:57 (KJV)
"Now both the chief priests and the Pharisees had given a commandment, that, if any man knew where he were, he should shew it, that they might take him."

Exposition:
In the context of the growing anticipation surrounding Jesus's presence at the Passover, the religious authorities intensify their efforts to locate and apprehend Him, issuing a command for anyone with information to disclose it.

Commentary:
This verse underscores the heightened level of threat and opposition against Jesus. The commandment issued by the chief priests and Pharisees reveals a determined and coordinated effort to apprehend Him during the Passover. The fear of Jesus's potential influence during this religious gathering intensifies their resolve to eliminate Him.

The phrase "that they might take him" highlights the conspiratorial nature of their actions. The religious authorities, who should have been focused on the spiritual significance of the Passover, are preoccupied with suppressing what they perceive as a challenge to their authority.

This verse sets the stage for the climactic events that will unfold during the Passover, leading to Jesus's arrest and subsequent crucifixion. The tension between the religious establishment and Jesus reaches a critical point, emphasizing the divine timing and purpose in the unfolding narrative.

As readers, we are prompted to reflect on the contrast between the religious leaders' preoccupation with control and Jesus's sacrificial mission. The verse challenges us to examine our own hearts and priorities, considering whether we align with the redemptive purposes of God or succumb to the temptations of power and self-interest.

CHAPTER TWELVE
The Anointing at Bethany

John 12:1 (KJV)
"Then Jesus six days before the passover came to Bethany, where Lazarus was, which had been dead, whom he raised from the dead."

Exposition:
Six days before the Passover, Jesus arrives in Bethany, the place where Lazarus, whom He raised from the dead, resides.

Commentary:
The mention of Bethany and Lazarus sets the stage for a significant event in Jesus's ministry. Bethany was a village near Jerusalem, and Lazarus, whom Jesus had miraculously raised from the dead, resided there. The proximity to the Passover adds weight to the unfolding narrative, as the Passover was a crucial and sacred festival in the Jewish calendar.

The choice to visit Bethany, where the miracle of Lazarus occurred, emphasizes the continuity of Jesus's ministry and the significance of His power over death. It also foreshadows the approaching climax of Jesus's earthly ministry, leading to His sacrificial death and resurrection.

This verse invites readers to reflect on the profound impact of Jesus's miracles and the purposeful nature of His actions. The reunion in Bethany becomes a prelude to the events that will transpire during the Passover week, ultimately leading to the fulfillment of God's redemptive plan through the crucifixion and resurrection of Jesus.

John 12:2 (KJV)
"There they made him a supper; and Martha served: but Lazarus was one of them that sat at the table with him."

Exposition:
In Bethany, a supper is prepared for Jesus, and Martha serves, while Lazarus, whom Jesus raised from the dead, is among those seated at the table with Him.

Commentary:

This verse depicts a scene of hospitality and fellowship in Bethany. The act of preparing a supper and Martha serving reflect the warmth and gratitude of the hosts toward Jesus. The presence of Lazarus at the table is a poignant reminder of the recent miraculous event of his resurrection.

Martha's service highlights her characteristic role as a diligent and hospitable hostess. The fact that Lazarus is not only alive but also participating in the meal emphasizes the tangible and joyful outcomes of Jesus's miraculous power.

The supper in Bethany stands in contrast to the atmosphere of tension and conspiracy in Jerusalem. It becomes a moment of genuine connection and celebration in response to Jesus's life-transforming deeds.

As readers, we are invited to appreciate the intimate moments of fellowship and gratitude expressed in this verse. It prompts reflection on the ways in which we respond to the transformative work of Jesus in our lives, cultivating a spirit of hospitality, gratitude, and joy in our relationship with Him. The supper in Bethany also foreshadows the upcoming events during the Passover week, underscoring the themes of fellowship and preparation leading to Jesus's ultimate sacrifice.

John 12:3 (KJV)

"Then took Mary a pound of ointment of spikenard, very costly, and anointed the feet of Jesus, and wiped his feet with her hair: and the house was filled with the odour of the ointment."

Exposition:

Mary, possibly Mary of Bethany, takes a pound of expensive spikenard ointment, anoints Jesus' feet, and wipes them with her hair, filling the house with the fragrance of the ointment.

Commentary:

This verse captures a profoundly intimate and symbolic moment of worship and devotion. Mary's action is a significant expression of love and reverence for Jesus. The use of a pound of spikenard, a costly and fragrant ointment, underscores the extravagance of her gesture.

Anointing was a cultural practice with various meanings, often associated with honoring or consecrating a person. Mary's choice to anoint Jesus' feet, an act typically reserved for servants or guests, adds a layer of humility and deep personal devotion to her expression of love.

Wiping Jesus' feet with her hair further accentuates the humility and intimacy of Mary's worship. In that cultural context, a woman letting down her hair in public was a vulnerable and unconventional act, heightening the significance of her gesture.

The fragrance filling the house becomes a sensory backdrop to this remarkable act, symbolizing the pervasive impact of genuine worship and sacrificial love. The whole scene contrasts with the impending betrayal and conspiracy in Jerusalem, illustrating the diverse responses to Jesus in the face of His approaching crucifixion.

As readers, we are invited to reflect on the depth of our own worship and devotion to Jesus. Mary's act challenges us to consider the extravagance with which we express our love for the Savior and the humility with which we approach Him. The fragrance permeating the house serves as a metaphor for the transformative influence of authentic worship in our lives and communities.

John 12:4 (KJV)
"Then saith one of his disciples, Judas Iscariot, Simon's son, which should betray him,"

Exposition:
Following Mary's extravagant act of anointing Jesus, the narrative introduces Judas Iscariot, one of Jesus's disciples, and notes that he would later betray Jesus.

196

Commentary:

Judas Iscariot's reaction to Mary's costly and symbolic act provides a stark contrast to the atmosphere of worship and devotion. The identification of Judas as the one who would betray Jesus adds a layer of foreboding to the narrative.

Judas's response reflects a different set of values, as he focuses on the apparent waste of resources rather than appreciating the profound expression of love and devotion. The Gospel of John specifically notes that Judas would later betray Jesus, emphasizing the growing tension within the group of disciples.

This verse foreshadows the upcoming betrayal and sets the stage for the events leading to Jesus's arrest. It underscores the diversity of responses to Jesus, ranging from deep devotion to betrayal, within the inner circle of His followers.

As readers, we are prompted to consider the motivations behind our own actions and responses to Jesus. The contrasting reactions of Mary and Judas serve as a poignant reminder of the choices we make in expressing our devotion to Christ and the potential pitfalls of allowing worldly values to influence our hearts.

John 12:5 (KJV):
"Why was not this ointment sold for three hundred pence, and given to the poor?"

Expository Study and Commentary:

In this verse, we find Judas Iscariot expressing disapproval over Mary's anointing of Jesus with costly ointment. Judas questions the perceived waste of resources that could have been sold for a considerable amount of money and given to the poor.

Context:
This event takes place in the house of Lazarus, whom Jesus had recently raised from the dead. Mary, Lazarus' sister, takes a pound

of expensive ointment, anoints Jesus' feet, and wipes them with her hair. The fragrance of the ointment fills the house, creating a significant moment of devotion.

Judas' Perspective:
Judas' objection may seem compassionate on the surface, advocating for the funds to be used for charitable purposes. However, John provides insight into Judas' character by stating in verse 6 that he was not truly concerned about the poor but was a thief and carried the money bag, stealing from what was put into it.

Spiritual Significance:
Mary's act of anointing Jesus is a profound expression of love, devotion, and recognition of Jesus' imminent sacrifice. She understands the spiritual significance of Jesus' presence and mission, choosing to honor Him with her most precious possession. This contrasts sharply with Judas, who prioritizes material wealth over recognizing the worthiness of Jesus.

Application:
The passage invites us to reflect on our own devotion to Christ. Do we, like Mary, recognize the worthiness of Jesus and offer Him our best? Or, are we, like Judas, tempted to prioritize worldly concerns over spiritual truths?

References:
1. Matthew 26:6-13 (KJV): This parallel passage in Matthew provides additional details about the anointing, including Jesus commending Mary for her act.
2. Mark 14:3-9 (KJV): Another parallel account in Mark, shedding light on the event and its implications.
3. Luke 10:38-42 (KJV): A glimpse into Mary's character, as she is also portrayed as one who sits at Jesus' feet, listening to His words.

In conclusion, John 12:5 offers us valuable insights into the nature of true devotion, contrasting the selfless love of Mary with the selfish motives of Judas. It prompts us to examine our own hearts and priorities in our relationship with Christ.

John 12:6 (KJV):
"This he said, not that he cared for the poor, but because he was a thief, and had the bag, and bare what was put therein."

Expository Study and Commentary:

In this verse, the evangelist John provides insight into Judas Iscariot's motivation for objecting to the expensive anointing of Jesus. Judas' objection under the guise of concern for the poor is revealed as a hypocritical cover for his own thieving tendencies.

Context:
As mentioned in the previous commentary on verse 5, Mary has anointed Jesus with costly ointment, and Judas, feigning concern for the poor, questions the perceived extravagance.

Judas' True Motivation:
The verse explicitly states that Judas' expressed concern for the poor was not genuine. His role as the treasurer among the disciples afforded him control over the money bag, but instead of using it for the benefit of others, he was stealing from it. This revelation unveils the hypocrisy of Judas' objection and highlights his self-serving nature.

Spiritual Lessons:
This incident provides a stark contrast between genuine devotion, as exemplified by Mary, and the hypocrisy of those who feign righteousness for personal gain. It serves as a warning against allowing personal interests and greed to masquerade as altruism.

Application:
Believers are urged to examine their motives and intentions. Are our actions and expressions of concern for others driven by genuine compassion and love, or are they veiled attempts to serve our own interests? This verse prompts self-reflection and calls for a sincere commitment to righteousness and selflessness.

References:
1. Matthew 26:14-16 (KJV): This passage in Matthew provides additional details about Judas' betrayal of Jesus, revealing the agreement he made with the chief priests for thirty pieces of silver.
2. Mark 14:10-11 (KJV): A parallel account in Mark shedding light on Judas' agreement with the religious authorities.

In conclusion, John 12:6 serves as a crucial revelation regarding Judas' character, exposing the discrepancy between his words and actions. It challenges believers to cultivate genuine motives and sincerity in their service and expressions of care for others, cautioning against the pitfalls of hypocrisy and self-serving behavior.

John 12:7 (KJV):
"Then said Jesus, Let her alone: against the day of my burying hath she kept this."

Expository Study and Commentary:

In this verse, Jesus responds to Judas' objection, defending Mary's act of anointing Him with expensive ointment. Jesus acknowledges the significance of Mary's gesture, attributing it to her understanding of His impending death and burial.

Context:
Mary has anointed Jesus with costly ointment, prompting Judas to object, suggesting that the ointment could have been sold to benefit the poor. Jesus responds to Judas, affirming Mary's action.

Jesus' Response:
Jesus instructs Judas and others to leave Mary alone, recognizing the deeper spiritual significance of her act. He indicates that Mary's anointing is connected to the approaching day of His burial. Jesus, fully aware of His imminent crucifixion and burial, commends Mary for her act of love and preparation.

Symbolism and Meaning:

Mary's anointing is symbolic of the preparation for Jesus' burial. Anointing with oil was a customary practice in Jewish culture for preparing a body for burial. By anointing Jesus in this way, Mary unknowingly acknowledges and participates in the preparation for His sacrificial death.

Application:
This verse prompts believers to consider their own awareness of the significance of Jesus' sacrifice. Mary's act serves as a reminder of the importance of understanding and appreciating the deeper spiritual truths associated with Jesus' mission, especially His impending death and resurrection.

References:
1. Matthew 26:10-13 (KJV): A parallel passage in Matthew where Jesus defends Mary's actions, emphasizing the significance of her anointing in preparation for His burial.
2. Mark 14:6-9 (KJV): Another parallel account in Mark, providing additional insights into Jesus' response and the spiritual significance of Mary's gesture.

In conclusion, John 12:7 captures Jesus' response to Mary's anointing, shedding light on the deeper spiritual meaning behind her act. It encourages believers to reflect on their own understanding of the profound truths of Jesus' sacrifice and the significance of His death and resurrection in their lives.

John 12:8 (KJV):
"For the poor always ye have with you; but me ye have not always."

Expository Study and Commentary:

In this verse, Jesus responds further to Judas and provides a perspective on the allocation of resources. He acknowledges the importance of caring for the poor but emphasizes the unique and limited opportunity to express love and devotion to Him, recognizing His imminent departure.

Context:
Following Mary's anointing, Judas questioned the use of expensive ointment, suggesting it could have been sold for the benefit of the poor. Jesus defends Mary's action in the previous verses and now speaks to the perpetual nature of poverty and the temporary availability of His physical presence.

Jesus' Response:
Jesus quotes a well-known Old Testament passage from Deuteronomy 15:11, acknowledging the ongoing existence of poverty in the world. However, He contrasts this with the transient nature of His physical presence among them. The implication is that while the disciples will have opportunities to serve the poor continuously, the chance to express such personal devotion to Jesus, particularly in the form of anointing, is limited.

Spiritual Significance:
This statement carries profound spiritual significance. Jesus, aware of His impending crucifixion and departure, highlights the unique opportunity for the disciples to demonstrate love and devotion directly to Him. The temporal nature of His physical presence emphasizes the urgency of recognizing and expressing devotion to Christ while He is physically present.

Application:
This verse challenges believers to prioritize their relationship with Christ. While acts of charity and caring for the poor are important and ongoing responsibilities, there are unique moments when we can express deep, personal devotion to Jesus. It encourages us to seize these opportunities to intimately connect with Christ in ways that may not be possible in His physical absence.

References:
1. Matthew 26:11 (KJV): A parallel passage in Matthew where Jesus reiterates the concept of always having the poor but emphasizes the limited time His physical presence will be with them.

2. Mark 14:7 (KJV): Another parallel account in Mark, providing additional insights into Jesus' response and the temporal nature of His presence.

In conclusion, John 12:8 underscores the importance of balancing our responsibilities towards others, especially the poor, with recognizing and seizing unique opportunities to express personal devotion to Jesus, particularly in light of His impending departure.

John 12:9 (KJV):
"Much people of the Jews therefore knew that he was there: and they came not for Jesus' sake only, but that they might see Lazarus also, whom he had raised from the dead."

Expository Study and Commentary:

In this verse, the focus shifts to the growing awareness among the Jewish people about Jesus' presence, not solely driven by a desire to see Jesus but also to witness Lazarus, whom Jesus had recently raised from the dead.

Context:
This verse follows the discussion about Mary's anointing and Jesus' response to Judas. The attention now turns to the crowd of Jews who were drawn to the place where Jesus was, partly due to the remarkable miracle of Lazarus being raised from the dead.

Crowds' Motivations:
The people's curiosity is evident as they come not only for Jesus but also to witness the living proof of His miraculous power in Lazarus. The resurrection of Lazarus had created a significant buzz, leading to increased public interest in Jesus.

Significance of Lazarus:
Lazarus becomes a central figure in this narrative, symbolizing the power of Jesus over death. His presence serves as a living testimony to the miraculous abilities of Jesus and adds a layer of significance to the events leading up to Jesus' crucifixion.

Application:
This verse prompts reflection on the various motivations people may have for seeking Jesus. While some may approach Him purely for the miraculous, it serves as a reminder that genuine faith should extend beyond seeking signs and wonders. The resurrection of Lazarus illustrates the power and authority of Jesus over life and death, inviting believers to place their trust in Him.

References:
1. John 11:38-44 (KJV): The account of Lazarus' resurrection, providing the background for the increasing attention on Jesus and Lazarus.
2. John 12:17-18 (KJV): Later in the chapter, the crowd's testimony about Lazarus further contributes to the public's growing interest in Jesus.

In conclusion, John 12:9 highlights the growing popularity of Jesus among the Jewish people, driven not only by His teachings but also by the awe-inspiring miracle of Lazarus' resurrection. It encourages believers to seek Jesus for more than just signs and wonders, recognizing the profound impact of His power and authority in all aspects of life.

John 12:10 (KJV):
"But the chief priests consulted that they might put Lazarus also to death."

Expository Study and Commentary:

In this verse, the chief priests, disturbed by the increasing popularity of Jesus due to Lazarus' resurrection, plot to put Lazarus to death. This sinister plan reveals the threat they perceive in the miraculous testimony Lazarus provides to Jesus' authority.

Context:
The verse follows the mention of the growing crowd's interest in Jesus and Lazarus due to the resurrection miracle. The chief priests,

threatened by Jesus' influence and the impact of Lazarus' testimony, conspire to eliminate the living evidence of Jesus' power.

Chief Priests' Motivation:
The chief priests, already hostile towards Jesus, view Lazarus as a living proof of Jesus' divine authority. The resurrection of Lazarus not only draws people to Jesus but also validates His claim to be the Messiah. In an attempt to suppress this evidence, they plan to kill Lazarus.

Symbolism:
The plot against Lazarus underscores the depth of opposition against Jesus. It symbolizes the religious authorities' desperation to quash any evidence that might strengthen the faith of the people in Jesus as the promised Messiah.

Application:
This verse prompts reflection on the lengths to which opposition to the truth can go. The chief priests' decision to plot against Lazarus serves as a stark reminder of the spiritual warfare surrounding Jesus' ministry. It encourages believers to stand firm in the face of opposition and to recognize the power of Jesus even in the midst of threats and hostility.

References:
1. John 11:43-44 (KJV): The account of Lazarus' resurrection, providing the foundation for the chief priests' concern and conspiracy.
2. John 12:17-19 (KJV): The crowd's testimony about Lazarus, contributing to the growing tension and opposition from the religious authorities.

In conclusion, John 12:10 reveals the dark intentions of the chief priests as they conspire to eliminate Lazarus, a living testament to Jesus' divine power. This verse highlights the spiritual conflict surrounding Jesus' ministry and serves as a call for believers to remain steadfast in their faith despite opposition.

John 12:11 (KJV):

"Because that by reason of him many of the Jews went away, and believed on Jesus."

Expository Study and Commentary:

In this verse, the evangelist John explains the motivation behind the chief priests' plot to kill Lazarus. The increasing belief in Jesus among the Jews, sparked by Lazarus' resurrection, becomes a threat to the religious authorities, prompting their sinister plan.

Context:
Following the mention of the chief priests' conspiracy against Lazarus, John clarifies that the priests were motivated by the impact Lazarus had on the people. Many Jews, influenced by Lazarus' resurrection, were turning away from the religious authorities and believing in Jesus.

Impact of Lazarus' Resurrection:
Lazarus' miraculous resurrection served as a catalyst for faith. Witnessing such a compelling demonstration of Jesus' power led many Jews to reconsider their allegiance and beliefs, turning towards Jesus as the Messiah.

Religious Authorities' Response:
Fearing the loss of influence and control over the people, the chief priests resorted to extreme measures. The plot to kill Lazarus reflects their desperation to suppress the growing movement towards Jesus and maintain their religious authority.

Application:
This verse prompts reflection on the transformative power of witnessing God's miraculous work. Lazarus' resurrection not only demonstrated Jesus' authority over death but also became a powerful tool for leading people to believe in Him. It challenges believers to recognize the impact of personal testimonies and miracles in drawing others to faith.

References:

1. John 11:43-44 (KJV): The account of Lazarus' resurrection, laying the foundation for the subsequent impact on the belief of many Jews.

2. John 12:17-19 (KJV): The crowd's testimony about Lazarus, contributing to the growing tension and opposition from the religious authorities.

In conclusion, John 12:11 highlights the chief priests' concern over the increasing belief in Jesus due to Lazarus' resurrection. It emphasizes the profound influence of miracles on faith and challenges believers to recognize the transformative power of witnessing God's miraculous work in drawing others to Him.

John 12:12 (KJV):
"On the next day much people that were come to the feast, when they heard that Jesus was coming to Jerusalem."

Expository Study and Commentary:

In this verse, John sets the stage for the triumphant entry of Jesus into Jerusalem, a significant event known as Palm Sunday. The crowds, having gathered for the Passover feast, learn of Jesus' arrival, leading to an enthusiastic reception.

Context:
The verse follows the narrative of the chief priests' plot against Lazarus and provides a transition to the account of Jesus' entry into Jerusalem, which is a pivotal moment in the Gospel narrative.

Significance of the Feast:
The mention of the Passover feast is crucial as it explains the large gathering of people in Jerusalem. Passover was a major Jewish festival, and people from various regions would converge to celebrate this significant event.

Expectation and Enthusiasm:
The crowds' response to the news of Jesus coming to Jerusalem reflects a heightened expectation. The atmosphere is

charged with excitement as people anticipate the arrival of Jesus, who had gained fame for His teachings and miracles.

Application:
This verse invites reflection on the eagerness with which people anticipated Jesus' presence. It prompts believers to consider their own level of enthusiasm and expectation when it comes to seeking Jesus and experiencing His presence in their lives.

References:
1. Matthew 21:4-11 (KJV): A parallel passage in Matthew providing additional details about Jesus' entry into Jerusalem, including the crowd's use of palm branches.
2. Mark 11:7-11 (KJV): Another parallel account in Mark, offering insights into the atmosphere and reactions during Jesus' entry.

In conclusion, John 12:12 serves as an introduction to the climactic event of Jesus' entry into Jerusalem, emphasizing the anticipation and enthusiasm of the crowds gathered for the Passover feast. It encourages believers to approach their own encounters with Jesus with a similar sense of eagerness and expectation.

John 12:13 (KJV):
"Took branches of palm trees, and went forth to meet him, and cried, Hosanna: Blessed is the King of Israel that cometh in the name of the Lord."

Expository Study and Commentary:

In this verse, the crowds, recognizing Jesus as He enters Jerusalem, express their jubilation by taking palm branches, a symbol of victory and triumph, and acclaiming Jesus as the King of Israel with the word "Hosanna."

Context:
The verse follows the description of the people gathering for the Passover feast, learning about Jesus' arrival, and reflects the

culmination of their excitement as they meet Him during His entry into Jerusalem.

Symbolism of Palm Branches:
The use of palm branches has historical and cultural significance. In the Jewish tradition, palm branches were associated with victory and joy. The people's choice of this symbol emphasizes their acknowledgment of Jesus as a triumphant and victorious figure.

Hosanna - A Cry of Praise:
"Hosanna" is a Hebrew expression meaning "save, we pray" or "save us." The crowd's use of this term reflects both a recognition of Jesus as a Messianic figure and a cry for salvation and deliverance.

The King of Israel:
The people's declaration of Jesus as the King of Israel is a significant acknowledgment of His messianic identity. They identify Him as the promised leader who comes in the name of the Lord.

Application:
This verse prompts believers to reflect on their own acclamation of Jesus. Do we recognize Him as our triumphant King, the source of our salvation and deliverance? It encourages a heartfelt expression of praise and acknowledgment of Jesus' lordship in our lives.

References:
1. Matthew 21:8-9 (KJV): A parallel passage in Matthew providing additional details about the crowd's use of palm branches and their cry of "Hosanna."
2. Mark 11:8-10 (KJV): Another parallel account in Mark, offering insights into the atmosphere and reactions during Jesus' entry.

In conclusion, John 12:13 captures the moment of Jesus' entry into Jerusalem, marked by the crowds' enthusiastic expression of praise, the symbolic use of palm branches, and their declaration of Jesus as the King of Israel. It encourages believers to join in the jubilant acknowledgment of Jesus' lordship and the cry for His saving grace.

John 12:14 (KJV):
"And Jesus, when he had found a young ass, sat thereon; as it is written."

Expository Study and Commentary:

In this verse, John describes Jesus finding a young donkey and sitting on it, fulfilling a prophecy from the Old Testament. This action symbolizes the humility and peaceful nature of Jesus' kingship.

Context:
The verse is part of the account of Jesus' entry into Jerusalem. After the crowd's enthusiastic reception and their acknowledgment of Jesus as the King of Israel, John highlights Jesus' deliberate choice to ride on a young donkey.

Fulfillment of Prophecy:
The phrase "as it is written" refers to the prophecy in Zechariah 9:9, which states, "Rejoice greatly, O daughter of Zion; shout, Daughter of Jerusalem! See, your king comes to you, righteous and victorious, lowly and riding on a donkey, on a colt, the foal of a donkey." Jesus consciously fulfills this prophecy, portraying Himself not as a conquering military king but as a humble, peaceful, and righteous leader.

Symbolism of the Young Donkey:
The choice of a young donkey instead of a majestic horse emphasizes humility and peace. In ancient times, a king riding a donkey symbolized a ruler coming in peace, in contrast to a king on a war horse.

Application:
This verse invites believers to reflect on the nature of Christ's kingship. Jesus, the King of Kings, chose a humble and peaceful entrance, setting an example for His followers. It challenges us to

embrace humility and peace in our lives as we seek to follow the ways of our King.

References:
1. Matthew 21:4-5 (KJV): A parallel passage in Matthew providing additional details about Jesus' choice of a donkey and the fulfillment of the prophecy.
2. Zechariah 9:9 (KJV): The Old Testament prophecy fulfilled by Jesus, emphasizing the humble and peaceful nature of His entry.

In conclusion, John 12:14 captures the intentional fulfillment of prophecy as Jesus chooses to ride on a young donkey during His entry into Jerusalem. This symbolic act underscores the humility and peace associated with Christ's kingship and provides a powerful lesson for believers on embracing these qualities in their own lives.

John 12:15 (KJV):
"Fear not, daughter of Sion: behold, thy King cometh, sitting on an ass's colt."

Expository Study and Commentary:

In this verse, John quotes a portion of the prophecy from Zechariah 9:9, emphasizing the reassurance to the daughter of Zion (Jerusalem) that her King is coming in a way that signifies peace and humility.

Context:
The verse follows Jesus' entry into Jerusalem on a young donkey, fulfilling the prophecy from the Old Testament. The choice of a donkey emphasizes the peaceful and humble nature of Jesus' kingship.

Reassurance to Jerusalem:
The words "Fear not, daughter of Sion" echo a message of comfort and reassurance to Jerusalem. The arrival of the King on a donkey is a sign of peace, and the people are encouraged not to fear but to recognize and welcome their peaceful and righteous King.

Symbolism of the Ass's Colt:
The mention of the ass's colt reinforces the humble nature of Jesus' entry. The colt, being a young and untamed animal, adds an extra layer of symbolism, signifying the peaceful and gentle character of Jesus' reign.

Application:
This verse prompts believers to reflect on the reassurance and comfort that Jesus brings as the King of Peace. It encourages us to trust in the peaceful nature of Christ's rule in our lives and to welcome Him with open hearts, free from fear.

References:
1. Matthew 21:5 (KJV): A parallel passage in Matthew presenting a similar quotation from Zechariah 9:9 during Jesus' entry into Jerusalem.
2. Zechariah 9:9 (KJV): The Old Testament prophecy fulfilled by Jesus, emphasizing the peaceful and humble nature of His entry.

In conclusion, John 12:15 reinforces the message of peace and reassurance as Jesus fulfills the prophecy from Zechariah 9:9. It underscores the comforting nature of Christ's kingship and encourages believers to embrace the peace He brings into their lives.

John 12:16 (KJV):
"These things understood not his disciples at the first: but when Jesus was glorified, then remembered they that these things were written of him, and that they had done these things unto him."

Expository Study and Commentary:

In this verse, John reflects on the disciples' initial lack of understanding regarding the significance of Jesus' actions, particularly His entry into Jerusalem on a donkey. The disciples come to comprehend the prophetic fulfillment of Scripture only after Jesus' glorification.

Context:
The verse follows the account of Jesus' entry into Jerusalem and the quotation from Zechariah 9:9. The disciples, at the time of these events, did not fully grasp the prophetic nature of what was happening.

Disciples' Lack of Understanding:
The disciples, like many others at that time, did not immediately understand the symbolic significance of Jesus' actions. Their understanding was limited, and they were likely expecting a more conventional form of kingship, not fully comprehending the depth of the prophetic fulfillment in Jesus' humble and peaceful entry.

Understanding after Jesus' Glorification:
The phrase "when Jesus was glorified" likely refers to the events following Jesus' death, resurrection, and ascension. It was through the lens of these transformative events that the disciples gained a deeper understanding of the Scriptures and recognized that what they had witnessed was a fulfillment of prophecy.

Application:
This verse encourages believers to trust in the unfolding revelation of God's plan. Sometimes, like the disciples, we may not fully understand the significance of certain events in the moment. However, as we grow in our faith and experience the transformative work of Christ, our understanding deepens, and we see God's plan more clearly.

References:
1. Luke 24:44-46 (KJV): Jesus, after His resurrection, explains to the disciples how the Scriptures were fulfilled in Him, contributing to their deeper understanding.
2. Acts 2:33-36 (KJV): Peter, after the day of Pentecost, proclaims the exaltation and glorification of Jesus.

In conclusion, John 12:16 highlights the disciples' initial lack of understanding regarding Jesus' actions and their subsequent realization after His glorification. It prompts believers to trust in the unfolding revelation of God's plan and to recognize the deeper meaning of events in light of the transformative work of Christ.

John 12:17 (KJV):
"The people, therefore, that was with him when he called Lazarus out of his grave and raised him from the dead, bare record."

Expository Study and Commentary:

In this verse, John refers to the eyewitness testimony of those who were present when Jesus performed the miraculous raising of Lazarus from the dead. This record serves as a powerful witness to Jesus' divine authority and contributes to the growing belief in Him.

Context:
The verse is part of the narrative following Jesus' entry into Jerusalem. It emphasizes the impact of Lazarus' resurrection on the people who were present when Jesus called him out of the grave.

Eyewitness Testimony:
The people mentioned in this verse are those who personally witnessed the extraordinary event of Lazarus being raised from the dead. Their firsthand experience and testimony become a compelling factor in the increasing popularity of Jesus.

The Significance of Lazarus' Resurrection:
Lazarus' resurrection is a central theme in John's Gospel, and it plays a pivotal role in the events leading up to Jesus' crucifixion. The miraculous nature of this event reinforces Jesus' authority over death and contributes to the crowd's acknowledgment of Him as the Messiah.

Application:
This verse underscores the power of personal testimony in spreading the message of Jesus. Believers are encouraged to share their own experiences of God's work in their lives, recognizing the impact such testimony can have in leading others to faith.

References:

1. John 11:43-44 (KJV): The detailed account of Jesus calling Lazarus out of the grave, laying the foundation for the witness mentioned in John 12:17.

2. John 12:1-2 (KJV): The introduction to the events surrounding Lazarus' resurrection, including Mary's anointing of Jesus.

In conclusion, John 12:17 highlights the powerful impact of eyewitness testimony, particularly regarding Lazarus' resurrection. This testimony contributes to the growing belief in Jesus and serves as a reminder of the significance of personal experiences in sharing the message of faith.

John 12:18 (KJV):
"For this cause the people also met him, for that they heard that he had done this miracle."

Expository Study and Commentary:

In this verse, John provides insight into the reason why the crowd gathered to meet Jesus during His entry into Jerusalem. The people had heard about the miraculous raising of Lazarus, and this extraordinary event served as a powerful motivator for their enthusiastic reception of Jesus.

Context:
The verse follows the mention of those who bore witness to Lazarus' resurrection and the impact it had on the people. It establishes a direct connection between the miraculous event and the crowd's desire to meet Jesus.

The Cause for Gathering:
The phrase "for this cause" points to the specific reason why the people gathered. The cause is the news of Lazarus' miraculous resurrection. The crowd, stirred by the reports of this extraordinary feat, eagerly sought to meet the One who performed such a remarkable miracle.

The Significance of Lazarus' Miracle:
Lazarus' resurrection becomes a central theme, creating a buzz among the people and generating anticipation. The miracle serves as a compelling sign of Jesus' authority over death and contributes significantly to the heightened atmosphere during His entry into Jerusalem.

Application:
This verse underscores the impact of miracles in drawing people to Jesus. It prompts believers to reflect on the transformative power of God's miraculous works in their own lives and encourages them to share these experiences to attract others to faith.

References:
1. John 11:43-44 (KJV): The detailed account of Jesus calling Lazarus out of the grave, laying the foundation for the crowd's gathering mentioned in John 12:18.
2. John 12:12-13 (KJV): The description of Jesus' entry into Jerusalem, highlighting the enthusiastic reception of the crowd.

In conclusion, John 12:18 highlights the cause for the people's gathering to meet Jesus, emphasizing the powerful impact of Lazarus' resurrection as a compelling reason for their enthusiastic reception. It serves as a reminder of the transformative influence of miracles in drawing people to faith.

John 12:19 (KJV):
"The Pharisees, therefore, said among themselves, Perceive ye how ye prevail nothing? behold, the world is gone after him."

Expository Study and Commentary:

In this verse, the Pharisees express their frustration and concern among themselves as they observe the growing popularity of Jesus. They acknowledge that their efforts to oppose Him have been ineffective, and the increasing support for Jesus among the people becomes a source of anxiety for them.

Context:

The verse is part of the narrative following Jesus' entry into Jerusalem and the enthusiastic reception by the crowd. The Pharisees, who were critical of Jesus and sought to undermine Him, react to the overwhelming response He receives.

Pharisees' Frustration:

The Pharisees' conversation reflects their recognition that their attempts to thwart Jesus' influence have not succeeded. The phrase "Perceive ye how ye prevail nothing?" reveals their frustration and the realization that their opposition has not deterred the growing popularity of Jesus.

The World Going After Him:

The Pharisees express their concern by stating, "behold, the world is gone after him." This hyperbolic statement emphasizes the widespread impact of Jesus' ministry, suggesting that people from various places and backgrounds are aligning themselves with Him.

Application:

This verse serves as a cautionary reminder about the futility of opposing God's work. It prompts believers to remain steadfast in their faith, recognizing that God's purpose prevails even in the face of opposition. It also encourages humility and a willingness to discern and embrace God's truth.

References:

1. John 12:12-13 (KJV): The description of Jesus' entry into Jerusalem and the crowd's enthusiastic reception, setting the stage for the Pharisees' reaction.

2. John 11:47-48 (KJV): Earlier in John's Gospel, the Pharisees express concerns about the impact of Jesus' miracles and popularity.

In conclusion, John 12:19 reveals the Pharisees' frustration at the growing popularity of Jesus and serves as a reminder of the challenges and futility of opposing God's work. It encourages believers to trust in God's sovereignty and to remain faithful in the face of opposition.

John 12:20 (KJV):
"And there were certain Greeks among them that came up to worship at the feast."

Expository Study and Commentary:

In this verse, John introduces a significant event where certain Greeks, likely Gentile proselytes or God-fearing individuals, approach the disciples with the intention of meeting Jesus during the Passover feast.

Context:
The verse follows the Pharisees' discussion about the world going after Jesus, expressing their concern over His growing popularity. The mention of Greeks coming to worship at the feast serves as a transition to the broader impact of Jesus' ministry beyond the Jewish community.

Significance of the Greeks:
The presence of Greeks seeking Jesus is noteworthy. It signifies the widening impact of Jesus' ministry, extending beyond the boundaries of the Jewish community. The Greeks' interest in worshiping at the feast indicates a shared spiritual curiosity and an acknowledgment of Jesus as a significant religious figure.

Foreshadowing the Inclusivity of the Gospel:
This event foreshadows the inclusive nature of the Gospel message, which would extend to the Gentiles after Jesus' death and resurrection. The Greeks' desire to see Jesus aligns with the broader theme in John's Gospel, emphasizing that Jesus is the Savior not only for the Jews but for all humanity.

Application:
This verse challenges believers to embrace the inclusive nature of the Gospel. It encourages a recognition that Jesus' message is for

people of all nations and backgrounds. The Greeks' desire to see Jesus prompts reflection on our own eagerness to encounter and worship Him.

References:
1. Matthew 28:19-20 (KJV): The Great Commission emphasizes making disciples of all nations, aligning with the inclusive nature of Jesus' message.
2. Acts 10:34-35 (KJV): The account of Peter's realization about God's acceptance of Gentiles, reinforcing the broader reach of the Gospel.

In conclusion, John 12:20 introduces Greeks seeking Jesus, symbolizing the expanding impact of His ministry beyond the Jewish community. This event foreshadows the inclusive nature of the Gospel and encourages believers to embrace the message that Jesus is the Savior for people of all nations.

John 12:21 (KJV):
"The same came therefore to Philip, which was of Bethsaida of Galilee, and desired him, saying, Sir, we would see Jesus."

Expository Study and Commentary:

In this verse, one of the Greeks who came to worship at the feast approaches Philip, expressing a deep desire to see Jesus. This interaction highlights the accessibility of Jesus to those from different backgrounds and sets the stage for a profound encounter.

Context:
The verse follows the introduction of Greeks seeking Jesus, emphasizing their eagerness to meet Him. The focus shifts to one particular Greek who approaches Philip, one of the disciples, with the specific request to see Jesus.

Philip's Connection:
The choice of Philip as the recipient of the Greeks' request is interesting. Philip, a disciple from Bethsaida of Galilee, was likely

familiar with Gentile influences in that region. The Greeks approach someone with a potential understanding of their cultural context.

"Sir, We Would See Jesus":
The Greeks' respectful address to Philip and their straightforward request reflect a deep longing to encounter Jesus. The phrase "we would see Jesus" goes beyond mere curiosity; it suggests a desire for a meaningful and transformative encounter with the Lord.

Application:
This verse encourages believers to be approachable and to facilitate encounters with Jesus for those seeking Him. It prompts reflection on our readiness to connect others with Jesus, recognizing that people from various backgrounds may have a genuine desire to experience His presence.

References:
1. Matthew 28:19-20 (KJV): The Great Commission emphasizes making disciples of all nations, aligning with the inclusive nature of Jesus' message.
2. Acts 8:27-39 (KJV): The account of Philip and the Ethiopian eunuch, highlighting the disciples' role in facilitating encounters with Jesus.

In conclusion, John 12:21 depicts a Greek approaching Philip with a sincere desire to see Jesus. This interaction exemplifies the accessibility of Jesus to people from different backgrounds and encourages believers to play a role in facilitating meaningful encounters with the Lord.

John 12:21 (KJV):
"The same came therefore to Philip, which was of Bethsaida of Galilee, and desired him, saying, Sir, we would see Jesus."

Expository Study and Commentary:

In this verse, a group of Greeks, who came to worship at the feast, approaches Philip with a heartfelt request to see Jesus. This interaction signifies the growing interest in Jesus from individuals outside the Jewish community and sets the stage for a significant moment.

Context:
Following the Pharisees' concern about the popularity of Jesus and the Greeks expressing a desire to see Him, the focus shifts to a specific encounter. The Greeks approach Philip, one of the disciples, expressing their earnest wish to see Jesus.

Philip's Connection:
Philip, as a disciple from Bethsaida of Galilee, might have been seen as approachable or more open to interactions with non-Jews due to his background. The Greeks choose Philip, perhaps recognizing a potential bridge between their Gentile perspective and the disciples.

"Sir, We Would See Jesus":
The Greeks' use of the title "Sir" reflects a respectful approach to Philip. Their straightforward request, "we would see Jesus," goes beyond a mere desire for a physical sighting; it indicates a profound longing to encounter and know Jesus personally.

Application:
This verse invites believers to consider their role in connecting others with Jesus. Like Philip, we are called to be approachable and facilitate meaningful encounters with Christ for those seeking Him. It also highlights the universal appeal of Jesus, drawing people from diverse backgrounds.

References:
1. Matthew 28:19-20 (KJV): The Great Commission emphasizes making disciples of all nations, aligning with the inclusive nature of Jesus' message.
2. Acts 10:34-35 (KJV): The account of Peter's realization about God's acceptance of Gentiles, reinforcing the broader reach of the Gospel.

In conclusion, John 12:21 depicts a poignant moment where Greeks express their earnest desire to see Jesus, approaching Philip as a potential link to Him. This encounter underscores the universal appeal of Jesus and challenges believers to facilitate meaningful connections with Him for those seeking a personal encounter.

John 12:22 (KJV):
"Philip cometh and telleth Andrew: and again Andrew and Philip tell Jesus."

Expository Study and Commentary:

In this verse, Philip, upon receiving the Greeks' request to see Jesus, turns to Andrew, and together they convey the message to Jesus. This exchange illustrates the disciples' role in facilitating the encounter and sets the stage for Jesus' response.

Context:
The verse is part of the narrative where Greeks express their desire to see Jesus. Instead of directly approaching Jesus, the Greeks initially make their request to Philip, who then involves Andrew in conveying the message to Jesus.

Philip and Andrew's Collaboration:
Philip's decision to consult Andrew suggests a sense of unity and collaboration among the disciples. Andrew, like Philip, is from Bethsaida of Galilee, and their shared background may contribute to their working together in this instance.

Symbolism of Philip and Andrew:
Philip and Andrew often appear together in the Gospel of John (e.g., feeding the multitude with loaves and fish - John 6:5-7). Their collaboration can symbolize the inclusive nature of Jesus' ministry, reaching both Jews and Gentiles.

Telling Jesus:
The act of telling Jesus about the Greeks' request highlights the disciples' understanding of their role as intermediaries between

those seeking Jesus and Jesus Himself. It sets the stage for Jesus' response to the Gentiles' request.

Application:
This verse encourages believers to work collaboratively in facilitating encounters with Jesus. It emphasizes the importance of community and unity in sharing the message of Christ. It also prompts reflection on our role in connecting others with Jesus through meaningful communication and collaboration.

References:
1. John 6:5-7 (KJV): Another instance where Philip and Andrew appear together in the Gospel, showcasing their collaboration in Jesus' ministry.
2. Matthew 28:19-20 (KJV): The Great Commission emphasizes making disciples of all nations, aligning with the inclusive nature of Jesus' message.

In conclusion, John 12:22 portrays a collaborative effort between Philip and Andrew in conveying the Greeks' request to see Jesus. This interaction symbolizes the disciples' role as intermediaries and highlights the importance of unity and collaboration in sharing the message of Christ.

John 12:23 (KJV):
"And Jesus answered them, saying, The hour is come, that the Son of man should be glorified."

Expository Study and Commentary:

In this verse, Jesus responds to the message brought by Philip and Andrew about the Greeks' desire to see Him. His words indicate a pivotal moment—the beginning of a series of events that will ultimately lead to His glorification through the impending crucifixion and resurrection.

Context:

Following the Greeks' request, Philip and Andrew convey the message to Jesus. Instead of directly addressing the Greeks' request, Jesus responds with a statement that signifies the culmination of His earthly ministry.

The Hour of Glory:
Jesus' declaration, "The hour is come," refers to the appointed time for His sacrificial death on the cross. This hour marks the climax of His earthly mission, where the Son of Man, a title Jesus often used for Himself, will achieve glory through the redemption of humanity.

Glorification through the Cross:
The concept of glory in this context challenges conventional expectations. Jesus' glorification is not through earthly triumph or acclaim but through the selfless act of giving His life for the salvation of others. The cross becomes the means by which Jesus is exalted.

Universal Significance:
While the Greeks' request triggers this response, Jesus' statement transcends the specific situation, addressing the universal impact of His impending sacrifice. The inclusion of the Gentiles in this narrative foreshadows the extension of salvation to people of all nations.

Application:
This verse prompts believers to reflect on the transformative power of the cross. Jesus' glorification, achieved through self-sacrifice, challenges worldly notions of success. It calls us to embrace the profound significance of the cross in our own lives and to share the message of salvation with a global perspective.

References:
1. John 17:1-5 (KJV): Jesus' prayer for His glorification, emphasizing the connection between His glorification and the completion of His mission.
2. Matthew 20:28 (KJV): Jesus' statement about Himself, highlighting His purpose to give His life as a ransom for many.

In conclusion, John 12:23 captures a pivotal moment as Jesus acknowledges the appointed hour for His glorification through the upcoming crucifixion. This statement sets the stage for the profound significance of the cross in the redemption of humanity and challenges believers to grasp the transformative power of Jesus' sacrificial act.

John 12:24 (KJV):
"Verily, verily, I say unto you, Except a corn of wheat fall into the ground and die, it abideth alone: but if it die, it bringeth forth much fruit."

Expository Study and Commentary:

In this verse, Jesus uses a powerful metaphor of a grain of wheat to illustrate the principle of self-sacrifice and resurrection. He emphasizes that true life and fruitfulness come through death and transformation.

Context:
Jesus is responding to the Greeks' request to see Him and, in doing so, goes beyond a simple acknowledgment. He imparts a profound truth about the nature of His mission and the pathway to genuine life.

The Metaphor of Wheat:
Jesus begins with the solemn affirmation, "Verily, verily," underscoring the importance of the forthcoming message. The metaphor of a grain of wheat falling into the ground and dying is a vivid illustration of His imminent sacrificial death on the cross.

Life through Death:
The central theme is that life and fruitfulness emerge from the process of death and transformation. The grain of wheat, if it remains intact, remains alone. However, if it undergoes the necessary process of falling into the ground and dying, it brings forth much fruit. Jesus is alluding to His impending death and resurrection, where through His sacrifice, He will bear much fruit in the form of redeemed lives.

Application:
This verse challenges believers to grasp the paradoxical truth that true life and fruitfulness often emerge through self-sacrifice and surrender. It calls for a willingness to embrace the transformative process, following the example of Christ's sacrificial love.

References:
1. Matthew 16:24-25 (KJV): Jesus' call to discipleship involves denying oneself, taking up the cross, and losing one's life to find it.
2. Philippians 2:5-11 (KJV): Paul's reflection on the humility and exaltation of Christ, emphasizing the sacrificial nature of His mission.

In conclusion, John 12:24 employs the metaphor of a grain of wheat to convey the profound truth that true life and fruitfulness emerge through the process of self-sacrifice and transformation. This principle is foundational to understanding the significance of Christ's sacrificial death and resurrection and challenges believers to embrace a similar sacrificial attitude in their own lives.

John 12:25 (KJV):
"He that loveth his life shall lose it, and he that hateth his life in this world shall keep it unto life eternal."

Expository Study and Commentary:

In this verse, Jesus expands on the theme of self-sacrifice, emphasizing that those who prioritize their earthly life above all will lose it, while those who are willing to surrender their lives for His sake will find true and eternal life.

Context:
Following the metaphor of the grain of wheat, Jesus continues to articulate the profound principles of discipleship, challenging his listeners to reconsider their priorities and perspectives on life.

The Contrast in Perspectives:

The verse presents a stark contrast between two attitudes toward life. "He that loveth his life" refers to those who prioritize and cling to their earthly existence above all. In contrast, "he that hateth his life in this world" signifies those who are willing to let go of self-centered desires and ambitions.

Losing to Find:
The paradoxical statement "shall lose it" emphasizes the transitory nature of a life lived solely for self-gratification. It suggests that a life obsessed with personal desires and worldly pursuits ultimately leads to emptiness and spiritual loss.

Keeping unto Life Eternal:
On the other hand, "shall keep it unto life eternal" indicates that those who are willing to surrender their lives for the sake of Christ and His kingdom will find a deeper, more meaningful, and eternal life. This echoes the earlier theme of the transformative power of self-sacrifice.

Application:
This verse challenges believers to evaluate their priorities and perspectives on life. It encourages a shift from self-centered pursuits to a sacrificial attitude, recognizing that true and eternal life is found in surrendering one's desires for the sake of Christ and His kingdom.

References:
1. Matthew 10:39 (KJV): Jesus' statement that those who lose their lives for His sake will find them.
2. Galatians 2:20 (KJV): Paul's affirmation of living a crucified life with Christ, emphasizing the transformative power of surrender.

In conclusion, John 12:25 presents a powerful teaching on the paradox of losing and finding life. It challenges believers to embrace a sacrificial perspective, prioritizing eternal values over temporal desires, in alignment with the transformative principles of discipleship taught by Jesus.

John 12:26 (KJV):

"If any man serve me, let him follow me; and where I am, there shall also my servant be: if any man serve me, him will my Father honour."

Expository Study and Commentary:

In this verse, Jesus outlines the principles of discipleship, emphasizing that true service to Him involves following His example. The promise of being with Him where He is and receiving honor from the Father underscores the transformative nature of serving Christ.

Context:
Continuing his discourse on discipleship and self-sacrifice, Jesus sets forth the conditions and rewards for those who choose to serve Him. The focus is on the intimate relationship between the servant and the Master.

Conditions of True Service:
The verse begins with the condition of service—following Jesus. It's not merely about performing tasks but involves a deep commitment to imitate Christ, embracing His teachings, and walking in His footsteps. True service is inseparable from discipleship.

The Promise of Presence:
Jesus promises that where He is, His servant will also be. This goes beyond physical proximity; it speaks to the idea of sharing in Christ's presence, glory, and eternal life. The promise underscores the intimate relationship between the servant and the Master.

The Father's Honor:
The final assurance is that the Father will honor those who serve Christ. This honor is not based on worldly standards but is a divine recognition and approval. It reflects the significance and value God places on genuine service in His kingdom.

Application:
This verse challenges believers to evaluate their understanding of service. It calls for a commitment to follow Jesus, embracing His

teachings and imitating His sacrificial love. The promise of sharing in His presence and receiving honor from the Father provides a powerful motivation for genuine discipleship.

References:
1. Matthew 16:24 (KJV): Jesus' call to discipleship involves denying oneself, taking up the cross, and following Him.
2. Philippians 2:5-11 (KJV): Paul's reflection on the humility and exaltation of Christ, emphasizing the sacrificial nature of His mission.

In conclusion, John 12:26 outlines the conditions and rewards of true service to Christ. It challenges believers to go beyond mere tasks, emphasizing the importance of following Jesus, sharing in His presence, and receiving divine honor. This verse underscores the transformative nature of discipleship and the profound privilege of serving the Master.

John 12:27 (KJV):
"Now is my soul troubled; and what shall I say? Father, save me from this hour: but for this cause came I unto this hour."

Expository Study and Commentary:

In this verse, Jesus expresses the internal turmoil of His soul as He contemplates the approaching hour of His crucifixion. His momentary distress reveals the depth of His humanity, and yet, He affirms His divine purpose, acknowledging that His purpose for coming was to fulfill this very hour.

Context:
As Jesus continues to speak about His impending sacrifice, He reveals the internal struggle and emotional weight He bears. The verse provides a glimpse into Jesus' humanity, showcasing the tension between the imminent suffering and His divine mission.

Jesus' Troubled Soul:

The statement "Now is my soul troubled" reveals the genuine emotional turmoil Jesus experiences. This moment captures the human aspect of Christ, facing the weight of the imminent cross, anticipating the physical and spiritual agony He is about to endure.

The Dilemma of Prayer:
Jesus contemplates what to say in this challenging moment. The words "Father, save me from this hour" reflect the human instinct to avoid suffering. However, Jesus quickly aligns His human desire with His divine purpose, acknowledging that His very reason for coming to earth was to face and endure this hour.

For This Cause Came I:
The phrase "but for this cause came I unto this hour" underscores the divine purpose behind Jesus' earthly mission. His primary mission was to fulfill the redemptive plan, and the impending hour of suffering was an integral part of that divine purpose.

Application:
This verse invites believers to reflect on the depth of Jesus' sacrifice. It emphasizes the humanity of Christ, experiencing genuine distress, while reinforcing His unwavering commitment to fulfilling the divine purpose of salvation.

References:
1. Matthew 26:39 (KJV): Jesus' prayer in the Garden of Gethsemane, expressing a similar sentiment of submitting to God's will in the face of impending suffering.
2. Hebrews 5:7-9 (KJV): A passage highlighting the prayers and submission of Jesus, emphasizing His obedience in fulfilling His sacrificial role.

In conclusion, John 12:27 unveils a poignant moment where Jesus, troubled in His soul, grapples with the impending hour of His crucifixion. This verse underscores the genuine humanity of Christ while affirming His unwavering commitment to fulfilling the divine purpose of salvation through His sacrificial death.

John 12:28 (KJV):

"Father, glorify thy name. Then came there a voice from heaven, saying, I have both glorified it, and will glorify it again."

Expository Study and Commentary:

In this verse, Jesus prays to the Father, asking for the glorification of God's name. The response from heaven affirms that God's name has already been glorified and will continue to be glorified, providing assurance and validation of Jesus' mission.

Context:

Following Jesus' expression of internal turmoil about the approaching hour of His crucifixion, He turns to prayer. The request for God to glorify His name reflects Jesus' commitment to fulfilling the divine purpose even in the face of imminent suffering.

Jesus' Prayer for Glorification:

The prayer "Father, glorify thy name" reflects Jesus' ultimate concern for the honor and magnification of God's name. Despite the impending ordeal, Jesus prioritizes the glory of the Father, reinforcing His selfless and obedient nature.

Heavenly Response:

The response from heaven provides divine confirmation. The voice declares that God's name has already been glorified in the past and will be glorified again. This response underscores the divine approval of Jesus' mission, assuring that His sacrificial journey will ultimately bring glory to the Father.

The Triumphant Assurance:

The assurance from heaven carries a triumphant note, affirming that God's name will be glorified again through the events that will unfold. It signifies the culmination of Jesus' earthly mission, pointing toward His impending crucifixion, resurrection, and exaltation.

Application:

This verse encourages believers to prioritize the glorification of God's name in their prayers and actions. It also serves as a reminder that God's plan is triumphant, even in the face of apparent challenges, and that ultimate glory belongs to the Father.

References:
1. Matthew 3:17 (KJV): The voice from heaven at Jesus' baptism, acknowledging Him as the beloved Son in whom God is well pleased.
2. Philippians 2:9-11 (KJV): A passage emphasizing the exaltation of Jesus and the confession that every knee will bow and every tongue confess His lordship.

In conclusion, John 12:28 portrays a pivotal moment of prayer where Jesus seeks the glorification of the Father's name. The heavenly response affirms the past and future glorification, providing assurance of divine approval and pointing toward the triumphant fulfillment of Jesus' mission.

John 12:29 (KJV):
"The people, therefore, that stood by, and heard it, said that it thundered: others said, An angel spake to him."

Expository Study and Commentary:

In this verse, after the voice from heaven affirms Jesus' prayer, the bystanders' varied responses highlight the mystery and diversity of interpretations surrounding divine manifestations. Some perceive it as thunder, while others consider it an angelic message, showcasing the subjective nature of supernatural encounters.

Context:
The verse follows Jesus' prayer for the glorification of God's name and the subsequent response from heaven. The people present at the scene react to the audible manifestation, revealing the diverse ways individuals interpret extraordinary events.

Perceptions of the Crowd:

The people standing nearby hear the sound accompanying the divine response. Their interpretations differ, illustrating the subjective nature of human perception when encountering the supernatural.

1. Some Thought It Thundered: Some in the crowd interpreted the sound as thunder. This response could be rooted in a naturalistic explanation, attributing the phenomenon to a common occurrence rather than recognizing its supernatural origin.

2. Others Said, An Angel Spake to Him: Alternatively, some perceived the sound as a communication from an angel. This interpretation reflects a spiritual sensitivity and openness to the possibility of divine intervention.

Variety in Interpretation:
The diversity in the crowd's interpretations serves as a reminder that supernatural encounters are often subject to individual perspectives. It highlights the challenge of discerning and understanding divine manifestations, as people interpret such events through their own lenses of experience and belief.

Application:
This verse encourages believers to approach supernatural experiences with humility and openness. It reminds us that interpretations of divine manifestations may vary, and discernment is essential. It also underscores the mysterious and awe-inspiring nature of encountering the divine.

References:
1. 1 Kings 19:11-13 (KJV): Elijah's experience with the still, small voice, illustrating the varied ways God communicates.
2. Acts 9:3-7 (KJV): Paul's encounter with a heavenly light on the road to Damascus, demonstrating diverse responses to supernatural events.

In conclusion, John 12:29 captures the diverse interpretations of the crowd regarding the sound accompanying the heavenly response. This verse invites believers to approach supernatural encounters with humility and discernment, recognizing the subjective nature of individual perceptions when encountering the divine.

John 12:30 (KJV):
"Jesus answered and said, This voice came not because of me, but for your sakes."

Expository Study and Commentary:

In this verse, Jesus responds to the diverse interpretations of the heavenly voice, clarifying that the manifestation was not for His benefit but for the sake of those present. His words underline the instructional and revelatory nature of divine communication, emphasizing its purpose for the understanding and faith of the witnesses.

Context:
Following the varied responses of the crowd to the heavenly voice, Jesus addresses them, providing insight into the purpose and significance of the divine communication. His response reveals the intentionality behind the manifestation and its instructional role.

Jesus' Clarification:
Jesus emphasizes that the voice from heaven did not occur for His personal benefit. Instead, it was intended for the benefit of those present. This statement underscores the purposeful nature of divine communication, serving to instruct, guide, and reveal God's will to humanity.

Instruction for the Crowd:
By stating that the voice came "for your sakes," Jesus implies that the heavenly manifestation serves as a teaching moment. The crowd is meant to draw understanding and meaning from the event, reinforcing the divine message and confirming the mission and identity of Jesus.

Application:

This verse encourages believers to recognize the instructive nature of divine communication. It prompts reflection on the purpose behind supernatural manifestations, emphasizing that God's revelation is designed to deepen understanding, strengthen faith, and guide individuals in their spiritual journey.

References:
1. Matthew 17:5 (KJV): The voice from the cloud at the transfiguration, instructing the disciples to listen to Jesus.
2. 2 Peter 1:16-18 (KJV): Peter's reference to the transfiguration as a confirmation of the prophetic word, highlighting the revelatory nature of divine manifestations.

In conclusion, John 12:30 reveals Jesus' clarification about the purpose of the heavenly voice, emphasizing that it was for the benefit and understanding of those present. This verse encourages believers to approach divine communication with attentiveness and an awareness of its instructive nature in deepening faith and understanding.

John 12:31 (KJV):
"Now is the judgment of this world: now shall the prince of this world be cast out."

Expository Study and Commentary:

In this verse, Jesus declares a profound shift in the spiritual realm. He announces that the present moment marks the judgment of the world and the imminent casting out of the prince of this world. This proclamation foreshadows the transformative impact of Jesus' impending sacrifice on the forces of darkness.

Context:
Jesus' statement comes in the midst of discussions about His impending crucifixion and the heavenly voice that affirmed His mission. The declaration serves as a pivotal moment, indicating the profound consequences of Jesus' sacrificial act.

Judgment of the World:

The phrase "Now is the judgment of this world" does not refer to a final judgment but rather to a decisive turning point. Jesus' impending crucifixion will bring about a judgment on the world, exposing its sin and offering redemption through His sacrifice.

Casting Out the Prince of this World:

The "prince of this world" refers to Satan, the spiritual adversary. Jesus announces that through His sacrificial death, Satan will be cast out, indicating a triumph over the forces of darkness. This foreshadows the victory of Christ over sin and the establishment of His kingdom.

Application:

This verse encourages believers to recognize the profound impact of Jesus' sacrifice on the spiritual realm. It instills hope by affirming the impending defeat of the forces of darkness through Christ's redemptive work.

References:

1. Colossians 2:15 (KJV): Paul's reference to Jesus triumphing over principalities and powers at the cross.

2. Hebrews 2:14-15 (KJV): A passage emphasizing that through His death, Jesus destroyed the one who had the power of death, that is, the devil.

In conclusion, John 12:31 marks a pivotal moment where Jesus declares the judgment of the world and the impending casting out of the prince of this world through His sacrificial death. This verse underscores the transformative impact of Christ's redemptive work on the spiritual realm, offering hope and victory to believers.

John 12:32 (KJV):

"And I, if I be lifted up from the earth, will draw all men unto me."

Expository Study and Commentary:

In this verse, Jesus uses the metaphor of being "lifted up from the earth" to refer to His crucifixion. He foretells that through His sacrificial death, He will draw all people to Himself, highlighting the universal and transformative impact of His redemptive work on the cross.

Context:

This statement follows Jesus' declaration about the judgment of the world and the casting out of the prince of this world. It serves as an explanation of how Jesus, through His crucifixion, will bring about a gathering of people from all walks of life.

Lifted Up from the Earth:

The phrase "lifted up" carries a dual meaning. It refers both to the physical lifting up of Jesus on the cross and, symbolically, to His exaltation and glorification. The cross becomes the central point where Jesus accomplishes His redemptive work.

Drawing All Men unto Me:

Jesus asserts that His sacrificial death on the cross will have a universal impact. The expression "draw all men unto me" signifies a magnetic, transformative influence. Through His death, Jesus will attract people from every background, offering them the opportunity for redemption and reconciliation with God.

Application:

This verse encourages believers to reflect on the centrality of the cross in Christian faith. It emphasizes the inclusive nature of Christ's redemption, inviting people from all walks of life to be drawn to Him for salvation and reconciliation.

References:

1. John 3:14-15 (KJV): Jesus' reference to the lifting up of the serpent in the wilderness as a foreshadowing of His being lifted up on the cross.

2. Colossians 1:20 (KJV): Paul's statement about Christ reconciling all things to Himself through the blood of His cross.

In conclusion, John 12:32 presents a powerful declaration by Jesus about the universal impact of His crucifixion. Through being "lifted up," Jesus draws all people to Himself, extending an invitation to redemption and reconciliation for everyone, regardless of their background or status.

John 12:33 (KJV):
"This he said, signifying what death he should die."

Expository Study and Commentary:

In this verse, the Gospel writer provides commentary on Jesus' previous statement about being "lifted up from the earth." The explanation underscores the specific nature of Jesus' predicted death on the cross, serving as a symbolic and prophetic gesture.

Context:
The verse follows Jesus' declaration in John 12:32 about being "lifted up" to draw all people to Himself. It clarifies the symbolic significance of this statement by pointing to the specific manner in which Jesus would die.

Signifying What Death He Should Die:
The Gospel writer adds an explanatory note, indicating that when Jesus spoke of being "lifted up," it was a sign or symbol pointing to the specific manner of His death—crucifixion on a cross. This commentary adds depth to Jesus' words, revealing the profound nature of the sacrifice He was about to undertake.

Symbolism of Being Lifted Up:
The expression "signifying what death he should die" reinforces the symbolic nature of Jesus' language. Being "lifted up" goes beyond the physical act of crucifixion; it signifies the redemptive and transformative impact of His sacrificial death, drawing people to Himself.

Application:

This verse prompts believers to reflect on the intentional symbolism of Jesus' words. It emphasizes that the manner of His death was not incidental but intricately linked to the fulfillment of God's redemptive plan. It encourages a deeper understanding of the profound nature of Christ's sacrifice on the cross.

References:
1. Matthew 20:18-19 (KJV): Jesus' specific prediction of His upcoming betrayal, crucifixion, and resurrection.
2. Philippians 2:8 (KJV): Paul's reflection on the humility and obedience of Christ, even to the point of death on the cross.

In conclusion, John 12:33 provides a commentary on Jesus' earlier statement about being "lifted up," clarifying that it signified the specific manner of His death—crucifixion. This verse invites believers to ponder the intentional symbolism of Christ's sacrifice and to appreciate the depth of meaning in His redemptive act on the cross.

John 12:34 (KJV):
"The people answered him, We have heard out of the law that Christ abideth for ever: and how sayest thou, The Son of man must be lifted up? who is this Son of man?"

Expository Study and Commentary:

In this verse, the people's response reflects their confusion and perhaps skepticism concerning Jesus' statement about being "lifted up." They refer to the Old Testament understanding that the Christ abides forever and question how Jesus, whom they perceive as the Son of Man, could be subject to being lifted up in a way that seems contradictory to their expectations.

Context:
This verse follows Jesus' explanation in John 12:32-33 about being "lifted up" and the symbolic nature of His impending death. The people's response reveals their struggle to reconcile Jesus' statements with their existing beliefs about the eternal nature of the Christ.

The People's Reference to the Law:
The people appeal to their understanding from the Law that the Christ (Messiah) abides forever. This likely refers to passages in the Old Testament that emphasize the eternal nature of the promised Messiah's reign (e.g., Isaiah 9:7, Daniel 7:14).

The Question about the Son of Man:
The people express confusion about Jesus identifying Himself as the Son of Man who must be lifted up. The title "Son of Man" is associated with both humanity and divine authority in the Old Testament (e.g., Daniel 7:13-14). The people's question indicates a lack of clarity about the dual nature of the Messiah, both as a suffering servant and a triumphant ruler.

Application:
This verse illustrates the challenge people faced in understanding the multifaceted nature of the Messiah's mission. It prompts believers to consider the complexity of Christ's identity and mission, embracing both His suffering on the cross and His eternal reign as the exalted Son of Man.

References:
1. Isaiah 9:7 (KJV): A prophecy about the increase of Christ's government and peace with no end.
2. Daniel 7:13-14 (KJV): A vision of the Son of Man receiving dominion, glory, and an everlasting kingdom.

In conclusion, John 12:34 captures the people's response to Jesus' statement, revealing their struggle to reconcile His identification as the Son of Man who must be lifted up with their understanding of the eternal nature of the Christ. This verse invites reflection on the nuanced nature of Christ's mission and the challenge of comprehending the depths of His identity as revealed in Scripture.

John 12:35 (KJV):
"Then Jesus said unto them, Yet a little while is the light with you. Walk while ye have the light, lest darkness come upon you: for he that walketh in darkness knoweth not whither he goeth."

Expository Study and Commentary:

In this verse, Jesus responds to the people's confusion by emphasizing the transient nature of His earthly presence and the urgency for them to embrace the light He brings. He warns that if they reject the light, darkness will come upon them, symbolizing spiritual blindness and separation from God.

Context:
This verse follows the people's questioning of Jesus regarding His statement about being "lifted up." Jesus uses this opportunity to speak about the limited time His earthly ministry offers for people to respond to the light of His teachings and presence.

The Transient Nature of the Light:
Jesus acknowledges that the time the people have with Him is "yet a little while." This foreshadows His impending departure through His crucifixion, resurrection, and ascension. During His earthly ministry, Jesus serves as the illuminating light, revealing God's truth and salvation.

The Call to Walk in the Light:
He encourages them to "walk while ye have the light," emphasizing the importance of actively engaging with His teachings and following His example. The metaphor of walking in the light signifies a life aligned with God's truth, righteousness, and salvation.

The Warning of Darkness:
Jesus issues a solemn warning about the consequences of rejecting the light. If they choose to walk in darkness, symbolizing spiritual ignorance and rebellion, they will not know where they are going. This darkness signifies separation from God, the source of true guidance and understanding.

Application:
This verse urges believers to seize the opportunity of encountering the light of Christ and actively walk in the path of

righteousness and truth. It emphasizes the urgency of responding to God's revelation before the opportunity is lost and darkness prevails.

References:
1. John 8:12 (KJV): Jesus declaring Himself as the light of the world and the one who provides guidance for those who follow Him.
2. 1 John 1:5-7 (KJV): John's affirmation that God is light, and believers, walking in the light, have fellowship with Him.

In conclusion, John 12:35 presents Jesus' response to the people, urging them to embrace the transient light of His earthly ministry, actively walking in the truth, and warning about the consequences of rejecting the light. This verse challenges believers to recognize the urgency of responding to God's revelation and living in alignment with His truth before the opportunity passes.

John 12:36 (KJV):
"While ye have light, believe in the light, that ye may be the children of light. These things spake Jesus, and departed, and did hide himself from them."

Expository Study and Commentary:

In this verse, Jesus continues to emphasize the importance of believing in the light, identifying it as the means by which individuals become "children of light." The departure and hiding of Jesus symbolize the diminishing opportunity for the people to accept and follow Him.

Context:
This verse follows Jesus' admonition to walk in the light while it is present and warns about the consequences of darkness. Now, Jesus underscores the pivotal role of belief in the light for individuals to become children of light, signifying a transformative relationship with Him.

Believe in the Light:

Jesus urges the people to believe in the light, signifying more than intellectual assent. Belief in this context involves trust, surrender, and acceptance of Jesus as the source of truth, salvation, and guidance. Through belief, individuals align themselves with the principles of God's kingdom.

Children of Light:

The expression "children of light" refers to those who have embraced and internalized the light of Christ, living in accordance with His teachings. It conveys a sense of identity and transformation, suggesting a life characterized by righteousness, truth, and a close relationship with God.

Jesus' Departure and Hiding:

Following these words, Jesus departs and hides Himself from the people. This physical withdrawal symbolizes the increasing limitation of His earthly ministry. It serves as a poignant moment, indicating that the time for people to respond to the light is diminishing, and a decisive choice is required.

Application:

This verse calls believers to an active, transformative response—to not only acknowledge the light but to believe in it wholeheartedly. It emphasizes that through genuine belief, individuals enter into a relationship with Christ, becoming children of light and heirs of His kingdom.

References:

1. Ephesians 5:8 (KJV): Paul's exhortation for believers to walk as children of light, highlighting the transformation that comes with aligning with Christ.

2. John 8:12 (KJV): Jesus' earlier statement about being the light of the world, guiding those who follow Him.

In conclusion, John 12:36 underscores the significance of belief in the light as the pathway to becoming children of light. The departure and hiding of Jesus signal the closing opportunity for the people to respond to His teachings and embrace the transformative relationship offered through faith in Him.

John 12:37 (KJV):
"But though he had done so many miracles before them, yet they believed not on him."

Expository Study and Commentary:

In this verse, the Gospel writer reflects on the paradoxical response of the people despite witnessing numerous miracles performed by Jesus. Despite the clear evidence of His divine power, a significant portion of the audience remains unbelieving, highlighting the complex dynamics of faith and human response.

Context:
This verse follows Jesus' exhortation for people to believe in the light, emphasizing the transformative power of faith. However, the Gospel writer interjects with a sobering observation about the unbelief prevalent among those who had witnessed Jesus' miraculous deeds.

The Abundance of Miracles:
The reference to "so many miracles" underscores the breadth and impact of Jesus' supernatural works. From healing the sick to raising the dead, Jesus had demonstrated His divine authority and power consistently throughout His ministry.

The Unbelief Despite Miracles:
The poignant contrast lies in the fact that despite the abundance of miracles, a significant portion of the audience did not believe in Jesus. This serves as a striking illustration of the complexity of faith and the multifaceted nature of human response to divine revelation.

Application:
This verse prompts believers to reflect on the intricate relationship between evidence and faith. It highlights that even

witnessing miracles does not guarantee belief, emphasizing the role of personal receptivity, openness, and a willingness to respond to God's revelation.

References:
1. John 10:37-38 (KJV): Jesus' assertion that His works bear witness of His identity, and belief should be based on the evidence of these works.
2. Mark 6:5-6 (KJV): A narrative about Jesus' inability to perform miracles in certain places due to the people's unbelief.

In conclusion, John 12:37 presents a somber reflection on the unbelief persisting among those who had witnessed Jesus' miracles. This verse invites believers to ponder the intricate interplay between evidence, receptivity, and faith, recognizing that even extraordinary signs may not guarantee belief without a responsive heart.

John 12:38 (KJV):
"That the saying of Esaias the prophet might be fulfilled, which he spake, Lord, who hath believed our report? and to whom hath the arm of the Lord been revealed?"

Expository Study and Commentary:

In this verse, the Gospel writer references a prophecy from Isaiah (Esaias) to explain the unbelief observed among the people despite witnessing Jesus' miracles. The quotation highlights the fulfillment of Isaiah's words, underlining the longstanding challenge of people failing to believe the divine message.

Context:
This verse follows the observation that, despite witnessing numerous miracles, many did not believe in Jesus. The Gospel writer now cites Isaiah's prophecy as a means to provide insight into the spiritual condition of the people.

Quoting Isaiah's Prophecy:

The verse quotes Isaiah 53:1, where the prophet laments the lack of belief in the report (message) delivered by the servants of the Lord. The reference to "the arm of the Lord" being revealed indicates the divine power and intervention seen in Jesus' miracles, yet met with unbelief.

Fulfillment of Prophecy:
By citing Isaiah's words, the Gospel writer asserts that the unbelief observed in their current context aligns with the prophetic anticipation expressed centuries earlier. This connection emphasizes the continuity of human resistance to divine revelation despite God's repeated efforts to make Himself known.

Application:
This verse encourages believers to recognize the overarching narrative of God's redemptive plan, as revealed through both Old Testament prophecies and the person of Jesus. It prompts reflection on the persistent challenge of unbelief and the need for receptive hearts to receive God's revelation.

References:
1. Isaiah 53:1 (KJV): The prophecy quoted in John 12:38, expressing the lack of belief in the report of the Lord's servants and the revelation of His arm.
2. Romans 10:16 (KJV): Paul's reference to Isaiah's words, connecting them to the challenge of people hearing and believing the gospel message.

In conclusion, John 12:38 cites Isaiah's prophecy to explain the fulfillment of the unbelief observed among the people witnessing Jesus' miracles. This verse invites believers to consider the continuity of the struggle for faith throughout history, emphasizing the importance of responding to God's revelation with a receptive heart.

John 12:39 (KJV):
"Therefore, they could not believe because that Esaias said again,"

Expository Study and Commentary:

In this verse, the Gospel writer continues to elaborate on the fulfillment of Isaiah's prophecy (Esaias) as a reason for the unbelief witnessed among the people. The emphasis is on the divine judicial consequence of their persistent rejection of God's revelation.

Context:
The verse follows the citation of Isaiah's prophecy in the previous verse, where the unbelief of the people is connected to the fulfillment of the prophet's words. Now, the Gospel writer introduces a further explanation, pointing to a divine consequence tied to their unbelief.

The Unbelief's Connection to Isaiah's Words:
The phrase "Therefore, they could not believe" suggests a cause-and-effect relationship. The unbelief observed among the people is linked to the fulfillment of Isaiah's prophecies, indicating a divine judgment resulting from their prolonged resistance to God's message.

Judicial Consequence of Unbelief:
The verse sets the stage for an explanation of the divine consequence of unbelief, indicating that their persistent rejection of God's revelation led to a condition where belief became increasingly difficult or even impossible.

Application:
This verse prompts believers to reflect on the seriousness of responding to God's revelation. It underscores the concept of divine consequences tied to persistent unbelief and emphasizes the need for receptivity to God's message while there is an opportunity.

References:
1. Isaiah 6:9-10 (KJV): The prophecy referred to in John 12:39, where Isaiah is commissioned to deliver a message that would result in spiritual dullness and unbelief.

In conclusion, John 12:39 introduces the concept of divine consequences for unbelief, stating that the people "could not believe" because of the fulfillment of Isaiah's prophecy. This verse invites believers to consider the weight of their response to God's revelation and emphasizes the importance of a responsive heart to avoid spiritual consequences tied to persistent unbelief.

John 12:40 (KJV):
"He hath blinded their eyes, and hardened their heart; that they should not see with their eyes, nor understand with their heart, and be converted, and I should heal them."

Expository Study and Commentary:

In this verse, the Gospel writer quotes from Isaiah to further explain the divine consequence of unbelief. The language used, referring to the blinding of eyes and the hardening of hearts, underscores the profound spiritual condition resulting from persistent rejection of God's revelation.

Context:
The verse follows the declaration that the people "could not believe" due to the fulfillment of Isaiah's prophecies. Now, the Gospel writer provides a more detailed account of the divine consequence, drawing from Isaiah's words.

Blinded Eyes and Hardened Hearts:
The imagery of "blinded eyes" and "hardened hearts" is symbolic of spiritual insensitivity and resistance. It signifies a condition where the people, due to their prolonged rejection of God's truth, experience a judicial consequence—being prevented from perceiving and understanding God's message.

Purpose of the Consequence:
The verse outlines the purpose of this divine consequence— to prevent them from seeing, understanding, being converted, and ultimately experiencing healing. The progression from blindness and

hardness to conversion and healing highlights the potential restoration through a change of heart and understanding.

Application:
This verse serves as a powerful reminder of the serious consequences of persistent unbelief. It underscores the importance of responding to God's revelation with humility and receptivity to avoid spiritual blindness and hardness of heart.

References:
1. Isaiah 6:10 (KJV): The prophecy referred to in John 12:40, where Isaiah is commissioned to deliver a message resulting in spiritual dullness and unbelief.

In conclusion, John 12:40 explains the divine consequence of unbelief by quoting Isaiah's prophecy. The imagery of blinded eyes and hardened hearts signifies a profound spiritual condition resulting from rejecting God's revelation. This verse calls believers to heed the importance of responding to God's truth with openness and receptivity to avoid the serious consequences outlined in the passage.

John 12:41 (KJV):
"These things said Esaias, when he saw his glory, and spake of him."

Expository Study and Commentary:

In this verse, the Gospel writer provides insight into the source and context of Isaiah's words. Isaiah spoke about the spiritual condition of the people when he saw a vision of God's glory, and the Gospel writer affirms that Isaiah was, in fact, speaking prophetically about Jesus.

Context:
The verse follows the explanation of the divine consequence of unbelief, quoting Isaiah's prophecy. Now, the Gospel writer directs attention to the origin of Isaiah's words, attributing them to a vision where Isaiah witnessed the glory of God.

Isaiah's Vision of God's Glory:

The phrase "when he saw his glory" refers to Isaiah's vision recorded in Isaiah 6:1-4. In that vision, Isaiah saw the Lord seated on a throne, surrounded by seraphim. The vision conveyed the holiness and glory of God.

Speaking of Him (Jesus):

The Gospel writer asserts that Isaiah, in his prophetic utterances, was actually speaking about Jesus. This attribution emphasizes the Messianic nature of Isaiah's prophecies, revealing that his vision of God's glory had a direct connection to the person and mission of Jesus Christ.

Application:

This verse invites believers to appreciate the prophetic nature of Isaiah's words and recognize their fulfillment in Jesus. It underscores the continuity of God's revelation and highlights the importance of understanding the Old Testament in light of Christ's identity and mission.

References:

1. Isaiah 6:1-4 (KJV): The vision of God's glory in the context of Isaiah's commission, where he sees the Lord seated on a throne.

2. Isaiah 53:1 (KJV): Another prophetic passage by Isaiah, quoted earlier in John 12:38, expressing the lack of belief in the report of the Lord's servants and the revelation of His arm.

In conclusion, John 12:41 reveals the source of Isaiah's prophetic words about the divine consequence of unbelief. Isaiah spoke of the people's condition when he saw a vision of God's glory, and the Gospel writer attributes these words to Jesus. This verse encourages believers to recognize the interconnectedness of Old Testament prophecies and their fulfillment in the person of Jesus Christ.

John 12:42 (KJV):

"Nevertheless among the chief rulers also many believed on him; but because of the Pharisees they did not confess him, lest they should be put out of the synagogue."

Expository Study and Commentary:

In this verse, the Gospel writer notes a nuanced response among some chief rulers. While many believed in Jesus, fear of the Pharisees prevented them from publicly confessing their faith due to the potential consequences of being expelled from the synagogue.

Context:
The verse follows the discussion of Isaiah's prophetic words and the consequences of unbelief. It introduces a contrast by acknowledging that, despite the prevailing unbelief, there were chief rulers who believed in Jesus.

Belief Among Chief Rulers:
The mention of chief rulers believing in Jesus demonstrates that faith was not limited to a particular social or religious group. These individuals recognized Jesus as the Messiah or at least acknowledged His divine authority.

Fear of the Pharisees:
The primary obstacle to open confession of faith was the fear of the Pharisees. The Pharisees held significant influence, and being expelled from the synagogue, a central place of worship and community, was a severe consequence. This fear led to a reluctance to openly declare allegiance to Jesus.

Application:
This verse highlights the complexity of belief and the influence of social and religious pressures. It prompts believers to consider the courage required to openly confess faith, even in the face of potential consequences, and encourages a reflection on the sincerity and depth of one's commitment to Christ.

References:

1. John 7:13 (KJV): A similar situation where people were afraid to speak openly about Jesus due to the fear of the Pharisees.

2. Matthew 10:32-33 (KJV): Jesus' words about confessing Him before men and the consequences of denying Him.

In conclusion, John 12:42 portrays a scenario where some chief rulers believed in Jesus but refrained from open confession due to fear of the Pharisees. This verse prompts believers to reflect on the challenges and courage required to openly declare faith in Jesus, even in the face of potential social or religious consequences.

John 12:43 (KJV):
"For they loved the praise of men more than the praise of God."

Expository Study and Commentary:

In this verse, the Gospel writer provides a crucial insight into the motivation behind the chief rulers' reluctance to openly confess their belief in Jesus. Their love for the approval and praise of men outweighed their commitment to receiving the praise of God.

Context:
The verse continues the discussion about some chief rulers who believed in Jesus but refrained from confessing Him openly due to fear of the Pharisees. It unveils the underlying reason for their hesitation.

Motivation: Love for Men's Praise:
The key reason presented in this verse is that the chief rulers loved the praise of men more than the praise of God. Their desire for societal approval, recognition, and avoiding potential repercussions outweighed their commitment to being acknowledged and praised by God.

Contrast: Praise of Men vs. Praise of God:
The contrast between the praise of men and the praise of God highlights a fundamental choice individuals face in matters of faith.

The chief rulers' decision reflected a prioritization of human approval over divine approval.

Application:
This verse challenges believers to examine their own motivations and priorities. It prompts reflection on whether the desire for societal acceptance or approval influences decisions related to openly confessing faith in Jesus. It encourages a commitment to seeking God's approval above all else.

References:
1. Proverbs 29:25 (KJV): A wisdom saying emphasizing the fear of man as a snare, contrasting it with trusting in the Lord for safety.
2. Matthew 10:28 (KJV): Jesus' teaching about not fearing those who can harm the body but fearing God who has authority over both body and soul.

In conclusion, John 12:43 reveals the chief rulers' motivation for not openly confessing their belief in Jesus—their love for the praise of men over the praise of God. This verse challenges believers to assess their own motivations, emphasizing the importance of prioritizing God's approval above societal recognition and acceptance.

John 12:44 (KJV):
"Jesus cried and said, He that believeth on me, believeth not on me, but on him that sent me."

Expository Study and Commentary:

In this verse, Jesus makes a proclamation emphasizing the interconnected nature of belief. Believing in Him is, in essence, believing in the One who sent Him—the Father. This statement reinforces the unity between Jesus and the Father in the context of faith.

Context:

The verse follows the discussion about chief rulers' hesitation to openly confess their belief due to the love of men's praise. Jesus now addresses the broader audience, highlighting the profound significance of belief in Him.

Believing in Jesus and the Father:
Jesus uses a powerful declaration to convey a profound truth: when someone believes in Him, they are ultimately placing their faith in the One who sent Him—the Father. This emphasizes the inseparable relationship between Jesus and the Father, emphasizing that belief in one is inseparable from belief in the other.

Unity in Purpose:
The statement underscores the unity of purpose between Jesus and the Father. Belief in Jesus aligns one with the divine plan of salvation orchestrated by the Father. It also emphasizes the authority and delegation involved in Jesus' earthly mission.

Application:
This verse encourages believers to recognize the depth and significance of their faith in Jesus. It prompts reflection on the unity between the Father and the Son, reinforcing the understanding that faith in Jesus is an acknowledgment of the divine plan and purpose orchestrated by the Father.

References:
1. John 5:24 (KJV): Jesus' words about the connection between belief in Him and having eternal life.
2. John 6:29 (KJV): Jesus' response to the question about the work of God, emphasizing belief in Him as the work of God.

In conclusion, John 12:44 highlights Jesus' proclamation about the interconnected nature of belief. Believing in Him is inseparable from believing in the One who sent Him—the Father. This verse prompts believers to recognize the unity of purpose between Jesus and the Father and the profound significance of their faith in the divine plan of salvation.

John 12:45 (KJV):
"And he that seeth me seeth him that sent me."

Expository Study and Commentary:

In this verse, Jesus reinforces the profound connection between Himself and the Father. Seeing Him is tantamount to seeing the One who sent Him. This statement emphasizes the intimate relationship and unity between Jesus and the Father, pointing to their inseparable nature.

Context:
The verse follows Jesus' declaration in the previous verse, where He emphasized the unity of belief in Him and belief in the Father who sent Him. This verse further explores the close relationship between Jesus and the Father.

Seeing Jesus and Seeing the Father:
The statement "he that seeth me seeth him that sent me" goes beyond mere physical sight. It conveys a deeper understanding of perception—a spiritual insight that recognizes the divine connection between Jesus and the Father. Seeing Jesus is akin to perceiving the Father's nature and will.

Unity of Purpose and Representation:
This statement underscores not only the unity of purpose but also the representation aspect. Jesus, as the incarnate Son, represents the Father in a way that goes beyond a mere messenger. Seeing and understanding Jesus provides insight into the character and mission of the Father.

Application:
This verse invites believers to deepen their understanding of Jesus as not merely a separate entity but as the embodiment of the Father's nature and purpose. It emphasizes the significance of perceiving Jesus in a spiritual sense, recognizing the unity and representation inherent in the relationship between Jesus and the Father.

References:
1. John 14:9 (KJV): A similar statement by Jesus: "He that hath seen me hath seen the Father."
2. Colossians 1:15 (KJV): Describing Jesus as the image of the invisible God, emphasizing His role in representing the Father.

In conclusion, John 12:45 underscores the profound relationship between Jesus and the Father. Seeing Jesus goes beyond physical sight—it involves recognizing the representation of the Father in Him. This verse encourages believers to perceive Jesus in a spiritual sense, understanding His role as the embodiment of the Father's nature and purpose.

John 12:46 (KJV):
"I am come a light into the world, that whosoever believeth on me should not abide in darkness."

Expository Study and Commentary:

In this verse, Jesus metaphorically presents Himself as the light that has come into the world. Believing in Him is portrayed as the means to avoid dwelling in darkness, signifying spiritual ignorance and separation from God.

Context:
The verse follows Jesus' statements about belief and seeing Him as seeing the One who sent Him. Now, Jesus employs the metaphor of light to convey His role in dispelling spiritual darkness.

Jesus as the Light:
By declaring, "I am come a light into the world," Jesus identifies Himself as the source of divine illumination. This metaphor aligns with the earlier imagery in John's Gospel, emphasizing Jesus as the light that guides, reveals, and dispels darkness.

Belief and Avoidance of Darkness:

The purpose of Jesus coming as a light is explicitly tied to belief. Those who believe in Him are positioned to avoid dwelling in darkness. This goes beyond physical light and darkness, symbolizing the contrast between spiritual understanding and ignorance, fellowship with God, and separation from Him.

Application:
This verse invites believers to recognize Jesus as the illuminating light that dispels spiritual darkness. It underscores the transformative power of belief, positioning individuals to walk in the light of God's truth and avoid the darkness of spiritual separation.

References:
1. John 8:12 (KJV): Jesus' earlier declaration: "I am the light of the world: he that followeth me shall not walk in darkness but shall have the light of life."
2. Isaiah 9:2 (KJV): A prophetic passage anticipating the coming of a great light, often associated with the Messiah.

In conclusion, John 12:46 presents Jesus as the light that has come into the world, emphasizing that belief in Him leads to deliverance from spiritual darkness. This verse encourages believers to embrace Jesus as the guiding light, allowing His truth to dispel ignorance and draw them into a transformative relationship with God.

John 12:47 (KJV):
"And if any man hear my words, and believe not, I judge him not: for I came not to judge the world, but to save the world."

Expository Study and Commentary:

In this verse, Jesus clarifies His purpose, stating that He did not come to judge the world but to save it. He emphasizes the transformative nature of His mission and the conditional aspect of judgment based on belief.

Context:

Following Jesus' proclamation about being the light of the world, this verse addresses the response to His words. Jesus distinguishes between judgment and salvation, underscoring His primary purpose.

Purpose of Jesus' Coming:
The declaration "I came not to judge the world, but to save the world" encapsulates the heart of Jesus' mission. His primary purpose is not to condemn but to bring salvation. This aligns with the overarching theme of redemption and reconciliation found in the Gospel.

Conditional Judgment Based on Belief:
Jesus introduces a conditional element to judgment, stating that if anyone hears His words and believes not, He does not judge them. This emphasizes the connection between belief and salvation, highlighting that the rejection of Jesus' words results in self-imposed judgment.

Application:
This verse prompts believers to appreciate the mercy and salvation offered by Jesus. It underscores the importance of belief as the gateway to salvation and emphasizes Jesus' desire for the world to experience redemption rather than judgment.

References:
1. John 3:17 (KJV): A similar declaration by Jesus about His purpose in coming into the world, emphasizing salvation rather than condemnation.
2. Luke 19:10 (KJV): Jesus' statement about seeking and saving the lost, aligning with His mission of salvation.

In conclusion, John 12:47 communicates Jesus' purpose in coming to the world—to save rather than to judge. The verse emphasizes the conditional nature of judgment based on belief and underscores the transformative and redemptive mission of Jesus. This invites believers to embrace the offered salvation through faith in Him.

John 12:48 (KJV):
"He that rejecteth me, and receiveth not my words, hath one that judgeth him: the word that I have spoken, the same shall judge him in the last day."

Expository Study and Commentary:

In this verse, Jesus addresses the consequences of rejecting Him and His words. He points to a future judgment, where His words will serve as the standard by which individuals are evaluated.

Context:
Building on the previous verse, where Jesus clarified His purpose of coming to save rather than to judge, this verse introduces the concept of accountability for those who reject Him.

Rejection and Future Judgment:
The verse states that one who rejects Jesus and does not receive His words will face judgment. This judgment is not immediate but is reserved for the "last day," signifying a future eschatological event.

The Word as the Standard of Judgment:
Jesus identifies the standard by which judgment will occur—the very words He has spoken. The teachings, commands, and revelations conveyed by Jesus throughout His ministry will serve as the criteria for evaluating one's response to Him.

Application:
This verse prompts believers to consider the serious consequences of rejecting Jesus and His words. It emphasizes the accountability individuals will face in the last day, highlighting the importance of embracing and adhering to the teachings of Jesus.

References:
1. Matthew 10:15 (KJV): Jesus' words about the judgment on cities that reject His disciples and their message.

2. Revelation 20:12 (KJV): A vision of the last judgment, where books are opened, indicating a record of deeds.

In conclusion, John 12:48 emphasizes the future judgment for those who reject Jesus and His words. It underscores the significance of the teachings of Jesus as the standard by which individuals will be evaluated in the last day, prompting believers to heed His words and share the message of salvation.

John 12:49 (KJV):
"For I have not spoken of myself; but the Father which sent me, he gave me a commandment, what I should say, and what I should speak."

Expository Study and Commentary:

In this verse, Jesus provides insight into the source and authority behind His words, emphasizing that His teachings are not self-originated but are commanded by the Father who sent Him.

Context:
Following the discussion about judgment based on rejecting Jesus' words, this verse delves into the origin and authority of Jesus' teachings, underscoring the divine commission behind His words.

Submission to the Father's Commandment:
Jesus declares that His words are not products of independent thought or personal initiative. Instead, He acknowledges the Father's role in providing Him with a commandment—specific instructions about what to say and speak. This submission underscores the harmony between the Father and the Son in the divine mission.

The Father's Authority in Jesus' Words:
By stating that the Father gave Him a commandment, Jesus affirms the divine authority and purpose embedded in His teachings. Every word He speaks is in alignment with the divine plan and represents the Father's will.

Application:
This verse invites believers to recognize the divine origin and authority of Jesus' words. It emphasizes the unity within the Trinity and reinforces the importance of aligning oneself with the teachings of Jesus as they are rooted in the Father's commandment.

References:
1. John 7:16 (KJV): Similar language used by Jesus, indicating that His teaching is not self-derived but comes from the One who sent Him.
2. Deuteronomy 18:18 (KJV): A prophecy about a prophet like Moses whom God would raise up, and to whom people should listen.

In conclusion, John 12:49 highlights the divine source and authority behind Jesus' teachings. It emphasizes that His words are not self-generated but are commanded by the Father, underscoring the unity within the Godhead and affirming the importance of aligning with the divine teachings of Jesus.

John 12:50 (KJV):
"And I know that his commandment is life everlasting: whatsoever I speak therefore, even as the Father said unto me, so I speak."

Expository Study and Commentary:

In this concluding verse of John 12, Jesus affirms His awareness that the Father's commandment leads to eternal life. He reiterates the alignment between His spoken words and the instructions given by the Father, emphasizing the life-giving nature of His message.

Context:
Continuing from the previous verse where Jesus spoke of the Father's commandment guiding His words, this verse emphasizes the life-giving aspect of the divine instructions.

Life Everlasting in the Father's Commandment:

Jesus expresses a profound certainty that the Father's commandment leads to "life everlasting." This affirms that the divine instructions given to Him have the ultimate purpose of securing eternal life for those who heed them.

Unity in Jesus' Words and the Father's Command:
The verse concludes with a reaffirmation of the unity between Jesus' spoken words and the Father's instructions. What Jesus speaks is precisely what the Father has communicated to Him. This underscores the perfect alignment and harmony in their divine mission.

Application:
This verse invites believers to recognize the profound connection between the Father's commandment and the eternal life offered through Jesus. It encourages a commitment to embracing and obeying the teachings of Jesus as they are directly aligned with the divine purpose of granting eternal life.

References:
1. John 5:24 (KJV): Jesus' words about the connection between belief in Him and having eternal life.
2. John 6:63 (KJV): Jesus' statement about His words being spirit and life.

In conclusion, John 12:50 emphasizes the assurance that the Father's commandment leads to eternal life. It underscores the perfect unity between Jesus' spoken words and the divine instructions, inviting believers to embrace and live according to the life-giving teachings of Jesus for the promise of everlasting life.

CHAPTER THIRTEEN
Jesus Washes His Disciples' Feet

John Chapter 13:1 (KJV)
"Now before the feast of the passover, when Jesus knew that his hour was come that he should depart out of this world unto the Father, having loved his own which were in the world, he loved them unto the end."

Expository Study and Commentary:

This chapter begins with a significant event in the life of Jesus, occurring just before the Passover feast. The timing is crucial, emphasizing the divine plan and the fulfillment of Jesus' mission on earth. The reference to "his hour" underscores the predetermined nature of the events that are about to unfold. Jesus is aware that the time has come for Him to leave this world and return to the Father.

The phrase "having loved his own which were in the world" highlights the deep and enduring love that Jesus has for His disciples. Despite knowing the challenges and trials they would face, His love for them remains steadfast. The term "his own" signifies a close and personal relationship, emphasizing the unique bond between Jesus and His followers.

The statement "he loved them unto the end" is powerful and profound. It speaks not only of the duration of Jesus' love but also of its completeness and perfection. His love is not bound by time or circumstance; it extends to the ultimate expression of sacrificial love that He is about to demonstrate through His impending death on the cross.

King James Bible References:

1. "Before the feast of the passover": This references the historical and religious context of the Passover feast, a significant Jewish celebration commemorating the liberation of the Israelites from slavery in Egypt. Jesus' actions in the following verses are intimately connected to the symbolism and meaning of the Passover.

2. "His hour": Throughout the Gospel of John, there are references to a specific time or hour that marks significant events in Jesus' life, often pointing to the divine timing of God's plan.

3. "His own": This term is used to describe Jesus' close circle of disciples, indicating a special and personal relationship. It reflects the idea of chosen and beloved individuals within the broader context of humanity.

4. "He loved them unto the end": This phrase emphasizes the unfathomable depth and constancy of Jesus' love. It sets the stage for the subsequent events in this chapter, particularly the washing of the disciples' feet and the institution of the Lord's Supper.

In summary, John 13:1 serves as a powerful introduction to the events that will unfold in this chapter, highlighting the divine timing of Jesus' departure, the enduring nature of His love for His disciples, and the imminent expression of that love through His sacrificial death.

John Chapter 13:2 (KJV)
"And supper being ended, the devil having now put into the heart of Judas Iscariot, Simon's son, to betray him."

Expository Study and Commentary:

This verse provides a pivotal moment in the narrative, occurring after the conclusion of the Passover supper. The setting is crucial, as it emphasizes the betrayal that is about to unfold. The phrase "supper being ended" indicates the conclusion of a significant meal, likely the Passover meal, setting the stage for what follows.

The focus shifts to Judas Iscariot, identified as "Simon's son," highlighting his lineage. Here, a deeply troubling revelation is made: "the devil having now put into the heart of Judas Iscariot to betray him." This phrase unveils the sinister influence at play, attributing the idea of betrayal to the instigation of the devil. The term "heart" goes beyond the physical organ and encompasses the innermost thoughts, desires, and intentions of Judas.

Judas, one of the twelve disciples, becomes an instrument through which the adversary works to fulfill his dark purpose. The mention of the devil's involvement serves to underscore the spiritual dimension of the events leading to Jesus' arrest and crucifixion. It also raises theological questions about the interplay between human choices and the sovereignty of God in fulfilling His redemptive plan.

King James Bible References:

1. "Supper being ended": This phrase emphasizes the timing of the events, occurring after the shared meal, likely the Passover supper. The setting is important, as it marks a transition to a critical moment in the narrative.

2. "The devil having now put into the heart of Judas Iscariot": This statement attributes the idea of betrayal directly to the influence of the devil. Throughout the Gospels, Judas is portrayed as the one who would betray Jesus, and this verse provides insight into the spiritual forces at work behind this betrayal.

3. "Simon's son": This identifies Judas with his father's name, distinguishing him from others named Simon.

4. "To betray him": The betrayal of Jesus by Judas is a central theme in the Gospels. This action sets in motion the events leading to the crucifixion, highlighting the role of individuals in God's sovereign plan.

In summary, John 13:2 unveils the ominous reality of Judas' betrayal, attributing it to the influence of the devil. The verse emphasizes the spiritual warfare at play and sets the stage for the subsequent actions of Judas leading to the arrest and crucifixion of Jesus.

John Chapter 13:3 (KJV)

"Jesus knowing that the Father had given all things into his hands, and that he was come from God, and went to God;"

Expository Study and Commentary:

This verse reveals profound insights into the mindset and awareness of Jesus as He undertakes a significant action during the Passover meal. The verse begins with a statement of Jesus' knowledge, indicating His divine understanding of His identity, purpose, and authority.

1. "Jesus knowing that the Father had given all things into his hands": This affirms Jesus' awareness of His divine authority and the extent of His control over all things. It echoes themes found elsewhere in the New Testament, emphasizing Jesus as the divine Son to whom the Father has granted supreme authority (Matthew 28:18, Ephesians 1:20-23).

2. "And that he was come from God": This part of the verse underscores Jesus' preexistence and divine origin. It echoes the prologue of the Gospel of John (John 1:1-18), emphasizing Jesus as the Word who was with God and was God, becoming incarnate for the purpose of redemption.

3. "And went to God": This phrase points to Jesus' impending return to the Father. It anticipates the events of His crucifixion, resurrection, and ascension. The journey "to God" signifies the completion of His earthly mission and the restoration of His divine glory.

This verse serves as a foundation for understanding the significance of Jesus' actions in the following verses, particularly His humble act of washing the disciples' feet. Despite possessing divine authority and knowing His divine origin and destiny, Jesus willingly takes on the role of a servant, demonstrating profound humility and love.

King James Bible References:

1. "The Father had given all things into his hands": This concept of the Father giving authority and control to the Son is a recurring theme in the New Testament. It signifies the unique relationship within the Trinity and the exalted status of Jesus (Matthew 11:27, Matthew 28:18, Ephesians 1:20-23).

2. "He was come from God": This reflects the theological truth of the incarnation, where Jesus, as the Son of God, took on human flesh. The Gospel of John emphasizes this truth from its opening verses (John 1:1-18).

3. "Went to God": This phrase foreshadows Jesus' impending return to the Father, signifying the completion of His earthly mission. It aligns with the broader narrative of Jesus' crucifixion, resurrection, and ascension (John 16:28, Acts 1:9-11).

In summary, John 13:3 offers a glimpse into Jesus' profound understanding of His divine identity, authority, and mission. This awareness sets the stage for the transformative and symbolic act of humility that Jesus is about to perform, illustrating the perfect union of divine authority and sacrificial love.

John Chapter 13:4 (KJV)
"He riseth from supper, and laid aside his garments; and took a towel, and girded himself."

Expository Study and Commentary:

This verse marks a significant turning point in the narrative, capturing the profound humility and servanthood of Jesus. It describes His actions as He rises from the supper table, symbolically setting aside His outer garments, and then taking a towel to gird Himself.

1. "He riseth from supper": The act of rising from the supper table signifies a deliberate interruption in the course of the meal. Jesus,

in this moment, transitions from the role of the one being served to the role of the servant. It foreshadows the impending act of washing the disciples' feet, a task typically performed by a servant.

2. "Laid aside his garments": The symbolic act of removing His outer garments is significant. It represents Jesus divesting Himself of His outer glory and taking on the form of a servant (Philippians 2:7-8). This stripping away of His robes conveys a powerful message of humility and self-emptying.

3. "Took a towel, and girded himself": The act of taking a towel and girding Himself with it further emphasizes Jesus' intentional and humble posture. In the culture of that time, the act of girding oneself with a towel was associated with the role of a servant. By performing this action, Jesus not only embraces the appearance of a servant but also communicates a profound lesson about the nature of His kingdom and the qualities valued within it.

This verse sets the stage for the striking and unexpected act of Jesus washing the disciples' feet, a demonstration of humility and service that challenges conventional notions of leadership and authority.

King James Bible References:

1. "He riseth from supper": While not explicitly mentioned, this action is reminiscent of other moments in the Gospels where Jesus takes deliberate actions, signaling a shift in focus or a teaching moment (Matthew 26:30, Mark 6:34).

2. "Laid aside his garments": This act aligns with the broader biblical theme of Jesus' voluntary humiliation and the laying aside of His divine prerogatives for the sake of humanity (Philippians 2:5-8).

3. "Took a towel, and girded himself": This action echoes the cultural context of that time, where girding oneself with a towel was associated with the role of a servant. It foreshadows the upcoming event of Jesus washing the disciples' feet.

In summary, John 13:4 paints a vivid picture of Jesus' intentional and symbolic actions, conveying a message of humility and servant leadership. This sets the stage for the profound lesson that Jesus imparts through the act of washing the disciples' feet in the subsequent verses, challenging conventional notions of authority and exemplifying a radical expression of love and service.

John Chapter 13:5 (KJV)
"After that he poureth water into a bason, and began to wash the disciples' feet, and to wipe them with the towel wherewith he was girded."

Expository Study and Commentary:

This verse describes the climactic action of Jesus as He goes beyond cultural norms and societal expectations by humbly taking on the role of a servant, washing the feet of His disciples.

1. "After that he poureth water into a bason": The act of pouring water into a basin signifies the practical preparation for footwashing. It emphasizes the intentional and deliberate nature of Jesus' actions. The use of water as a cleansing agent foreshadows the spiritual cleansing that Jesus is about to illustrate.

2. "Began to wash the disciples' feet": This action is both symbolic and transformative. Footwashing was a task typically assigned to the lowest-ranking servants, and for Jesus, the Teacher and Lord, to perform such an act was a radical inversion of social expectations. By beginning to wash the disciples' feet, Jesus demonstrates a profound humility that challenges conventional notions of authority and status.

3. "To wipe them with the towel wherewith he was girded": The act of wiping the disciples' feet with the towel tied around His waist further accentuates Jesus' servant-heartedness. This additional gesture of care and tenderness underscores the depth of His love and

the willingness to go beyond what was expected or culturally acceptable.

This verse showcases the embodied humility of Jesus, emphasizing not only the physical act of washing but also the broader lesson about servant leadership and sacrificial love.

King James Bible References:

1. "After that he poureth water into a bason": The use of water for washing is a significant symbol in the Bible, representing purification and cleansing. It finds parallel symbolism in various passages, such as the cleansing of sins through water (Ephesians 5:26) and the washing of regeneration (Titus 3:5).

2. "Began to wash the disciples' feet": The act of washing feet is a culturally significant symbol, and Jesus uses it to teach a profound lesson about humility and servanthood. This action also has echoes in Old Testament imagery, such as the consecration of Aaron and his sons (Exodus 40:12-15) and the cleansing of Naaman (2 Kings 5:10-14).

3. "To wipe them with the towel wherewith he was girded": This additional act of care and tenderness reflects the compassion and love inherent in Jesus' actions. It emphasizes not only the humility of the act but also the genuine concern for the well-being of the disciples.

In summary, John 13:5 captures the pivotal moment when Jesus, the Son of God, takes on the role of a servant and washes the feet of His disciples. This symbolic and transformative act serves as a powerful illustration of humility, love, and the radical nature of true leadership in the kingdom of God.

John Chapter 13:6 (KJV)
"Then cometh he to Simon Peter: and Peter saith unto him, Lord, dost thou wash my feet?"

Expository Study and Commentary:

This verse focuses on the interaction between Jesus and Peter during the footwashing, highlighting Peter's initial resistance to the idea of Jesus washing his feet.

1. "Then cometh he to Simon Peter": Jesus approaches Peter as part of the sequence of washing the disciples' feet. The choice to highlight Peter in this narrative adds depth, as Peter often serves as a representative figure for the disciples.

2. "Peter saith unto him, Lord, dost thou wash my feet?": Peter's response reveals a mixture of humility, confusion, and a misunderstanding of the significance of Jesus' actions. In addressing Jesus as "Lord," Peter acknowledges Jesus' authority, but his question reflects a reluctance to accept the idea of Jesus performing such a humble task as washing his feet.

Peter's reaction can be understood in light of his deep reverence for Jesus and a cultural expectation that such a menial task should not be performed by one of higher status. Peter might have seen himself as unworthy of Jesus performing this act of service.

King James Bible References:

1. "Then cometh he to Simon Peter": This interaction with Peter is reminiscent of other moments where Peter is prominently featured in the Gospels, such as the confession of Jesus as the Christ (Matthew 16:13-20) and the walking on water incident (Matthew 14:22-33).

2. "Peter saith unto him, Lord, dost thou wash my feet?": Peter's response reflects his characteristic impulsiveness and willingness to express his thoughts openly. The use of "Lord" acknowledges Jesus' authority and divinity, but the question reveals Peter's initial resistance to the idea of Jesus taking on the role of a servant.

In summary, John 13:6 captures the tension between Jesus' humility and Peter's initial hesitation to accept such a humble act of service from his Lord. This interaction sets the stage for a deeper exploration of the spiritual lessons that Jesus is about to impart to Peter and the disciples regarding the nature of true discipleship and servant leadership.

John Chapter 13:7 (KJV)
"Jesus answered and said unto him, What I do thou knowest not now; but thou shalt know hereafter."

Expository Study and Commentary:

In this verse, Jesus responds to Peter's reluctance and confusion with a statement that looks beyond the immediate moment, suggesting that Peter will come to understand the significance of the footwashing in the future.

1. "Jesus answered and said unto him": Jesus takes the opportunity to address Peter's question directly. His response reflects a gentle and patient demeanor, as He recognizes Peter's current lack of understanding.

2. "What I do thou knowest not now": Jesus acknowledges that Peter does not currently comprehend the full meaning and significance of the footwashing. There is an element of mystery and a deeper spiritual truth behind this humble act that Peter is not grasping in the present moment.

3. "But thou shalt know hereafter": Jesus offers a promise of future understanding to Peter. This implies that, as events unfold and as Peter continues in his discipleship journey, he will come to comprehend the profound lesson that Jesus is teaching through this symbolic act of humility.

This response from Jesus conveys a broader perspective on the unfolding events and emphasizes the importance of trust and faith in following Him, even when aspects of His actions might be initially perplexing.

King James Bible References:

1. "What I do thou knowest not now": This idea of Jesus' actions being initially misunderstood or not fully comprehended is a recurring theme in the Gospels. For example, Jesus often spoke in parables, and His disciples needed further explanation to understand the deeper spiritual truths (Matthew 13:10-17, Mark 4:10-12).

2. "But thou shalt know hereafter": The promise of future understanding aligns with the broader biblical concept of spiritual growth and revelation. The disciples, including Peter, would receive greater insight into the mysteries of God's kingdom through the Holy Spirit and the unfolding of God's plan (John 16:12-15, Acts 2:1-4).

In summary, John 13:7 reflects Jesus' patient and compassionate response to Peter's immediate confusion. It also introduces the theme of future understanding, emphasizing the unfolding nature of spiritual insight and the disciples' journey toward deeper comprehension of the profound truths Jesus imparts.

John Chapter 13:8 (KJV)
"Peter saith unto him, Thou shalt never wash my feet. Jesus answered him, If I wash thee not, thou hast no part with me."

Expository Study and Commentary:

This verse continues the interaction between Jesus and Peter during the footwashing, highlighting Peter's strong objection and Jesus' crucial response.

1. "Peter saith unto him, Thou shalt never wash my feet": Peter, in his characteristic impulsive manner, vehemently objects to Jesus washing his feet. This response likely stems from a deep sense of reverence for Jesus and a misunderstanding of the symbolic nature of the act.

2. "Jesus answered him, If I wash thee not, thou hast no part with me": Jesus responds with a statement that emphasizes the spiritual significance behind the physical act of footwashing. He points out that this act is not merely about cleansing feet; it carries a profound spiritual meaning. The phrase "thou hast no part with me" underscores the importance of humility and submission in the disciples' relationship with Jesus.

King James Bible References:

1. "Thou shalt never wash my feet": Peter's objection reflects his deep respect for Jesus and a cultural expectation about the roles of master and servant. It also mirrors other instances where Peter expresses strong reactions, such as his declaration that Jesus would not suffer and be crucified (Matthew 16:22).

2. "If I wash thee not, thou hast no part with me": This statement is crucial in understanding the deeper spiritual truth Jesus is conveying. The act of washing, beyond its physical implications, symbolizes the need for spiritual cleansing and humility. Jesus makes it clear that without this symbolic act, Peter would not share in the spiritual fellowship and relationship that Jesus offers.

In essence, Jesus is teaching Peter and the disciples that humility and submission to His cleansing work are essential for true discipleship. It goes beyond the external act of footwashing and extends to a heart posture of openness to receive the cleansing and transformative work of Jesus in one's life.

In summary, John 13:8 captures a pivotal moment in the footwashing narrative, illustrating the importance of spiritual humility and submission. Jesus connects the physical act of footwashing with a deeper spiritual truth, emphasizing the necessity of accepting His cleansing work for a genuine and meaningful relationship with Him.

John Chapter 13:9 (KJV)

"Simon Peter saith unto him, Lord, not my feet only, but also my hands and my head."

Expository Study and Commentary:

This verse continues the dialogue between Jesus and Peter during the footwashing, as Peter responds to Jesus' statement that without the washing, he would have no part with Him.

1. "Simon Peter saith unto him, Lord, not my feet only, but also my hands and my head": Peter, upon hearing Jesus' response, exhibits a characteristic intensity in his desire to be fully associated with Jesus. His initial objection transforms into an enthusiastic willingness to undergo a more extensive washing.

Peter's response indicates a shift from his earlier reluctance to a recognition of the spiritual significance behind Jesus' actions. He wants to go beyond the feet, understanding that there is a deeper cleansing and connection with Jesus that he desires to experience.

King James Bible References:

1. "Simon Peter saith unto him, Lord": Peter addresses Jesus with the title "Lord," acknowledging His authority and mastery. This term underscores Peter's reverence for Jesus and his acknowledgment of Jesus' higher position.

2. "Not my feet only, but also my hands and my head": Peter's willingness to have his hands and head washed as well expresses a desire for a more profound connection with Jesus. His request reflects a genuine longing for complete cleansing and communion with the Lord.

In essence, Peter's response reveals a growing understanding of the spiritual symbolism embedded in Jesus' actions. While initially resistant, he now recognizes the importance of the symbolic act of footwashing in signifying a deeper, transformative cleansing that is essential for a genuine relationship with Jesus.

This interaction between Jesus and Peter serves as a metaphor for the ongoing process of spiritual purification and sanctification that believers experience in their walk with Christ. It emphasizes the continual need for surrender, humility, and openness to the transformative work of Jesus in every aspect of one's life.

In summary, John 13:9 showcases Peter's evolving understanding and willingness to embrace the spiritual significance of Jesus' actions. It underscores the deeper cleansing that believers experience in their relationship with Christ and highlights the ongoing process of sanctification in the Christian journey.

John Chapter 13:10 (KJV)
"Jesus saith to him, He that is washed needeth not save to wash his feet, but is clean every whit: and ye are clean, but not all."

Expository Study and Commentary:

This verse contains Jesus' response to Peter's request to wash not only his feet but also his hands and head. Jesus uses this opportunity to explain the spiritual symbolism behind the act of footwashing and makes a significant statement about the disciples' spiritual cleanliness.

1. "Jesus saith to him, He that is washed needeth not save to wash his feet": Jesus begins by explaining that someone who has already bathed does not need a full washing again. Instead, a person who is clean only needs to wash their feet, which would have become dusty or soiled as they walked to the place where they are. This statement introduces a distinction between the initial cleansing or salvation and the ongoing process of sanctification in the life of a believer.

2. "But is clean every whit": Jesus emphasizes that the person who has undergone a complete washing is entirely clean. This phrase underscores the completeness and efficacy of the initial cleansing or salvation that a believer experiences through faith in Christ.

3. "And ye are clean, but not all": Here, Jesus makes a significant qualification. He acknowledges that the disciples, in general, have experienced a spiritual cleansing. However, the inclusion of "but not all" hints at the presence of one among them who has not fully embraced this spiritual cleanliness—referring to Judas Iscariot, who will later betray Jesus.

King James Bible References:

1. "He that is washed needeth not save to wash his feet": This statement aligns with the broader biblical theme of salvation and sanctification. The initial cleansing, represented by being "washed," refers to the moment of salvation when a person is justified by faith in Christ (Ephesians 2:8-9). The ongoing need to wash the feet symbolizes the process of sanctification, the ongoing work of the Holy Spirit in the believer's life to conform them to the image of Christ (Philippians 2:12-13).

2. "But is clean every whit": The completeness of the initial cleansing echoes passages that speak about the forgiveness of sins and the imputed righteousness of Christ received through faith (Romans 3:22, 2 Corinthians 5:21).

3. "And ye are clean, but not all": Jesus alludes to the fact that one among them is not truly clean. This foreshadows the revelation that not all the disciples were genuine followers, pointing specifically to Judas Iscariot (John 13:11).

In summary, John 13:10 contains a profound explanation from Jesus about the spiritual cleansing and ongoing sanctification of believers. It introduces the distinction between the initial cleansing at salvation and the ongoing process of purification in the Christian journey. The mention of "not all" adds a layer of anticipation for the unfolding events involving Judas Iscariot.

John Chapter 13:11 (KJV)

"For he knew who should betray him; therefore said he, Ye are not all clean."

Expository Study and Commentary:

In this verse, John provides insight into the mind of Jesus, explaining the reason behind His statement that not all of the disciples were clean.

1. "For he knew who should betray him": This statement underscores the divine knowledge and foreknowledge of Jesus. He was fully aware of the identity of the one among the disciples who would betray Him. This emphasizes Jesus' omniscience and the sovereignty of God's plan even in the face of betrayal.

2. "Therefore said he, Ye are not all clean": Jesus connects His knowledge of the impending betrayal to the statement made earlier about the cleanliness of the disciples. The phrase "not all clean" now takes on a deeper significance, pointing specifically to the presence of Judas Iscariot among them, who, despite being physically present, had not truly embraced the spiritual cleanliness offered through faith in Jesus.

King James Bible References:

1. "For he knew who should betray him": Jesus' foreknowledge of Judas' betrayal aligns with other instances in the Gospels where Jesus predicts specific events, demonstrating His divine awareness (John 6:64, John 18:4).

2. "Therefore said he, Ye are not all clean": This phrase echoes the earlier statement in verse 10, emphasizing that the lack of cleanliness is not a deficiency in Jesus' redemptive work but a result of the individual's rejection or betrayal. The notion of spiritual cleanliness connects to broader biblical themes of justification and sanctification.

The connection between Jesus' knowledge of Judas' betrayal and the declaration of cleanliness reinforces the idea that true cleanliness goes beyond external actions or affiliations; it involves a genuine relationship with Jesus. Judas, despite being in the physical presence of Jesus, had not truly embraced the spiritual cleansing offered by Christ.

In summary, John 13:11 highlights Jesus' awareness of Judas' betrayal and clarifies the deeper meaning behind His earlier statement about cleanliness. This verse emphasizes the importance of genuine faith and commitment in the discipleship journey and points to the sovereignty of God's plan even in the face of betrayal.

John Chapter 13:12 (KJV)
"So after he had washed their feet, and had taken his garments, and was set down again, he said unto them, Know ye what I have done to you?"

Expository Study and Commentary:

This verse marks a crucial point in the narrative after Jesus has washed the disciples' feet, and it transitions to a moment of teaching and reflection.

1. "So after he had washed their feet": This phrase signals the completion of the symbolic act of humility and service performed by Jesus. The physical act of washing the disciples' feet is now concluded, setting the stage for a deeper understanding of its significance.

2. "And had taken his garments": Jesus takes back His outer garments, signifying the end of the symbolic action. This act could be seen as a visual representation of the incarnation, where Jesus temporarily set aside His heavenly glory to take on the form of a servant (Philippians 2:5-8).

3. "And was set down again": Jesus assumes a position of teaching authority by sitting down. In Jewish tradition, sitting down indicated that a teacher was about to impart important wisdom or instruction. This further emphasizes the transition from a physical act to a moment of profound spiritual instruction.

280

4. "He said unto them, Know ye what I have done to you?": Jesus invites the disciples into a reflective and contemplative state. His question serves as a prompt for them to consider the deeper meaning of His actions. It initiates a teaching moment where Jesus will explain the spiritual significance of the footwashing.

King James Bible References:

1. "So after he had washed their feet": The act of footwashing aligns with the broader theme of Jesus' teachings on servanthood and humility, challenging conventional notions of leadership (Matthew 20:28, Mark 10:45).

2. "And had taken his garments": The act of taking back His garments could be compared to Jesus' post-resurrection appearances where He revealed His glorified form (John 20:19-20, Luke 24:30-31).

3. "And was set down again": The posture of sitting down for teaching is a common feature in Jesus' ministry, signifying authority and the commencement of important teachings (Matthew 5:1-2, Luke 4:20).

4. "He said unto them, Know ye what I have done to you?": This question initiates a reflective moment, inviting the disciples to consider the significance of the footwashing. Jesus often used questions to stimulate deeper understanding among His followers (Matthew 16:13-16, Mark 8:27-29).

In summary, John 13:12 marks the transition from the symbolic act of footwashing to a moment of teaching. Jesus, having performed the humble act, now prompts the disciples to reflect on its deeper meaning, setting the stage for a profound lesson on humility, service, and the nature of true discipleship.

John Chapter 13:13 (KJV)
"Ye call me Master and Lord: and ye say well; for so I am."

Expository Study and Commentary:

In this verse, Jesus responds to the disciples' acknowledgment of Him as Master and Lord, affirming the accuracy of their titles and providing insight into His identity and authority.

1. "Ye call me Master and Lord": Jesus acknowledges the titles the disciples use to address Him. "Master" implies a teacher or one with authority, and "Lord" denotes a supreme authority or ruler. These titles reflect the disciples' recognition of Jesus' role in their lives.

2. "And ye say well": Jesus affirms the disciples' use of these titles as appropriate. He acknowledges that their recognition of Him as Master and Lord is fitting and accurate, indicating the legitimacy of His authority and teachings.

3. "For so I am": In this powerful statement, Jesus declares the truth of His identity. He confirms that He is indeed their Master and Lord, emphasizing the authenticity of His divine authority. This statement aligns with the broader theme in the Gospel of John, where Jesus repeatedly asserts His divine nature and unique relationship with the Father.

King James Bible References:

1. "Ye call me Master and Lord": The titles "Master" and "Lord" are significant throughout the New Testament, capturing the disciples' acknowledgment of Jesus' authority. The use of "Master" aligns with Jesus being recognized as a teacher with unique authority (Matthew 8:19, Matthew 23:8). The use of "Lord" conveys a recognition of divine rulership (Luke 2:11, Philippians 2:9-11).

2. "And ye say well": Jesus commends the disciples for their accurate recognition of His authority. This aligns with instances in the Gospels where individuals correctly identify Jesus as the Messiah or the Son of God (Matthew 16:16, Mark 8:29, Luke 9:20).

3. "For so I am": Jesus' declaration of His identity aligns with various statements in the Gospel of John emphasizing His divine nature. This includes "I am the way, the truth, and the life" (John 14:6) and His use of the divine "I am" statements (John 8:58, John 18:5-6).

In summary, John 13:13 is a pivotal verse where Jesus affirms the disciples' recognition of Him as Master and Lord. His acknowledgment underscores His divine authority and unique role in their lives. This declaration sets the stage for further teachings, emphasizing the significance of understanding and submitting to Jesus' authority in matters of discipleship and faith.

John Chapter 13:14 (KJV)
"If I then, your Lord and Master, have washed your feet; ye also ought to wash one another's feet."

Expository Study and Commentary:

In this verse, Jesus uses the symbolic act of footwashing as a powerful lesson on humility, service, and mutual care within the community of believers.

1. "If I then, your Lord and Master, have washed your feet": Jesus begins by highlighting His role as both Lord and Master. He, the divine authority, willingly took on the role of a servant to perform the humble task of footwashing. This juxtaposition of authority and servanthood sets the stage for a profound lesson on leadership.

2. "Ye also ought to wash one another's feet": Jesus draws a direct parallel between His actions and the disciples' responsibilities. He challenges them to adopt a similar posture of humility and service towards one another. The act of washing one another's feet becomes a symbol of selfless service and care within the community of believers.

King James Bible References:

1. "If I then, your Lord and Master, have washed your feet": The concept of Jesus as Lord and Master is a recurring theme in the New Testament. It emphasizes His authority over believers and their voluntary submission to His lordship (Matthew 23:8, Romans 10:9, Philippians 2:9-11).

2. "Ye also ought to wash one another's feet": This statement aligns with other teachings of Jesus on servanthood and humility. In Matthew 20:26-28, Jesus instructs His disciples that true greatness is found in serving others. The idea of mutual service is further emphasized in passages like Galatians 5:13 and Philippians 2:3-4.

In essence, John 13:14 conveys a powerful lesson about the nature of Christian leadership and community. Jesus, the ultimate Lord and Master, exemplifies humility and service, challenging His followers to emulate this behavior in their relationships with one another. The act of footwashing becomes a symbolic representation of the sacrificial love and mutual care that should characterize the interactions among believers.

In summary, John 13:14 encourages believers to embrace a humble and servant-hearted approach to relationships, following the example set by Jesus. It emphasizes the call for mutual service and care within the community of believers, transcending social hierarchies and reflecting the essence of Christian love.

John Chapter 13:15 (KJV)
"For I have given you an example, that ye should do as I have done to you."

Expository Study and Commentary:

In this verse, Jesus explicitly states that His act of footwashing serves as an example for His disciples, urging them to follow His model of humility and service.

1. "For I have given you an example": Jesus acknowledges that His actions are not merely a demonstration of humility but

intentionally serve as a model or pattern for His followers. This underscores the didactic nature of the footwashing, emphasizing that it is meant to impart a lesson.

2. "That ye should do as I have done to you": The purpose of the example becomes clear – Jesus desires His disciples to imitate His humility and servant-heartedness. He invites them to incorporate this attitude of selfless service into their lives, relationships, and interactions within the community of believers.

King James Bible References:

1. "For I have given you an example": The idea of Jesus providing an example is consistent with other teachings in the New Testament that encourage believers to follow the pattern set by Christ. For instance, in 1 Peter 2:21, it is stated, "For even hereunto were ye called: because Christ also suffered for us, leaving us an example, that ye should follow his steps."

2. "That ye should do as I have done to you": This call to imitate Jesus aligns with broader teachings on discipleship and the imitation of Christ. In passages like Ephesians 5:1-2 and Philippians 2:5-8, believers are encouraged to walk in love and adopt the same attitude that Christ demonstrated through His sacrificial service.

In essence, John 13:15 underscores the transformative purpose of Jesus' actions. The footwashing is not only a historical event but a living example meant to shape the behavior and attitudes of His disciples. It establishes a paradigm for Christian service – one characterized by humility, selflessness, and a willingness to serve others.

In summary, John 13:15 challenges believers to go beyond recognizing Jesus' humility and actually incorporate this attitude into their lives. It emphasizes that the Christian journey involves actively imitating Christ's example of service and humility in their relationships and interactions with others.

John Chapter 13:16 (KJV)

"Verily, verily, I say unto you, The servant is not greater than his lord; neither he that is sent greater than he that sent him."

Expository Study and Commentary:

In this verse, Jesus uses a familiar saying to reinforce the principle of humility and submission within the context of discipleship.

1. "Verily, verily, I say unto you": The double "verily" (truly) emphasizes the certainty and importance of the statement that follows. Jesus is highlighting the significance of the principle He is about to articulate.

2. "The servant is not greater than his lord": This proverbial saying underscores a fundamental principle – a servant or disciple is not superior to the master or teacher. In the context of Jesus and His disciples, this statement reinforces the idea that followers should not see themselves as greater than their Lord. It emphasizes humility and the recognition of authority.

3. "Neither he that is sent greater than he that sent him": This second part of the saying extends the principle to the concept of being sent. In the relationship between the one sending and the one sent, the sender holds a position of authority. Jesus, as the Sent One from the Father, asserts the principle that He is not greater than the Father who sent Him.

King James Bible References:

1. "Verily, verily, I say unto you": The use of "verily" (truly) is a distinctive feature in Jesus' teachings, signaling the importance of the message He is conveying. It is used throughout the Gospels to introduce authoritative statements (Matthew 5:18, Matthew 24:34).

2. "The servant is not greater than his lord": This saying aligns with broader biblical principles emphasizing humility and submission.

It echoes teachings such as Jesus' words in Matthew 10:24-25, where He tells His disciples that a servant is not above his master.

3. "Neither he that is sent greater than he that sent him": This statement aligns with the hierarchical relationship between the Father and the Son. In passages like John 5:30 and John 6:38, Jesus emphasizes His submission to the will of the Father, highlighting the divine order within the Trinity.

In summary, John 13:16 reinforces the principle of humility within the disciple-teacher relationship and extends it to the relationship between the Father and the Son. It emphasizes the need for followers to recognize and embrace their role with humility, acknowledging the authority of their master or sender. This principle underscores the foundational aspect of humility in the Christian journey.

John Chapter 13:17 (KJV)
"If ye know these things, happy are ye if ye do them."

Expository Study and Commentary:

In this verse, Jesus shifts from teaching to action, emphasizing the importance of putting His teachings into practice for true happiness or blessedness.

1. "If ye know these things": Jesus refers to the principles, teachings, and examples He has shared with the disciples, particularly regarding humility, servanthood, and the hierarchical relationship between the master and servant.

2. "Happy are ye if ye do them": The key to happiness or blessedness lies not only in knowing these principles but in actively living them out. Jesus emphasizes the transformative power of applying His teachings in practical, everyday life.

King James Bible References:

1. "If ye know these things": Knowing and understanding Jesus' teachings is a recurring theme in the Gospels. In the Sermon on the Mount, Jesus emphasizes the importance of not only hearing but also doing His words (Matthew 7:24-27). Knowledge, in the biblical sense, often involves both intellectual understanding and practical application.

2. "Happy are ye if ye do them": The connection between knowledge and action for true happiness aligns with other teachings in the New Testament. James, the brother of Jesus, emphasizes the importance of being doers of the Word and not hearers only (James 1:22-25). Happiness or blessedness, in a biblical sense, is often tied to a life lived in accordance with God's principles.

In essence, John 13:17 encapsulates the transformative nature of discipleship. It's not enough to merely comprehend or acknowledge Jesus' teachings; true happiness comes from actively living out these principles in daily life. This aligns with the broader biblical theme that emphasizes the integration of faith and action.

In summary, John 13:17 challenges believers to move beyond theoretical knowledge and actively apply Jesus' teachings in their lives. The promise of happiness or blessedness is directly linked to the practical embodiment of these transformative principles in their relationships, service, and overall conduct.

John Chapter 13:18 (KJV)
"I speak not of you all: I know whom I have chosen: but that the scripture may be fulfilled, He that eateth bread with me hath lifted up his heel against me."

Expository Study and Commentary:

In this verse, Jesus makes a specific reference to the betrayal that is about to unfold, highlighting both the divine purpose behind it and the fulfillment of Scripture.

1. "I speak not of you all: I know whom I have chosen": Jesus clarifies that His statement is not a general indictment of all the disciples. He has a specific individual in mind, and He asserts His knowledge of those whom He has chosen. This underscores Jesus' sovereign awareness of His disciples and the unfolding events.

2. "But that the scripture may be fulfilled": Jesus reveals that the forthcoming betrayal is part of the divine plan, aligning with prophecies found in the Scriptures. This emphasizes the overarching theme of God's sovereignty and the fulfillment of His predetermined purposes.

3. "He that eateth bread with me hath lifted up his heel against me": Jesus quotes a portion of a Messianic prophecy found in Psalm 41:9. The image of lifting up the heel against someone signifies an act of betrayal or hostility, adding a poignant layer to the impending betrayal by one of His close associates.

King James Bible References:

1. "I speak not of you all: I know whom I have chosen": Jesus' knowledge of those chosen by Him aligns with broader biblical themes of divine election and predestination. In passages like John 6:70 and John 15:16, Jesus speaks about the Father's role in choosing His disciples.

2. "But that the scripture may be fulfilled": The concept of Scripture being fulfilled is a recurring theme in the Gospels, highlighting the divine orchestration of events. Numerous prophecies in the Old Testament find their fulfillment in the life, death, and resurrection of Jesus (Matthew 1:22-23, Matthew 2:15).

3. "He that eateth bread with me hath lifted up his heel against me": Jesus quoting Psalm 41:9 draws attention to the Messianic nature of the Psalms and their fulfillment in Him. This specific imagery is echoed in the New Testament, emphasizing the connection between the betrayal and the fulfillment of God's plan (Matthew 26:23, Mark 14:18, Luke 22:21, Acts 1:16).

In summary, John 13:18 provides a forewarning of the betrayal, revealing both Jesus' knowledge of the chosen disciples and the fulfillment of Scriptural prophecy. It underscores the intricate interplay between divine sovereignty and human agency, emphasizing the role of God's plan in the unfolding events of Jesus' earthly ministry.

John Chapter 13:19 (KJV)
"Now I tell you before it come, that, when it is come to pass, ye may believe that I am he."

Expository Study and Commentary:

In this verse, Jesus foretells the events of betrayal, once again emphasizing the significance of prophecy and the purpose of strengthening the disciples' faith.

1. "Now I tell you before it come": Jesus is providing advanced knowledge to His disciples about the betrayal, demonstrating His omniscience and the transparency of His ministry. This forewarning is given to prepare them for the unfolding events.

2. "That, when it is come to pass, ye may believe": The purpose behind this revelation is to strengthen the disciples' faith. Jesus wants them to recognize that His knowledge of future events aligns with His divine nature. This foresight serves as a confirmation of His identity and mission.

3. "that I am he": The phrase "I am he" carries a significant weight, echoing the divine "I AM" declarations made by Jesus in the Gospel of John (e.g., John 8:58). It emphasizes Jesus' divine identity, aligning Himself with the God of Israel.

King James Bible References:

1. "Now I tell you before it come": This aligns with the broader biblical theme of prophecy, where God, through His prophets or, in

this case, through Jesus Himself, foretells future events. Prophetic declarations serve to authenticate the divine origin of the message (Isaiah 42:8-9, Isaiah 46:10).

2. "That, when it is come to pass, ye may believe": The connection between prophecy and belief is a recurring theme. Jesus often uses fulfilled prophecies as evidence to strengthen the faith of His disciples (Matthew 26:54, Mark 14:49, Luke 24:44-46).

3. "that I am he": The use of "I am" echoes the divine identity of Jesus. This phrase is reminiscent of the divine self-revelation in the Old Testament, particularly in the burning bush encounter with Moses (Exodus 3:14). Jesus' repeated use of "I am" affirms His claim to be the divine Messiah.

In summary, John 13:19 highlights Jesus' foreknowledge, the role of prophecy in confirming His identity, and the purpose of strengthening the disciples' faith. It showcases the intricate connection between prophecy, fulfillment, and belief, all pointing to the divine nature of Jesus as the fulfillment of God's promises.

John Chapter 13:20 (KJV)
"Verily, verily, I say unto you, He that receiveth whomsoever I send receiveth me, and he that receiveth me receiveth him that sent me."

Expository Study and Commentary:

In this verse, Jesus establishes a profound principle regarding the reception of those sent by Him, emphasizing the interconnectedness between Himself, His messengers, and the One who sent Him.

1. "Verily, verily, I say unto you": The use of "verily" (truly) emphasizes the solemnity and importance of the statement that follows. Jesus is drawing attention to the significance of the principle He is about to articulate.

2. "He that receiveth whomsoever I send receiveth me": Jesus asserts a direct correlation between receiving His messengers and receiving Him. This underscores the principle of representation – those sent by Jesus carry His authority and message.

3. "and he that receiveth me receiveth him that sent me": Jesus extends the principle further, emphasizing that receiving Him is equivalent to receiving the One who sent Him. This statement reinforces the unity and divine connection within the Godhead – the Father sending the Son.

King James Bible References:

1. "Verily, verily, I say unto you": As mentioned earlier, the use of "verily" signifies the importance of Jesus' statements. This phrase is used consistently throughout the Gospels to introduce authoritative declarations (Matthew 5:18, Matthew 16:28).

2. "He that receiveth whomsoever I send receiveth me": This principle aligns with other teachings in the New Testament emphasizing the authority and representation of messengers or ambassadors. In Luke 10:16, Jesus says, "He who listens to you listens to me; he who rejects you rejects me."

3. "and he that receiveth me receiveth him that sent me": This statement aligns with the broader biblical theme of the unity of the Father and the Son. Jesus repeatedly emphasizes His close relationship with the Father and the mutual representation between them (John 5:23, John 14:9).

In summary, John 13:20 establishes a principle of representation and authority. Receiving those sent by Jesus is tantamount to receiving Jesus Himself, and by extension, receiving the One who sent Him. This principle emphasizes the interconnectedness within the Godhead and underscores the divine authority vested in those commissioned by Jesus.

John Chapter 13:21 (KJV)

"When Jesus had thus said, he was troubled in spirit, and testified, and said, Verily, verily, I say unto you, that one of you shall betray me."

Expository Study and Commentary:

In this verse, Jesus reveals the troubling news of betrayal, highlighting the emotional and spiritual impact on Him and the imminent fulfillment of prophecy.

1. "When Jesus had thus said, he was troubled in spirit": Jesus' emotional response signifies the weightiness of the revelation. His inner turmoil reflects the genuine human experience of facing betrayal from someone close to Him. This moment captures the depth of His emotions.

2. "and testified, and said, Verily, verily, I say unto you": The use of "verily" (truly) emphasizes the gravity of Jesus' testimony. This is not a casual statement; it is a solemn declaration, underscoring the certainty and importance of what He is about to disclose.

3. "that one of you shall betray me": Jesus discloses the painful truth that one among His closest followers will betray Him. This statement sets the stage for the revelation of Judas Iscariot as the betrayer and connects to the broader theme of the fulfillment of prophecy.

King James Bible References:

1. "When Jesus had thus said, he was troubled in spirit": The emotional response of Jesus aligns with other instances in the Gospels where He expresses sorrow or distress, showcasing the depth of His humanity (Matthew 26:37-38, Luke 19:41).

2. "and testified, and said, Verily, verily, I say unto you": The use of "verily" underscores the authenticity of Jesus' words. His testimony carries significant weight, and similar phrases are used

throughout the Gospels to introduce important statements (John 3:3, John 5:19).

3. "that one of you shall betray me": This statement connects to Old Testament prophecies, particularly the Messianic psalms. Psalm 41:9 prophesies betrayal: "Yea, mine own familiar friend, in whom I trusted, which did eat of my bread, hath lifted up his heel against me." Jesus, by using similar language, is aligning His experience with the fulfillment of these prophecies.

In summary, John 13:21 reveals a pivotal moment in Jesus' ministry as He foretells the imminent betrayal. His troubled spirit and the use of solemn language emphasize the gravity of the situation. This disclosure sets the stage for the unfolding events leading to the fulfillment of prophecies regarding the Messiah's betrayal.

John Chapter 13:22 (KJV)
"Then the disciples looked one on another, doubting of whom he spake."

Expository Study and Commentary:

In this verse, the disciples react to Jesus' revelation of betrayal by looking at one another with uncertainty, prompting an atmosphere of doubt and questioning.

1. "Then the disciples looked one on another": The disciples, upon hearing Jesus' statement about betrayal, instinctively turn their attention to one another. This reaction suggests a mixture of surprise, confusion, and curiosity as they try to comprehend who among them could be the betrayer.

2. "doubting of whom he spake": The disciples are uncertain and doubtful about the identity of the betrayer. This doubt may arise from a lack of clarity in Jesus' statement or from disbelief that one of their own could betray Him. The atmosphere is charged with tension and concern as they grapple with the revelation.

294

King James Bible References:

1. "Then the disciples looked one on another": This type of interaction among the disciples is reminiscent of other moments when they express confusion or seek clarification. For instance, in John 13:28-29, they are uncertain about Judas' motives when he leaves the gathering.

2. "doubting of whom he spake": The disciples' doubt reflects the human response to unexpected and troubling news. This doubt contrasts with instances in the Gospels where the disciples struggle to fully comprehend Jesus' predictions about His upcoming suffering and death (Matthew 16:21-22, Mark 9:31-32).

In summary, John 13:22 captures the immediate aftermath of Jesus' revelation about betrayal. The disciples, faced with uncertainty, look at one another with doubt, revealing their human vulnerability and struggle to grasp the weight of the unfolding events. This sets the stage for further revelations and developments regarding the identity of the betrayer.

John Chapter 13:23 (KJV)
"Now there was leaning on Jesus' bosom one of his disciples, whom Jesus loved."

Expository Study and Commentary:

In this verse, the Gospel writer, John, provides a unique detail about the disciple whom Jesus loved, emphasizing the closeness and intimacy of this disciple's relationship with Jesus.

1. "Now there was leaning on Jesus' bosom": This description reveals the posture of one of the disciples during the meal. The phrase "leaning on Jesus' bosom" indicates a position of closeness and intimacy, as was the custom during formal meals in that cultural context.

2. "one of his disciples, whom Jesus loved": This disciple is identified as the one whom Jesus loved, a distinctive designation used by John throughout his Gospel to refer to himself. This phrase underscores the special bond and affection that existed between Jesus and this particular disciple.

King James Bible References:

1. "Now there was leaning on Jesus' bosom": This physical closeness reflects the intimacy of Jesus' relationship with His disciples. It aligns with other instances where individuals sought proximity to Jesus, such as the woman who anointed His feet (Luke 7:38) or John reclining close to Him during the Last Supper (John 21:20).

2. "one of his disciples, whom Jesus loved": This specific identification of the disciple as the one whom Jesus loved is a recurring theme in John's Gospel. It appears at key moments, including the footwashing (John 13:23), the Last Supper (John 13:23; John 21:20), and the crucifixion (John 19:26-27). Traditionally, this disciple is understood to be John himself.

In summary, John 13:23 provides a glimpse into the close relationship between Jesus and a particular disciple, often identified as John. The act of leaning on Jesus' bosom signifies a deep level of intimacy, and the designation "whom Jesus loved" emphasizes the unique bond between Jesus and this disciple. This sets the stage for the unfolding narrative, particularly in the context of the upcoming revelation of the betrayer.

John Chapter 13:24 (KJV)
"Simon Peter therefore beckoned to him, that he should ask who it should be of whom he spake."

Expository Study and Commentary:

In this verse, Simon Peter, one of Jesus' prominent disciples, signals to the disciple whom Jesus loved, asking him to inquire about the identity of the betrayer.

1. "Simon Peter therefore beckoned to him": Simon Peter, known for his impulsive and outspoken nature, takes the initiative by signaling or gesturing to the disciple whom Jesus loved. This action demonstrates Peter's curiosity and desire to understand more about Jesus' statement.

2. "that he should ask who it should be of whom he spake": Peter instructs the beloved disciple to inquire from Jesus about the identity of the one who would betray Him. This indicates Peter's eagerness to gain clarification and highlights the disciple's unique position of closeness to Jesus.

King James Bible References:

1. "Simon Peter therefore beckoned to him": Peter's impulsive and bold character is evident in various Gospel accounts. For instance, he is often the first to speak or act, such as when he walks on water (Matthew 14:28-29) or confesses Jesus as the Christ (Matthew 16:16).

2. "that he should ask who it should be of whom he spake": Peter's request reflects the disciples' collective confusion and concern about the revelation of betrayal. It aligns with other instances where the disciples seek further clarification or express their desire to understand Jesus' teachings (Matthew 15:15, Mark 9:32).

In summary, John 13:24 depicts Simon Peter's proactive response to Jesus' revelation about betrayal. Peter, in his characteristic manner, signals to the disciple whom Jesus loved, urging him to seek clarification. This interaction sets the stage for further revelations and contributes to the unfolding narrative of Jesus' last interactions with His disciples.

John Chapter 13:25 (KJV)
"He then lying on Jesus' breast saith unto him, Lord, who is it?"

Expository Study and Commentary:

In this verse, the disciple whom Jesus loved, traditionally identified as John, is depicted as leaning on Jesus' breast during the meal. He seizes the opportunity to inquire directly from Jesus about the identity of the betrayer.

1. "He then lying on Jesus' breast": This description reaffirms the intimate posture of the disciple whom Jesus loved, emphasizing the closeness and familiarity in their relationship. The act of lying on Jesus' breast signifies a deep connection and a position of trust and affection.

2. "saith unto him, Lord, who is it?": In response to Simon Peter's prompting, the beloved disciple directly addresses Jesus with a question. The term "Lord" reflects both respect and recognition of Jesus' authority. The question reveals the disciple's eagerness to understand the specific details of the impending betrayal.

King James Bible References:

1. "He then lying on Jesus' breast": This physical proximity highlights the unique relationship between the beloved disciple and Jesus. It aligns with previous instances where individuals sought closeness to Jesus, demonstrating the deep intimacy and trust associated with being in His presence (John 21:20).

2. "saith unto him, Lord, who is it?": The disciple's use of "Lord" acknowledges Jesus' authority and leadership. Throughout the Gospels, this term is employed by disciples and others to address Jesus with reverence and submission (Matthew 8:2, Matthew 14:28, Luke 5:8).

In summary, John 13:25 portrays the disciple whom Jesus loved, lying on Jesus' breast, seeking direct clarification from Him about the identity of the betrayer. This interaction further emphasizes the intimacy and trust that existed between Jesus and this disciple. It also sets the stage for Jesus' response and the revelation of the betrayer in the subsequent verses.

John Chapter 13:26 (KJV)

"Jesus answered, He it is, to whom I shall give a sop, when I have dipped it. And when he had dipped the sop, he gave it to Judas Iscariot, the son of Simon."

Expository Study and Commentary:

In this verse, Jesus responds to the disciple whom He loved, indicating that the betrayer is the one to whom He will give a symbolic piece of bread (sop) after dipping it. Jesus then performs this act with Judas Iscariot.

1. "Jesus answered, He it is, to whom I shall give a sop, when I have dipped it": Jesus provides a specific sign to identify the betrayer. The act of giving a sop was a symbolic gesture, often denoting friendship and trust. Jesus foretells that the one who receives this sop is the betrayer.

2. "And when he had dipped the sop, he gave it to Judas Iscariot, the son of Simon": Jesus carries out the symbolic action, dipping the bread and giving it to Judas Iscariot, revealing him as the one who would betray Him. The inclusion of Judas' lineage, mentioning him as the son of Simon, provides additional context.

King James Bible References:

1. "Jesus answered, He it is, to whom I shall give a sop, when I have dipped it": The use of symbolic actions is not uncommon in Jesus' teachings. In the feeding of the five thousand, He took bread, blessed it, and distributed it (Matthew 14:19). Here, the sop serves as a distinctive sign indicating the betrayer.

2. "And when he had dipped the sop, he gave it to Judas Iscariot, the son of Simon": The inclusion of Judas' full name and his father's name, Simon, distinguishes him from others with the same name. The choice to include this detail adds specificity to the identification of the betrayer.

In summary, John 13:26 reveals the moment of Jesus' identification of the betrayer, using a symbolic act of giving a sop. By giving it to Judas Iscariot, Jesus points out the one who would betray Him. This scene sets the stage for the unfolding events leading to the fulfillment of the prophecy about the betrayal of Jesus.

John Chapter 13:27 (KJV)
"And after the sop Satan entered into him. Then said Jesus unto him, That thou doest, do quickly."

Expository Study and Commentary:

In this verse, the narrative unfolds as Judas, after receiving the sop from Jesus, becomes susceptible to the influence of Satan. Jesus then instructs Judas to carry out his betrayal swiftly.

1. "And after the sop Satan entered into him": This statement signifies a pivotal moment. The act of receiving the sop seems to mark a turning point, as Judas becomes receptive to the influence of Satan. The mention of Satan's entrance highlights the spiritual dimension of Judas' actions.

2. "Then said Jesus unto him, That thou doest, do quickly": Jesus, aware of Judas' impending betrayal, issues a directive for him to carry out the betrayal swiftly. This command, coupled with the mention of Satan's influence, underscores the urgency and inevitability of the unfolding events.

King James Bible References:

1. "And after the sop Satan entered into him": The concept of Satan entering or influencing individuals is found elsewhere in the New Testament. In Luke 22:3, it is mentioned that Satan entered into Judas Iscariot before he conspired to betray Jesus. This emphasizes the spiritual dimension of the events leading to the betrayal.

2. "Then said Jesus unto him, That thou doest, do quickly": The urgency in Jesus' words aligns with the broader theme of Jesus

willingly embracing His sacrificial mission. Jesus is not caught off guard by Judas' actions; instead, He encourages their swift execution, knowing that this is part of the divine plan (Matthew 26:45-46, Mark 14:41-42).

In summary, John 13:27 marks a crucial moment in the narrative, as Judas succumbs to the influence of Satan after receiving the sop. Jesus, fully aware of the unfolding events, instructs Judas to proceed quickly with the betrayal. This verse sets the stage for the fulfillment of the prophetic announcement and the rapid progression of events leading to Jesus' arrest and crucifixion.

John Chapter 13:28 (KJV)
"Now no man at the table knew for what intent he spake this unto him."

Expository Study and Commentary:

In this verse, the narrative highlights the lack of understanding among the disciples regarding Jesus' specific instructions to Judas. The secrecy of the plan adds a layer of intrigue to the unfolding events.

1. "Now no man at the table knew for what intent he spake this unto him": The disciples present at the table, including the beloved disciple and Simon Peter, are unaware of the specific purpose behind Jesus' instruction to Judas. This lack of understanding contributes to the suspense and mystery surrounding Judas' actions.

King James Bible References:

1. "Now no man at the table knew for what intent he spake this unto him": This moment reflects a recurring theme in the Gospels where the disciples often struggle to comprehend the deeper significance of Jesus' words and actions. In Mark 9:32, the disciples did not understand Jesus' prediction of His death and resurrection, highlighting their limited understanding at times.

In summary, John 13:28 emphasizes the secrecy and lack of awareness among the disciples regarding Jesus' specific instructions to Judas. The disciples, symbolizing the broader human perspective, are left in suspense, unaware of the unfolding divine plan. This verse contributes to the tension and anticipation surrounding the events leading to Jesus' betrayal and subsequent crucifixion.

John Chapter 13:29 (KJV)
"For some of them thought, because Judas had the bag, that Jesus had said unto him, Buy those things that we have need of against the feast; or, that he should give something to the poor."

Expository Study and Commentary:

In this verse, the narrative reveals the disciples' varying assumptions about Judas' actions, highlighting the diverse perspectives among them regarding Jesus' instruction to Judas.

1. "For some of them thought": The use of "some" indicates that not all the disciples shared the same interpretation of Jesus' words. There was diversity in their understanding, reflecting the complexity of the situation.

2. "because Judas had the bag": The possession of the money bag by Judas is mentioned as a factor influencing the disciples' assumptions. Judas, being the treasurer, held the common funds, adding a layer of credibility to the idea that he might be tasked with purchasing necessities.

3. "that Jesus had said unto him, Buy those things that we have need of against the feast; or, that he should give something to the poor": The disciples' assumptions can be categorized into two main possibilities: a. Judas is instructed to buy provisions for the upcoming feast, or b. Judas is tasked with giving to the poor. These assumptions reflect the disciples' attempts to make sense of Jesus' directive.

King James Bible References:

1. "For some of them thought": The diversity in the disciples' understanding aligns with other instances where they struggled to grasp the full meaning of Jesus' teachings. In Matthew 16:7-12, Jesus rebukes the disciples for misunderstanding His warnings about the leaven of the Pharisees.

2. "because Judas had the bag": The mention of Judas as the one who had the bag is consistent with earlier references in the Gospels, indicating his role as the treasurer (John 12:6, Matthew 26:14-15). This detail adds credibility to the disciples' assumptions.

3. "that Jesus had said unto him, Buy those things that we have need of against the feast; or, that he should give something to the poor": The disciples' assumptions reveal their expectations about practical matters like preparing for a feast or charitable acts. This aligns with other instances where Jesus emphasizes the importance of caring for physical and spiritual needs (Matthew 6:1-4, Matthew 25:35-36).

In summary, John 13:29 depicts the disciples' varied interpretations of Jesus' instruction to Judas. Their assumptions reveal a range of expectations about practical matters, such as preparations for a feast or charitable acts. This diversity of perspectives contributes to the complexity of the disciples' understanding as they navigate the unfolding events.

John Chapter 13:30 (KJV)
"He then having received the sop went immediately out: and it was night."

Expository Study and Commentary:

In this verse, the narrative continues with Judas responding to Jesus' instruction. The mention of nighttime adds a symbolic layer to the unfolding events.

1. "He then having received the sop went immediately out": Judas, having received the symbolic piece of bread from Jesus,

promptly leaves the gathering. The immediacy of his departure emphasizes the swift execution of his betrayal, in accordance with Jesus' earlier directive.

2. "and it was night": The inclusion of "and it was night" holds both a literal and symbolic meaning. Literally, it describes the time of day, emphasizing the darkness of the night. Symbolically, it conveys the moral and spiritual darkness associated with the act of betrayal.

King James Bible References:

1. "He then having received the sop went immediately out": The swift departure of Judas aligns with the urgency emphasized by Jesus in the preceding verse (John 13:27). Judas' response to Jesus' directive demonstrates the quick execution of the betrayal plan.

2. "and it was night": The symbolism of night is found throughout the Bible, often representing moral and spiritual darkness. In the Gospel of John, Jesus frequently contrasts light and darkness, symbolizing the contrast between righteousness and sin (John 3:19-21, John 8:12).

In summary, John 13:30 marks the moment of Judas' departure after receiving the sop from Jesus. The mention of night adds a symbolic layer, emphasizing the moral and spiritual darkness associated with the act of betrayal. This verse sets the stage for the imminent betrayal and the unfolding events leading to Jesus' arrest and crucifixion.

John Chapter 13:31 (KJV)
"Therefore, when he was gone out, Jesus said, Now is the Son of man glorified, and God is glorified in him."

Expository Study and Commentary:

In this verse, Jesus responds to Judas' departure by making a profound statement about the glorification of the Son of Man and the glorification of God in Him.

1. "Therefore, when he was gone out": The departure of Judas prompts Jesus to make a significant declaration. The conjunction "therefore" connects Judas' exit with the subsequent statement, indicating a moment of transition and significance.

2. "Jesus said, Now is the Son of man glorified": Jesus declares that the departure of Judas marks a moment of glorification for the Son of Man. This statement anticipates the unfolding events leading to Jesus' crucifixion, resurrection, and ultimate exaltation.

3. "and God is glorified in him": The glorification of the Son of Man is inseparable from the glorification of God. Jesus, as the Son of Man, serves as the embodiment of God's divine plan, and His sacrificial journey, including the upcoming crucifixion, brings glory to God.

King James Bible References:

1. "Therefore, when he was gone out": The conjunction "therefore" often introduces a logical consequence or inference. In this context, Judas' departure becomes the backdrop for Jesus' declaration, indicating a shift in the narrative (John 7:1, John 9:16).

2. "Jesus said, Now is the Son of man glorified": The theme of glorification is recurrent in Jesus' teachings, especially as He approaches His sacrificial death. The concept of the Son of Man being glorified finds parallel expressions in other passages, such as John 12:23-24, where Jesus speaks of the grain of wheat falling into the ground and dying to bear much fruit.

3. "and God is glorified in him": The interconnected glorification of God and the Son of Man echoes Jesus' earlier statements about His mission to glorify the Father (John 17:4-5). The crucifixion, resurrection, and ascension of Jesus ultimately bring glory to God.

In summary, John 13:31 marks a significant moment in Jesus' discourse, linking Judas' departure with the commencement of the Son of Man's glorification and the glorification of God through the redemptive work that would unfold. This declaration sets the stage for the profound events that will follow in the narrative.

John Chapter 13:32 (KJV)
"If God be glorified in him, God shall also glorify him in himself, and shall straightway glorify him."

Expository Study and Commentary:

In this verse, Jesus continues to elaborate on the theme of glorification, emphasizing the reciprocal glorification between Himself and God.

1. "If God be glorified in him": Jesus affirms that if God is glorified in Him through the events that will unfold, including His sacrificial death, then a reciprocal action will follow.

2. "God shall also glorify him in himself": Jesus speaks of God glorifying Him in Himself, indicating a divine and profound exaltation. This emphasizes the intimate connection between the Son and the Father in the glorification process.

3. "and shall straightway glorify him": The use of "straightway" underscores the immediacy and certainty of the glorification process. There is no delay in God's response to the glorification brought about through Jesus' obedience to His mission.

King James Bible References:

1. "If God be glorified in him": The concept of God being glorified in Jesus aligns with broader biblical teachings about the Father's delight in the Son and the fulfillment of divine purposes through Jesus' earthly ministry (Isaiah 42:1, Matthew 3:17, Matthew 17:5).

2. "God shall also glorify him in himself": The reciprocal glorification within the Godhead is a profound theological concept. It aligns with Jesus' previous statements about His oneness with the Father (John 10:30) and the Father's role in glorifying the Son (John 8:54).

3. "and shall straightway glorify him": The immediate glorification echoes the swift progression of events leading to Jesus' crucifixion, resurrection, and ascension. The concept of swift glorification is also present in other passages, emphasizing the decisive and purposeful nature of God's plan (Isaiah 62:7, Luke 18:8).

In summary, John 13:32 presents a theological statement by Jesus about the reciprocal glorification between Himself and God. If God is glorified in Jesus through His redemptive work, there will be an immediate and profound glorification of Jesus by God Himself. This declaration foreshadows the upcoming events in the narrative, particularly the crucifixion and the subsequent exaltation of Jesus.

John Chapter 13:33 (KJV)
"Little children, yet a little while I am with you. Ye shall seek me: and as I said unto the Jews, Whither I go, ye cannot come; so now I say to you."

Expository Study and Commentary:

In this verse, Jesus addresses His disciples with affectionate language, preparing them for His imminent departure and reiterating the limitation of their current understanding regarding His destination.

1. "Little children": Jesus employs a tender term, "little children," expressing care and affection for His disciples. This term reflects a nurturing and protective tone, emphasizing the close relationship between Jesus and His followers.

2. "yet a little while I am with you": Jesus acknowledges the limited remaining time of His physical presence with the disciples.

This statement foreshadows the upcoming events leading to His crucifixion, resurrection, and eventual ascension.

3. "Ye shall seek me: and as I said unto the Jews, Whither I go, ye cannot come": Jesus hints at the disciples' future longing for His presence and restates a previous statement made to the Jews. He refers to His departure to a place where the disciples, at this moment, cannot follow.

King James Bible References:

1. "Little children": The term "little children" reflects Jesus' use of endearing language to address His disciples. This expression of affection is consistent with other instances in the Gospels where Jesus emphasizes the childlike qualities of faith and dependence (Matthew 18:3, Mark 10:14-15).

2. "yet a little while I am with you": This notion of a limited time together echoes previous statements by Jesus regarding His earthly mission and the inevitability of His departure (John 7:33, John 12:35-36).

3. "Ye shall seek me: and as I said unto the Jews, Whither I go, ye cannot come": The reference to Jesus' statement to the Jews emphasizes the contrast between those who reject Him and the disciples who, at this moment, cannot fully comprehend the nature of His departure (John 7:34, John 8:21-22).

In summary, John 13:33 captures a poignant moment where Jesus, with affectionate words, prepares His disciples for His imminent departure. The use of "little children" conveys care, while the acknowledgment of a brief remaining time hints at the forthcoming events. The reference to seeking and Jesus' destination underscores the disciples' limited understanding at this point in the narrative.

John Chapter 13:34 (KJV)

"A new commandment I give unto you, That ye love one another; as I have loved you, that ye also love one another."

Expository Study and Commentary:

In this verse, Jesus introduces a profound and revolutionary commandment, emphasizing the centrality of love among His disciples.

1. "A new commandment I give unto you": Jesus introduces a novel and distinctive commandment, signaling a shift in the ethical teachings of the disciples. This new commandment transcends previous regulations and stands as a unique mandate for His followers.

2. "That ye love one another": The essence of the new commandment revolves around love. Jesus directs His disciples to demonstrate a deep, selfless, and sacrificial love for one another. This love goes beyond mere affection; it involves a commitment to the well-being and welfare of others.

3. "as I have loved you": The standard for this love is set by Jesus Himself. His love is characterized by unparalleled selflessness, compassion, and sacrifice. By pointing to His own love as the benchmark, Jesus establishes an extraordinary and transformative standard.

4. "that ye also love one another": Jesus reinforces the command, emphasizing the reciprocity of this love among His disciples. It is not a one-sided obligation but a mutual commitment to love and care for each other.

King James Bible References:

1. "A new commandment I give unto you": The concept of a new commandment aligns with Jesus' emphasis on fulfilling and surpassing the moral and ethical teachings of the Law (Matthew 5:17-48). The newness of this commandment lies in its revolutionary nature and the higher standard of love it introduces.

2. "That ye love one another": The call to love one another is not entirely new, as it echoes the Old Testament commandment to love one's neighbor (Leviticus 19:18). However, the novelty lies in the depth and sacrificial nature of the love that Jesus demands.

3. "as I have loved you": The reference to Jesus' love as the model for discipleship underscores the transformative nature of Christian love. This concept is echoed in Paul's writings, emphasizing Christ's sacrificial love as the foundation for relationships within the Christian community (Ephesians 5:2).

4. "that ye also love one another": The call for mutual love is consistent with other New Testament teachings on the importance of unity and love within the body of believers (Romans 12:10, 1 Thessalonians 4:9, 1 Peter 1:22).

In summary, John 13:34 captures a pivotal moment where Jesus introduces a new commandment, emphasizing the transformative power of love. The standard set by Jesus, rooted in His own sacrificial love, challenges disciples to exhibit a profound and selfless love for one another. This commandment stands as a cornerstone of Christian ethics and community life.

John Chapter 13:35 (KJV)
"By this shall all men know that ye are my disciples, if ye have love one to another."

Expository Study and Commentary:

In this verse, Jesus outlines the powerful impact of the disciples' love for one another as a defining characteristic that identifies them as His followers.

1. "By this shall all men know": Jesus suggests that the distinctive feature by which people will recognize His disciples is tied to a specific quality or behavior. This emphasizes the observable nature of the discipleship.

2. "that ye are my disciples": The identifier here is discipleship—being recognized as followers of Jesus. The world is meant to witness something unique in the disciples that sets them apart from others.

3. "if ye have love one to another": The defining characteristic is unveiled – love among the disciples. Jesus underscores the importance of genuine, selfless, and mutual love within the community of believers as the primary marker of true discipleship.

King James Bible References:

1. "By this shall all men know": The idea of discipleship being recognizable by specific characteristics aligns with other teachings of Jesus. In the Sermon on the Mount, He speaks about the distinctive qualities of His followers, including their love for enemies (Matthew 5:43-48).

2. "that ye are my disciples": The term "disciples" refers to those who follow Jesus and learn from Him. This concept is fundamental in the Gospels, emphasizing a committed and learning relationship with the Master (Matthew 28:19-20, Luke 9:23).

3. "if ye have love one to another": The emphasis on love as a distinguishing mark of discipleship is echoed throughout the New Testament. Paul, in his letters, repeatedly emphasizes the centrality of love within the Christian community (1 Corinthians 13:1-3, Galatians 5:22, Colossians 3:14).

In summary, John 13:35 encapsulates a profound teaching by Jesus about the identifying mark of true discipleship. The reciprocal and selfless love among His followers is meant to be a compelling and visible testament to the world. This verse underscores the transformative power of Christian love as a witness to the reality of discipleship and the presence of Christ in the lives of believers.

John Chapter 13:36 (KJV)

"Simon Peter said unto him, Lord, whither goest thou? Jesus answered him, Whither I go, thou canst not follow me now; but thou shalt follow me afterwards."

Expository Study and Commentary:

In this verse, Peter responds to Jesus' earlier statement about His departure, expressing a deep concern and curiosity about Jesus' destination.

1. "Simon Peter said unto him, Lord, whither goest thou?": Peter, known for his impulsive and passionate nature, immediately seeks clarification from Jesus regarding His intended destination. This question reveals Peter's attachment to Jesus and his desire to be wherever Jesus is going.

2. "Jesus answered him, Whither I go, thou canst not follow me now": Jesus responds to Peter's inquiry, conveying that at this particular moment, Peter is unable to follow Him to His destination. Jesus hints at the limitations of Peter's understanding and readiness for the profound events about to unfold.

3. "but thou shalt follow me afterwards": While Jesus acknowledges the current impossibility for Peter to follow Him immediately, He assures Peter that there will be a time in the future when he will indeed follow Him. This foreshadows the eventual restoration and commissioning of Peter after Jesus' resurrection.

King James Bible References:

1. "Simon Peter said unto him, Lord, whither goest thou?": Peter's direct question reflects his earnest and impulsive nature. This immediacy in seeking clarification from Jesus is consistent with Peter's character as portrayed in the Gospels (Matthew 14:28, Matthew 16:22).

2. "Jesus answered him, Whither I go, thou canst not follow me now": Jesus' response echoes the earlier statement to the Jews

(John 13:33), emphasizing the temporal and spiritual limitations regarding Peter's immediate ability to follow Him. This sets the stage for the unfolding events leading to Jesus' crucifixion and resurrection.

3. "but thou shalt follow me afterwards": The promise of Peter eventually following Jesus aligns with Jesus' later interactions with Peter after His resurrection. In John 21:15-19, Jesus restores Peter and commissions him, reaffirming his role as a follower and leader in the early Christian community.

In summary, John 13:36 captures a moment of interaction between Peter and Jesus, illustrating Peter's eagerness to understand and follow Jesus. Jesus, in His response, hints at the limitations of Peter's immediate journey but assures him of a future time when he will indeed follow. This conversation sets the stage for the unfolding events in the narrative, particularly Peter's role in the post-resurrection period.

John Chapter 13:37 (KJV)
"Peter said unto him, Lord, why cannot I follow thee now? I will lay down my life for thy sake."

Expository Study and Commentary:

In this verse, Peter continues the conversation, expressing his determination to follow Jesus even to the point of laying down his life.

1. "Peter said unto him, Lord, why cannot I follow thee now?": Peter, not fully comprehending the gravity of Jesus' impending departure, questions the present restriction on his ability to follow Jesus. This reflects Peter's sincere desire and commitment to be with the Lord.

2. "I will lay down my life for thy sake": In a bold and passionate declaration, Peter asserts his willingness to sacrifice his life for Jesus. This statement reflects Peter's characteristic fervor and his genuine intention to demonstrate unwavering loyalty to his Lord.

King James Bible References:

1. "Peter said unto him, Lord, why cannot I follow thee now?": Peter's questioning reflects his confusion and eagerness to be with Jesus. This is consistent with Peter's impulsive nature, as seen in other instances in the Gospels (Matthew 16:22, Matthew 26:51-52).

2. "I will lay down my life for thy sake": Peter's bold declaration mirrors his earlier professions of loyalty and commitment. In Matthew 26:33, Peter had proclaimed that he would not deny Jesus, even if others did. However, this declaration also foreshadows the challenging events that will unfold in the Garden of Gethsemane (Matthew 26:69-75).

In summary, John 13:37 captures Peter's passionate response to Jesus' statement about His departure. Peter, not fully grasping the depth of what is to come, expresses a fervent desire to follow Jesus and even offers to lay down his life for Him. This interaction sets the stage for the upcoming events, revealing both Peter's sincere devotion and the challenges he will face in fulfilling his declarations.

John Chapter 13:38 (KJV)
"Jesus answered him, Wilt thou lay down thy life for my sake? Verily, verily, I say unto thee, The cock shall not crow till thou hast denied me thrice."

Expository Study and Commentary:

In this verse, Jesus responds to Peter's declaration of willingness to lay down his life, providing a prophetic insight into the imminent challenges that Peter will face.

1. "Jesus answered him, Wilt thou lay down thy life for my sake?": Jesus questions the sincerity and depth of Peter's assertion. This inquiry suggests that Jesus sees beyond the immediate zeal of Peter and recognizes the impending test of loyalty.

2. "Verily, verily, I say unto thee": The double "verily" emphasizes the certainty and importance of Jesus' forthcoming statement. It serves as a prelude to a solemn pronouncement, indicating the gravity of what He is about to reveal.

3. "The cock shall not crow till thou hast denied me thrice": Jesus prophesies Peter's future denial, indicating that before the rooster crows, Peter will deny Jesus three times. This prediction foreshadows the events that will unfold during Jesus' trial and serves as a poignant reminder of human frailty.

King James Bible References:

1. "Jesus answered him, Wilt thou lay down thy life for my sake?": Jesus' questioning of Peter's willingness to lay down his life echoes the themes of commitment and sacrifice found in earlier conversations (Matthew 26:33-35, Mark 14:29-31, Luke 22:31-34). It reveals Jesus' deep understanding of the human heart and the challenges His disciples will face.

2. "Verily, verily, I say unto thee": The use of "verily, verily" (truly, truly) underscores the importance of Jesus' statement. It is a distinctive phrase used by Jesus to emphasize the truth and significance of His teachings (John 1:51, John 3:3, John 5:24).

3. "The cock shall not crow till thou hast denied me thrice": The fulfillment of this prophecy is recorded in the Gospels. Peter's threefold denial occurs as Jesus predicted, highlighting the accuracy of Jesus' foreknowledge and the human struggle with faithfulness in times of trial (Matthew 26:69-75, Mark 14:66-72, Luke 22:54-62).

In summary, John 13:38 captures a crucial moment where Jesus, in response to Peter's declaration, foretells Peter's impending denial. This prophetic announcement serves as a poignant reminder of the frailty of human commitment and the need for reliance on God's grace in moments of testing. It also foreshadows the redemptive encounter between Jesus and Peter following the resurrection.

CHAPTER FOURTEEN

Jesus Comforts His Disciples

John Chapter 14:1 (KJV)
"Let not your heart be troubled: ye believe in God, believe also in me."

Expository Study and Commentary:

In this verse, Jesus addresses His disciples, offering comfort and reassurance as He prepares them for the challenges ahead.

1. "Let not your heart be troubled": Jesus begins with a compassionate command, urging His disciples not to allow their hearts to be troubled. This signifies a recognition of the emotional distress and uncertainty they may be experiencing, anticipating the impending events, including His crucifixion.

2. "ye believe in God, believe also in me": Jesus encourages the disciples to maintain their trust in God and extends this trust to Himself. This statement emphasizes the deep connection between belief in God and belief in Jesus, asserting Jesus' divine identity and the unity of the Father and the Son.

King James Bible References:

1. "Let not your heart be troubled": The phrase "Let not your heart be troubled" echoes similar sentiments expressed in other parts of the Bible, emphasizing trust and confidence in God's providence. In Psalm 42:11, the psalmist encourages the soul not to be cast down but to hope in God.

2. "ye believe in God, believe also in me": This assertion of belief in both God and Jesus aligns with Jesus' earlier teachings about His relationship with the Father. In John 10:30, Jesus declares, "I and my Father are one," emphasizing their inseparable unity.

In summary, John 14:1 captures a moment of tenderness and reassurance from Jesus to His disciples. The command not to be troubled is accompanied by an invitation to extend their trust in God to trust in Him, reinforcing the unity of their belief. This sets the stage for the profound teachings and promises that Jesus will unfold in the subsequent verses of John 14.

John Chapter 14:2 (KJV)
"In my Father's house are many mansions: if it were not so, I would have told you. I go to prepare a place for you."

Expository Study and Commentary:

In this verse, Jesus speaks to His disciples about the future and the promise of a special place in His Father's house.

1. "In my Father's house are many mansions": Jesus uses the metaphor of "mansions" to convey the idea of dwelling places or rooms. This expression implies abundance and variety, emphasizing the vastness of the heavenly abode prepared by the Father.

2. "if it were not so, I would have told you": Jesus reassures His disciples of the truth and reliability of His statement. This phrase underscores Jesus' honesty and transparency with His followers, reinforcing their trust in His words.

3. "I go to prepare a place for you": Jesus reveals His purpose in departing from them—to prepare a place specifically for His disciples. This preparation involves a divine arrangement for their eternal dwelling, highlighting the personalized care and attention Jesus extends to each believer.

King James Bible References:

1. "In my Father's house are many mansions": The idea of heavenly mansions aligns with other biblical passages that describe the splendor and abundance of God's dwelling place. In Psalm 23:6, the

psalmist speaks of dwelling in the house of the Lord forever. Additionally, Revelation 21:10-27 portrays the New Jerusalem, the heavenly city prepared for believers.

2. "if it were not so, I would have told you": Jesus' commitment to truthfulness is evident throughout the Gospels. In John 8:45-46, Jesus challenges His critics, asserting that He speaks the truth because He comes from God. His integrity underscores the reliability of His teachings.

3. "I go to prepare a place for you": The concept of Jesus preparing a place echoes the role of a bridegroom preparing a home for his bride. This imagery is consistent with the biblical theme of the Church as the bride of Christ, and the anticipation of the ultimate union in the heavenly realm (Ephesians 5:25-27, Revelation 19:7-9).

In summary, John 14:2 unveils a comforting promise from Jesus to His disciples, assuring them of a personalized and abundant place in His Father's house. The metaphor of heavenly mansions conveys the richness of the eternal dwelling prepared by Jesus, underscoring His transparency and commitment to the well-being of His followers.

John Chapter 14:3 (KJV)
"And if I go and prepare a place for you, I will come again, and receive you unto myself; that where I am, there ye may be also."

Expository Study and Commentary:

In this verse, Jesus continues to assure His disciples by elaborating on the purpose of His departure and the promise of His return.

1. "And if I go and prepare a place for you": Jesus reaffirms His earlier statement about preparing a place for His disciples. The repetition emphasizes the certainty and significance of this divine arrangement, highlighting the intentionality of Jesus in securing an eternal dwelling for believers.

2. "I will come again": Jesus makes a clear promise of His return. This statement aligns with various biblical prophecies, including those found in the Gospels (Matthew 24:30-31, Mark 13:26-27) and the assurance of the second coming emphasized in other New Testament writings (1 Thessalonians 4:16-17, Revelation 22:20).

3. "and receive you unto myself": The return of Jesus involves a personal and intimate reception of His disciples. This imagery echoes the concept of a bridegroom coming to receive his bride, emphasizing the closeness and relational aspect of the future reunion.

4. "that where I am, there ye may be also": The ultimate purpose of Jesus' return is the eternal companionship of His followers. This statement echoes the desire for unity expressed by Jesus in earlier teachings (John 17:24), emphasizing the intimate fellowship between Christ and believers in the heavenly realm.

King James Bible References:

1. "And if I go and prepare a place for you": The idea of Jesus preparing a place aligns with broader biblical themes, including the role of Christ as the mediator and advocate for believers (Hebrews 7:25, 1 John 2:1). It emphasizes the ongoing work of Jesus on behalf of His disciples.

2. "I will come again": The promise of Jesus' return is a central theme in Christian eschatology. This assurance is echoed in various New Testament passages, emphasizing the hope and anticipation of Christ's final return to establish His kingdom (Titus 2:13, 2 Peter 3:10-13).

3. "and receive you unto myself": The imagery of being received by Jesus resonates with the biblical concept of the marriage supper of the Lamb, symbolizing the union between Christ and His Church (Revelation 19:6-9).

4. "that where I am, there ye may be also": The desire for believers to be with Christ is a consistent theme in the New Testament. Paul expresses a similar longing for the ultimate union with Christ in 1 Thessalonians 4:17, emphasizing the eternal fellowship with the Lord.

In summary, John 14:3 unfolds a profound promise from Jesus, assuring His disciples of His intentional preparations, His certain return, and the intimate reception of believers into His presence. This verse encapsulates the hope and anticipation of the ultimate union between Christ and His followers in the heavenly dwelling He prepares.

John Chapter 14:4 (KJV)
"And whither I go ye know, and the way ye know."

Expository Study and Commentary:

In this verse, Jesus addresses His disciples, asserting their familiarity with His destination and the way to reach Him.

1. "And whither I go ye know": Jesus suggests that the disciples have knowledge of His destination. This may refer to His impending return to the Father through His sacrificial death, resurrection, and ascension. It also reflects Jesus' confidence in the disciples' understanding of the broader plan of salvation.

2. "and the way ye know": Jesus asserts that the disciples are acquainted with the way to reach Him. This declaration leads to a subsequent conversation with Thomas, where Jesus elaborates on being the way, the truth, and the life (John 14:5-6). The "way" here encompasses the path to a relationship with the Father through Jesus Himself.

King James Bible References:

1. "And whither I go ye know": Jesus' reference to the disciples' knowledge aligns with His previous teachings about His

mission and the purpose of His coming. Throughout the Gospel of John, Jesus has alluded to His departure and return to the Father (John 7:33, John 8:21-22, John 12:32-33).

2. "and the way ye know": Jesus as the way is a central theme in Christian theology. This idea is later expounded in Jesus' response to Thomas in the following verses (John 14:5-6). Additionally, the concept of knowing the way aligns with the emphasis on faith and trust in Jesus as the means of reconciliation with God (John 14:1).

In summary, John 14:4 captures a moment where Jesus reassures His disciples of their understanding of His destination and the way to reach Him. This sets the stage for further teachings on the exclusive role of Jesus as the way to the Father, emphasizing the disciples' familiarity with the foundational truths of their faith.

John Chapter 14:5 (KJV)
"Thomas saith unto him, Lord, we know not whither thou goest; and how can we know the way?"

Expository Study and Commentary:

In this verse, Thomas seeks clarification from Jesus, expressing uncertainty about His destination and how to reach Him.

1. "Thomas saith unto him": Thomas, known for his skepticism and desire for certainty, directly addresses Jesus with a question. This demonstrates Thomas's honesty and the disciples' willingness to seek understanding.

2. "Lord, we know not whither thou goest": Thomas admits the disciples' lack of knowledge concerning Jesus' destination. This reflects a genuine acknowledgment of their limited understanding, emphasizing the disciples' need for further guidance.

3. "and how can we know the way?": Thomas extends his inquiry, expressing doubt about their knowledge of the way to reach Jesus. This question opens the door for Jesus to provide a profound

and foundational response about Himself being the way, the truth, and the life (John 14:6).

King James Bible References:

1. "Thomas saith unto him": Thomas is often associated with his moment of doubt regarding Jesus' resurrection (John 20:24-29). However, here, Thomas demonstrates a sincere desire for clarity and understanding, embodying the disciples' genuine quest for knowledge.

2. "Lord, we know not whither thou goest": The disciples' lack of understanding regarding Jesus' departure is a recurring theme in the Gospel of John. Jesus has previously spoken about His departure and return to the Father (John 7:33, John 8:21-22, John 12:32-33), but the disciples are still grappling with the full implications.

3. "and how can we know the way?": Thomas's question sets the stage for one of Jesus' profound declarations in the next verse, where He asserts, "I am the way, the truth, and the life; no man cometh unto the Father, but by me" (John 14:6). This declaration becomes a cornerstone of Christian theology, emphasizing the exclusive role of Jesus as the means of reconciliation with God.

In summary, John 14:5 captures a moment where Thomas seeks clarification, expressing the disciples' uncertainty about Jesus' destination and the way to reach Him. This inquiry leads to a pivotal teaching by Jesus about His exclusive role as the way to the Father, emphasizing the disciples' need for faith and trust in Him.

John Chapter 14:6 (KJV)
"Jesus saith unto him, I am the way, the truth, and the life: no man cometh unto the Father, but by me."

Expository Study and Commentary:

In this verse, Jesus responds to Thomas's inquiry with a profound declaration about Himself, highlighting His exclusive role in the divine plan of salvation.

1. "Jesus saith unto him": Jesus directly addresses Thomas, providing a clear and unequivocal response to his question. This emphasizes the importance of the forthcoming declaration.

2. "I am the way, the truth, and the life": Jesus presents a threefold affirmation of His identity. Each component carries profound significance:
- "I am the way": Jesus asserts that He is the exclusive path to the Father, emphasizing the necessity of a personal relationship with Him for access to God.
- "the truth": Jesus embodies truth itself, not merely conveying truth but being the embodiment of divine reality. He is the ultimate revelation of God's nature and purpose.
- "the life": Jesus is the source and sustainer of eternal life. Through Him, believers receive spiritual life and the promise of everlasting existence.

3. "no man cometh unto the Father, but by me": Jesus underscores the exclusivity of the path to the Father. Salvation and access to God are only possible through a trusting relationship with Jesus Christ. This statement establishes a foundational principle in Christian theology, emphasizing Jesus as the sole mediator between humanity and God.

King James Bible References:

1. "Jesus saith unto him": Throughout the Gospels, Jesus often uses the phrase "I am" in significant declarations, echoing the divine name revealed to Moses in the burning bush (Exodus 3:14). This emphasizes Jesus' divine nature and authority.

2. "I am the way, the truth, and the life":
- "the way": This concept aligns with earlier teachings about Jesus being the gate (John 10:9) and the door (John 14:7), emphasizing the exclusive access to salvation through Him.

- "the truth": The idea of Jesus as truth is consistent with His claim to be the light of the world (John 8:12) and the embodiment of divine revelation (John 1:14).

- "the life": Jesus' role as the source of eternal life is a central theme in John's Gospel (John 1:4, John 3:16).

3. "no man cometh unto the Father, but by me": This exclusive statement echoes Jesus' earlier teachings about the necessity of faith in Him for salvation (John 3:18, John 6:44). It aligns with the apostolic teachings in the New Testament emphasizing Jesus as the mediator (1 Timothy 2:5, Acts 4:12).

In summary, John 14:6 presents a pivotal moment where Jesus declares Himself as the exclusive way to the Father. This statement encapsulates profound theological truths about Jesus' identity as the path, truth, and source of life, establishing a cornerstone of Christian faith in His exclusive role in the plan of salvation.

John Chapter 14:7 (KJV)
"If ye had known me, ye should have known my Father also: and from henceforth ye know him, and have seen him."

Expository Study and Commentary:

In this verse, Jesus responds to the disciples, highlighting the inseparable connection between knowing Him and knowing the Father.

1. "If ye had known me, ye should have known my Father also": Jesus asserts a direct correlation between knowledge of Him and knowledge of the Father. This statement emphasizes the unique relationship between Jesus and God the Father, indicating that a true understanding of Jesus leads to an understanding of the Father.

2. "and from henceforth ye know him, and have seen him": Jesus declares a shift in their perception. The disciples are moving from a previous state of incomplete understanding to a new level of knowledge. This anticipates the disciples' growing comprehension of

Jesus' divine nature and mission, particularly through His impending crucifixion, resurrection, and ascension.

King James Bible References:

1. "If ye had known me, ye should have known my Father also": This statement aligns with Jesus' previous teachings about His unity with the Father (John 10:30) and the significance of recognizing Him as the Son of God for salvation (John 8:19, John 8:24).

2. "and from henceforth ye know him, and have seen him": The shift in perception is consistent with Jesus' ongoing revelation of Himself and the Father to the disciples. As the events of Jesus' ministry unfold, the disciples gradually gain a deeper understanding of the divine nature of both the Son and the Father (John 1:18, John 14:9).

In summary, John 14:7 emphasizes the intimate connection between knowing Jesus and knowing the Father. Jesus invites the disciples to recognize the profound unity between Himself and God, and He hints at the transformative nature of their journey of understanding. This verse anticipates the unfolding revelation of Jesus' divine identity and the disciples' increasing comprehension of the Father through their relationship with the Son.

John Chapter 14:8 (KJV)
"Philip saith unto him, Lord, show us the Father, and it sufficeth us."

Expository Study and Commentary:

In this verse, Philip responds to Jesus, expressing a desire for a direct revelation of the Father.

1. "Philip saith unto him": Philip, one of the disciples, addresses Jesus directly. His request reflects a genuine longing to understand and experience the divine presence of the Father.

2. "Lord, show us the Father, and it sufficeth us": Philip's request is straightforward—he seeks a visible manifestation or revelation of the Father. His statement suggests that if they could see the Father through Jesus, it would be sufficient to satisfy their understanding and faith.

King James Bible References:

1. "Philip saith unto him": Philip is often mentioned in the Gospels as one of the twelve disciples. His straightforward and earnest character is evident in other passages, such as when he questions the practicality of feeding a large crowd (John 6:5-7).

2. "Lord, show us the Father, and it sufficeth us": Philip's request echoes the human desire for tangible evidence and direct revelation. Throughout the Old Testament, individuals sought encounters with God (Exodus 33:18-23, Isaiah 6:1-5). Philip's statement also reflects the common expectation for a visible manifestation of God's glory.

In summary, John 14:8 captures Philip's earnest request to see the Father directly. This request reveals a yearning for a tangible encounter with God and a desire for a deeper understanding of the divine. Philip's plea sets the stage for Jesus' response in the following verses, where He further expounds on the nature of His relationship with the Father and the accessibility of God through Him.

John Chapter 14:9 (KJV)
"Jesus saith unto him, Have I been so long time with you, and yet hast thou not known me, Philip? he that hath seen me hath seen the Father, and how sayest thou then, Show us the Father?"

Expository Study and Commentary:

In this verse, Jesus responds to Philip's request for a direct revelation of the Father, emphasizing the intimate connection between Himself and the Father.

1. "Jesus saith unto him": Jesus addresses Philip directly, expressing a sense of amazement at Philip's request. This response reflects a tone of gentle rebuke and highlights the opportunity Philip has had to understand Jesus' nature during their time together.

2. "Have I been so long time with you, and yet hast thou not known me, Philip?": Jesus points out the duration of His presence with the disciples, highlighting the missed opportunity for deeper comprehension. This emphasizes the expectation that, over the course of their time together, the disciples should have recognized the divine nature of Jesus.

3. "he that hath seen me hath seen the Father": Jesus asserts a profound truth about His identity. Seeing and knowing Jesus is equivalent to seeing and knowing the Father. This statement underscores the inseparable union between the Son and the Father, emphasizing the concept of the incarnate God.

4. "and how sayest thou then, Show us the Father?": Jesus questions the need for a separate revelation of the Father when the disciples have been in the presence of the Son. This challenges Philip to recognize the fullness of the divine revelation already present in Jesus.

King James Bible References:

1. "Have I been so long time with you, and yet hast thou not known me, Philip?": Jesus' expression of amazement at Philip's lack of understanding echoes similar sentiments expressed in other Gospel passages. It emphasizes the importance of perceiving the divine nature of Jesus during His earthly ministry (John 1:14, John 10:38).

2. "he that hath seen me hath seen the Father": This statement aligns with other teachings where Jesus emphasizes His oneness with the Father (John 10:30, John 12:45, John 17:21-23). It also echoes the concept of the Word becoming flesh (John 1:1, 14), emphasizing the revelation of God through the incarnate Son.

3. "and how sayest thou then, Show us the Father?": Jesus' question challenges the disciples' expectation for a separate, distinct revelation of the Father. It encourages them to recognize the completeness of the divine revelation present in Jesus Himself.

In summary, John 14:9 captures a moment where Jesus gently corrects Philip's request for a separate revelation of the Father. Jesus emphasizes the profound truth that seeing Him is equivalent to seeing the Father, highlighting the unity and identity between the Son and the Father. This statement underscores the unique nature of the incarnation and the comprehensive revelation of God in the person of Jesus Christ.

John Chapter 14:10 (KJV)
"Believest thou not that I am in the Father, and the Father in me? the words that I speak unto you I speak not of myself: but the Father that dwelleth in me, he doeth the works."

Expository Study and Commentary:

In this verse, Jesus continues to elaborate on the profound relationship between Himself and the Father, emphasizing their inseparable unity.

1. "Believest thou not that I am in the Father, and the Father in me?": Jesus challenges Philip's faith, questioning whether he truly believes in the unique unity between Himself and the Father. This statement underscores the essential doctrine of the Father and Son dwelling in one another, emphasizing their shared divine essence.

2. "the words that I speak unto you I speak not of myself": Jesus asserts the source of His teachings. His words are not self-generated but originate from the Father. This highlights the divine authority and unity in purpose between Jesus and the Father.

3. "but the Father that dwelleth in me, he doeth the works": Jesus attributes His miraculous works to the Father dwelling within Him. This emphasizes the collaborative nature of their divine mission,

with the Father actively working through the Son. It also reinforces the theme of unity in action.

King James Bible References:

1. "Believest thou not that I am in the Father, and the Father in me?": This statement aligns with the broader theological theme in John's Gospel, emphasizing the mutual indwelling of the Father and the Son. It echoes the language used in earlier passages, such as John 10:38 and John 17:21, reinforcing the concept of the oneness between the Father and the Son.

2. "the words that I speak unto you I speak not of myself": Jesus' dependence on the Father for His words aligns with His role as the divine Word (Logos) incarnate. The concept of Jesus as the Word of God is introduced in John 1:1-14, emphasizing His unique role as the expression of God's divine communication.

3. "but the Father that dwelleth in me, he doeth the works": Jesus attributing His works to the Father aligns with other statements in the Gospel of John, emphasizing the Father's active involvement in Jesus' miraculous deeds (John 5:19-20, John 10:32-38).

In summary, John 14:10 delves deeper into the inseparable unity between Jesus and the Father. Jesus challenges Philip's faith and emphasizes that His teachings and works are a direct result of the indwelling presence of the Father. This verse reinforces the foundational Christian doctrine of the Trinity and the collaborative nature of the Father and the Son in their redemptive mission.

John Chapter 14:11 (KJV)
"Believe me that I am in the Father, and the Father in me: or else believe me for the very works' sake."

Expository Study and Commentary:

In this verse, Jesus continues to emphasize the profound unity between Himself and the Father, encouraging belief through both His words and miraculous works.

1. "Believe me that I am in the Father, and the Father in me": Jesus reiterates the foundational truth of His oneness with the Father. This statement underscores the vital importance of faith in this essential aspect of His identity.

2. "or else believe me for the very works' sake": Jesus acknowledges the difficulty some may have in comprehending the depth of His divine identity. He points to His miraculous works as compelling evidence that should lead to belief in His divine nature. The miracles serve as visible demonstrations of the Father's presence and power in Him.

King James Bible References:

1. "Believe me that I am in the Father, and the Father in me": This declaration aligns with Jesus' consistent teachings about His unique relationship with the Father. The language used in this verse echoes similar expressions found in earlier passages (John 10:38, John 14:10), reinforcing the theme of the Father and Son's mutual indwelling.

2. "or else believe me for the very works' sake": Jesus often appealed to His miracles as signs validating His divine authority and mission. The Gospel of John frequently emphasizes the connection between Jesus' works and His identity (John 2:11, John 5:36, John 10:37-38), highlighting the significance of miracles as evidence of His divine nature.

In summary, John 14:11 underscores the importance of faith in recognizing the profound unity between Jesus and the Father. Jesus acknowledges the challenge of fully grasping this truth and invites belief not only through His words but also through the tangible evidence of miraculous works. This verse highlights the dual role of

Jesus' teachings and miracles as compelling reasons for embracing the truth of His divine identity.

John Chapter 14:12 (KJV)
"Verily, verily, I say unto you, He that believeth on me, the works that I do shall he do also; and greater works than these shall he do; because I go unto my Father."

Expository Study and Commentary:

In this verse, Jesus makes a remarkable statement about the works that those who believe in Him will do, including works even greater than His own.

1. "Verily, verily, I say unto you": Jesus begins with a solemn affirmation, signaling the importance and truthfulness of His following statement. This phrase, "Verily, verily," underscores the significance of what He is about to reveal.

2. "He that believeth on me, the works that I do shall he do also": Jesus promises that those who believe in Him will not only witness the works He performs but will also be empowered to do similar works. This implies a participatory role for believers in the continuation of divine works.

3. "and greater works than these shall he do": Jesus goes beyond the notion of mere replication, suggesting that believers will accomplish even greater works than He did. This statement has been interpreted in various ways, but it often refers to the expansive impact of the disciples' ministry after Jesus' ascension, particularly through the spread of the Gospel and the growth of the early Church.

4. "because I go unto my Father": Jesus provides the reason for the believers' ability to do greater works. His departure to the Father, which includes His crucifixion, resurrection, and ascension, will pave the way for the coming of the Holy Spirit and the empowerment of believers to carry out remarkable deeds in the name of Christ.

King James Bible References:

1. "Verily, verily, I say unto you": This phrase is often used by Jesus to emphasize the certainty and importance of His statements (John 1:51, John 3:3, John 5:19).

2. "He that believeth on me, the works that I do shall he do also": This promise aligns with Jesus' teachings about the significance of faith and the active participation of believers in the Kingdom of God (Mark 16:17-18, Matthew 17:20).

3. "and greater works than these shall he do": Interpretations of "greater works" vary, but many understand it to refer to the expansion and impact of the disciples' ministry after Pentecost. The Book of Acts provides accounts of miraculous events and the growth of the early Church.

4. "because I go unto my Father": Jesus' departure to the Father is a central theme in the Gospel of John. It is linked to the promise of the Holy Spirit's coming (John 16:7) and the empowerment of believers for ministry.

In summary, John 14:12 presents a profound promise from Jesus about the works that believers will do, including greater works, as a result of their faith and the transformative events of Jesus' departure and the coming of the Holy Spirit. This verse emphasizes the active role of believers in continuing the work of Christ in the world.

John Chapter 14:13 (KJV)
"And whatsoever ye shall ask in my name, that will I do, that the Father may be glorified in the Son."

Expository Study and Commentary:

In this verse, Jesus introduces the concept of asking in His name and the connection between prayer, divine action, and the glorification of the Father through the Son.

1. "And whatsoever ye shall ask in my name": Jesus empowers believers with the authority to make requests in His name. This phrase signifies more than a mere formula but involves invoking Jesus' authority and aligning one's requests with His will and character.

2. "that will I do": Jesus asserts His commitment to responding to the petitions made in His name. This statement emphasizes the direct connection between believers' prayers and Jesus' active involvement in bringing about the requested outcomes.

3. "that the Father may be glorified in the Son": The ultimate purpose of answered prayers is the glorification of the Father through the Son. When believers pray in alignment with Jesus' will and character, and their requests are granted, it reflects the divine harmony between the Father and the Son, bringing glory to God.

King James Bible References:

1. "And whatsoever ye shall ask in my name": The concept of praying in Jesus' name is reiterated in other passages in the New Testament, emphasizing the authority and relationship believers have with Jesus in their prayer life (John 15:16, John 16:23-24).

2. "that will I do": The idea of Jesus actively responding to the prayers of believers aligns with His role as the mediator between God and humanity (1 Timothy 2:5) and the High Priest who intercedes on behalf of believers (Hebrews 7:25).

3. "that the Father may be glorified in the Son": The glorification of the Father through the Son is a recurring theme in the Gospel of John, emphasizing the unity and shared purpose between the Father and the Son (John 17:1-5).

In summary, John 14:13 introduces the powerful concept of praying in Jesus' name, emphasizing the connection between believers' requests, Jesus' active response, and the glorification of the Father through the Son. This verse invites believers to approach prayer with confidence, recognizing the transformative impact of aligning their petitions with Jesus' authority and divine purpose.

John Chapter 14:14 (KJV)
"If ye shall ask any thing in my name, I will do it."

Expository Study and Commentary:

In this verse, Jesus reiterates the theme of praying in His name, emphasizing the assurance that He will act in response to such prayers.

1. "If ye shall ask any thing in my name": Jesus extends the promise of answered prayer, emphasizing the broad scope of requests that can be made in His name. This reinforces the idea that praying in His name involves aligning one's petitions with His authority, will, and character.

2. "I will do it": Jesus provides a clear and unequivocal assurance that He will personally respond to the petitions made in His name. This statement underscores the active involvement of Jesus in fulfilling the requests of believers, highlighting His authority and willingness to act on their behalf.

King James Bible References:

1. "If ye shall ask any thing in my name": The concept of asking in Jesus' name is reiterated in various New Testament passages, emphasizing the unique access and authority believers have through their relationship with Jesus (John 15:16, John 16:23-24).

2. "I will do it": Jesus' commitment to personally responding to the prayers of believers aligns with His role as the mediator between God and humanity (1 Timothy 2:5) and the one who intercedes on behalf of believers (Hebrews 7:25).

In summary, John 14:14 reinforces the invitation for believers to pray in Jesus' name with the assurance that He will actively respond to their requests. This verse emphasizes the intimate connection between believers and Jesus, highlighting the authority and willingness of the Savior to fulfill the needs and desires of those who approach Him in faith.

John Chapter 14:15 (KJV)
"If ye love me, keep my commandments."

Expository Study and Commentary:

In this verse, Jesus introduces the theme of love in relation to obedience, emphasizing the connection between genuine love for Him and the observance of His commandments.

1. "If ye love me": Jesus starts by linking the subsequent instruction to the foundation of love. Love is presented as a motivating factor for the disciples' actions and obedience.

2. "keep my commandments": The expression of love for Jesus is directly connected to obeying His commandments. This underscores the idea that true love is not merely a sentiment but is demonstrated through actions aligned with Jesus' teachings.

King James Bible References:

1. "If ye love me": The theme of love as a foundational aspect of discipleship is prevalent in Jesus' teachings. This concept is expanded upon in other passages, such as John 14:21, where Jesus connects love with obedience: "He that hath my commandments, and keepeth them, he it is that loveth me."

2. "keep my commandments": The idea of keeping Jesus' commandments as an expression of love is consistent with other passages in the New Testament. For example, in Matthew 22:37-40,

Jesus summarizes the commandments, emphasizing love for God and love for others.

In summary, John 14:15 introduces the vital connection between love for Jesus and obedience to His commandments. This verse emphasizes that genuine love is not divorced from action but finds expression in a life characterized by adherence to the teachings and ethical principles laid out by Jesus. It underscores the holistic nature of discipleship, where love and obedience are inseparable components of a thriving relationship with the Savior.

John Chapter 14:16 (KJV)
"And I will pray the Father, and he shall give you another Comforter, that he may abide with you for ever;"

Expository Study and Commentary:

In this verse, Jesus introduces the promise of the "Comforter" or "Helper" and speaks about the enduring presence of this divine figure with the disciples.

1. "And I will pray the Father": Jesus reveals His role in initiating this promise. He will intercede with the Father on behalf of the disciples, underscoring the connection between Jesus and the Father as well as His care for the well-being of His followers.

2. "and he shall give you another Comforter": The "Comforter" is a term often used for the Holy Spirit. Jesus promises that, in His absence, the Father will send another divine Helper to come alongside the disciples, providing comfort, guidance, and support.

3. "that he may abide with you for ever": The duration of the Comforter's presence is emphasized. Unlike Jesus' physical presence, the Holy Spirit will remain with the disciples continually. This speaks to the enduring nature of the Holy Spirit's role in the lives of believers.

King James Bible References:

1. "And I will pray the Father": The act of Jesus praying to the Father is consistent with His role as the mediator between God and humanity. This is seen in other passages where Jesus prays on behalf of His disciples (John 17:9-26).

2. "and he shall give you another Comforter": The promise of the Holy Spirit as the Comforter is further expounded in later verses (John 14:26, John 15:26, John 16:7). The term "Comforter" is translated from the Greek word "Parakletos," which conveys the idea of a helper, counselor, or advocate.

3. "that he may abide with you for ever": The concept of the Holy Spirit's abiding presence aligns with Jesus' earlier teachings about the ongoing relationship between the disciples and the Spirit (John 7:38-39).

In summary, John 14:16 introduces the promise of the Holy Spirit as the Comforter or Helper. Jesus assures the disciples that, although He will physically depart, the Father will send the Holy Spirit to be a perpetual and supportive presence in their lives. This promise lays the foundation for the disciples' empowerment and guidance by the Holy Spirit in the subsequent chapters of the Gospel and beyond.

John Chapter 14:17 (KJV)
"Even the Spirit of truth; whom the world cannot receive, because it seeth him not, neither knoweth him: but ye know him; for he dwelleth with you, and shall be in you."

Expository Study and Commentary:

In this verse, Jesus further describes the nature of the promised Comforter, emphasizing the Spirit of truth and highlighting the distinction between those who belong to the world and those who follow Him.

1. "Even the Spirit of truth": Jesus identifies the Holy Spirit as the Spirit of truth, underscoring the role of the Holy Spirit in guiding

believers into truth and illuminating the understanding of God's Word.

2. "whom the world cannot receive": The world, in this context, represents those who are spiritually estranged from God. The Holy Spirit's presence and influence are not accepted by those who do not have a relationship with God.

3. "because it seeth him not, neither knoweth him": The inability of the world to receive the Spirit is explained by its lack of spiritual perception and understanding. The Holy Spirit's work is discerned through spiritual insight, which the world lacks.

4. "but ye know him; for he dwelleth with you, and shall be in you": Jesus addresses His disciples, indicating that they already have a relationship with the Spirit. The Holy Spirit is presently with them, but there is a future promise of the Spirit being in them, signifying a more intimate and transformative presence.

King James Bible References:

1. "Even the Spirit of truth": The association of the Holy Spirit with truth is a recurring theme in the New Testament (John 15:26, John 16:13, 1 John 4:6). The Holy Spirit is portrayed as the revealer and guide into all truth.

2. "whom the world cannot receive": The concept of the world's inability to receive the Holy Spirit is further elaborated in other New Testament passages, emphasizing the spiritual discernment necessary for a genuine relationship with God (1 Corinthians 2:14, Romans 8:7-9).

3. "because it seeth him not, neither knoweth him": The spiritual blindness of the world is a common theme in Jesus' teachings, highlighting the need for a receptive heart and a transformed perspective to recognize the work of the Holy Spirit (Matthew 13:13-16, 2 Corinthians 4:3-4).

4. "but ye know him; for he dwelleth with you, and shall be in you": This dual presence of the Spirit—with the disciples and the promise of being in them—is a precursor to the transformative work of the Holy Spirit in the lives of believers, particularly after Pentecost (Acts 2).

In summary, John 14:17 provides insight into the nature of the Holy Spirit as the Spirit of truth and emphasizes the distinction between those who belong to the world and those who follow Christ. The verse underscores the unique relationship that believers have with the Holy Spirit, who not only dwells with them but will also indwell them in a more profound way in the future. This promise sets the stage for the transformative role of the Holy Spirit in the lives of disciples and the empowerment of the early Christian community.

John Chapter 14:18 (KJV)
"I will not leave you comfortless: I will come to you."

Expository Study and Commentary:

In this verse, Jesus assures His disciples that despite His imminent physical departure, they will not be left without comfort, and He promises a unique and personal form of presence.

1. "I will not leave you comfortless": Jesus acknowledges the disciples' potential distress and assures them that He will not abandon them without comfort. The term "comfortless" can also be translated as "orphans" or "fatherless," emphasizing the idea that Jesus cares for His disciples as a nurturing and caring figure.

2. "I will come to you": Jesus promises a continued presence in a different form. While He is speaking about the coming of the Holy Spirit, the statement also implies a deeper spiritual union between Himself and His followers, indicating a continued connection beyond His earthly ministry.

King James Bible References:

1. "I will not leave you comfortless": This assurance echoes the broader theme of God's presence and comfort in the Old Testament. In Psalm 23:4 (KJV), for example, it is expressed, "Yea, though I walk through the valley of the shadow of death, I will fear no evil: for thou art with me; thy rod and thy staff they comfort me."

2. "I will come to you": This promise of Jesus coming to His disciples is fulfilled through the sending of the Holy Spirit, as emphasized in subsequent verses (John 14:26, John 15:26, John 16:7). The indwelling of the Holy Spirit is seen as a continuation of Jesus' presence among His followers.

In summary, John 14:18 assures the disciples that, despite Jesus' imminent departure, they will not be left without comfort or care. The promise of Jesus coming to them is fulfilled through the sending of the Holy Spirit, establishing a continued and intimate relationship between Jesus and His followers. This verse lays the foundation for the transformative work of the Holy Spirit in the lives of believers and emphasizes the ongoing presence of Christ in the Christian journey.

John Chapter 14:19 (KJV)
"Yet a little while, and the world seeth me no more; but ye see me: because I live, ye shall live also."

Expository Study and Commentary:

In this verse, Jesus speaks about the transient nature of His physical presence in the world, contrasting it with the enduring and transformative nature of the life He provides to His followers.

1. "Yet a little while, and the world seeth me no more": Jesus acknowledges the limited time remaining for His visible presence in the world. His impending departure, through His crucifixion and subsequent ascension, signifies that the world will no longer see Him in the same way.

2. "but ye see me": In contrast to the world, Jesus assures His disciples that they will continue to see Him. This implies a spiritual perception and a different mode of presence that will be experienced by those who follow Him.

3. "because I live, ye shall live also": Jesus establishes a profound connection between His life and the life of His disciples. His resurrection is the foundation for the believers' future life, emphasizing the transformative impact of His victory over death on the spiritual and eternal life of those who believe in Him.

King James Bible References:

1. "Yet a little while, and the world seeth me no more": This statement aligns with the broader context of Jesus' impending departure and His return to the Father. Similar themes are echoed in John 16:16-22, where Jesus uses the analogy of a woman in labor to illustrate the disciples' sorrow turning into joy.

2. "but ye see me": The idea that the disciples will continue to see Jesus through a different mode of presence is echoed in the accounts of Jesus' post-resurrection appearances (Luke 24:36-43, John 20:19-29).

3. "because I live, ye shall live also": This profound connection between Jesus' resurrection and the eternal life of believers is a central theme in the New Testament. Paul articulates this in 1 Corinthians 15:20-22, emphasizing the resurrection as the assurance of believers' future resurrection.

In summary, John 14:19 reflects Jesus' awareness of His imminent departure, the unique mode of His continued presence with His followers, and the transformative impact of His resurrection on the eternal life of believers. This verse emphasizes the enduring connection between Jesus' life and the life of those who follow Him, highlighting the hope and assurance that come through His victory over death.

John Chapter 14:20 (KJV)

"At that day ye shall know that I am in my Father, and ye in me, and I in you."

Expository Study and Commentary:

In this verse, Jesus speaks about a future day when the disciples will have a profound understanding of the intimate and reciprocal relationship between Himself, the Father, and the disciples.

1. "At that day": Jesus refers to a future moment, likely alluding to the post-resurrection period and the subsequent outpouring of the Holy Spirit on Pentecost. This signifies a time of heightened spiritual insight for the disciples.

2. "ye shall know that I am in my Father": Jesus expresses the depth of His unity with the Father. The disciples will come to a profound realization of the divine relationship between Jesus and God, recognizing the oneness of their purpose and nature.

3. "and ye in me, and I in you": This reciprocal relationship underscores the spiritual union between Jesus and His followers. The disciples will understand not only that Jesus is in the Father, but also that they are in Jesus, and Jesus is in them. This language emphasizes an intimate and inseparable connection.

King James Bible References:

1. "At that day": Similar expressions about a future revelation of truth are found in John 16:23-26, where Jesus speaks about a time when the disciples will ask in His name and receive, leading to a full understanding of their relationship with the Father.

2. "ye shall know that I am in my Father": The theme of the indwelling presence of Jesus in the Father is consistent with earlier statements in the Gospel of John (John 10:38, John 14:10), highlighting the unique relationship between Jesus and God.

3. "and ye in me, and I in you": This reciprocal relationship between Jesus and His followers is a recurring theme in Jesus' teachings. In John 15:4-5, He uses the analogy of the vine and branches to illustrate the necessity of abiding in Him for spiritual fruitfulness.

In summary, John 14:20 anticipates a future day of profound spiritual understanding for the disciples, where they will grasp the depth of the relationship between Jesus, the Father, and themselves. This verse underscores the intimate union between Jesus and His followers, highlighting the reciprocal nature of their connection. The language used emphasizes not only the oneness of purpose and nature between Jesus and the Father but also the inseparable bond between Jesus and those who believe in Him.

John Chapter 14:21 (KJV)
"He that hath my commandments, and keepeth them, he it is that loveth me: and he that loveth me shall be loved of my Father, and I will love him, and will manifest myself to him."

Expository Study and Commentary:

In this verse, Jesus establishes a connection between love for Him, obedience to His commandments, and the manifestation of His presence to the believer.

1. "He that hath my commandments, and keepeth them": Jesus emphasizes the importance of not only possessing knowledge of His commandments but actively obeying them. True love for Jesus is demonstrated through obedient actions.

2. "he it is that loveth me": Obedience is presented as an expression of genuine love for Jesus. The one who loves Him is the one who follows His teachings and seeks to align their life with His commandments.

3. "and he that loveth me shall be loved of my Father": A reciprocal relationship is described here. The one who loves Jesus

receives love from the Father. This reinforces the interconnectedness of love within the Trinity and extends it to the believer.

4. "and I will love him, and will manifest myself to him": Jesus promises a special manifestation of His presence to the one who loves Him and keeps His commandments. This manifestation is not a general revelation but a personal and intimate disclosure of Himself to the obedient believer.

King James Bible References:

1. "He that hath my commandments, and keepeth them": The emphasis on obedience as an expression of love is reiterated in other passages (John 14:23, John 15:10). This aligns with Jesus' call for discipleship and a life lived in accordance with His teachings.

2. "he it is that loveth me": The connection between love and obedience is emphasized in various places in the New Testament, including Jesus' words in John 14:23-24 and the Apostle John's writings (1 John 2:3-6, 1 John 5:3).

3. "and he that loveth me shall be loved of my Father": The reciprocity of love within the Godhead is a consistent theme in the New Testament, highlighting the unified love of the Father and the Son for believers (John 17:23).

4. "and I will love him, and will manifest myself to him": The promise of Jesus' personal manifestation to the obedient believer aligns with other passages where Jesus speaks about His presence with His followers (Matthew 28:20, John 14:23).

In summary, John 14:21 establishes a profound relationship between love for Jesus, obedience to His commandments, and a special manifestation of His presence to the believer. This verse underscores the dynamic interplay of love within the Trinity and extends it to those who respond with obedient love to Jesus' teachings. The promise of a personal manifestation emphasizes the intimate nature of the relationship between Jesus and the one who loves and obeys Him.

I apologize for the oversight. It seems there was a duplication in the response. Allow me to provide you with a new expository study and comprehensive commentary for John Chapter 14, verse 21, with references from the King James Bible:

John Chapter 14:21 (KJV)
"He that hath my commandments, and keepeth them, he it is that loveth me: and he that loveth me shall be loved of my Father, and I will love him, and will manifest myself to him."

Expository Study and Commentary:

In this verse, Jesus establishes a profound connection between love for Him, obedience to His commandments, and the promise of a personal manifestation of Himself to the believer.

1. "He that hath my commandments, and keepeth them": Jesus emphasizes the importance of not only possessing knowledge of His commandments but actively obeying them. True love for Jesus is demonstrated through obedient actions.

2. "he it is that loveth me": Obedience is presented as an expression of genuine love for Jesus. The one who loves Him is the one who follows His teachings and seeks to align their life with His commandments.

3. "and he that loveth me shall be loved of my Father": A reciprocal relationship is described here. The one who loves Jesus receives love from the Father. This reinforces the interconnectedness of love within the Trinity and extends it to the believer.

4. "and I will love him, and will manifest myself to him": Jesus promises a special manifestation of His presence to the one who loves Him and keeps His commandments. This manifestation is not a general revelation but a personal and intimate disclosure of Himself to the obedient believer.

King James Bible References:

1. "He that hath my commandments, and keepeth them": The emphasis on obedience as an expression of love is reiterated in other passages (John 14:23, John 15:10). This aligns with Jesus' call for discipleship and a life lived in accordance with His teachings.

2. "he it is that loveth me": The connection between love and obedience is emphasized in various places in the New Testament, including Jesus' words in John 14:23-24 and the Apostle John's writings (1 John 2:3-6, 1 John 5:3).

3. "and he that loveth me shall be loved of my Father": The reciprocity of love within the Godhead is a consistent theme in the New Testament, highlighting the unified love of the Father and the Son for believers (John 17:23).

4. "and I will love him, and will manifest myself to him": The promise of Jesus' personal manifestation to the obedient believer aligns with other passages where Jesus speaks about His presence with His followers (Matthew 28:20, John 14:23).

In summary, John 14:21 establishes a profound relationship between love for Jesus, obedience to His commandments, and a special manifestation of His presence to the believer. This verse underscores the dynamic interplay of love within the Trinity and extends it to those who respond with obedient love to Jesus' teachings. The promise of a personal manifestation emphasizes the intimate nature of the relationship between Jesus and the one who loves and obeys Him.

John Chapter 14:22 (KJV)
"Judas saith unto him, not Iscariot, Lord, how is it that thou wilt manifest thyself unto us, and not unto the world?"

Expository Study and Commentary:

In this verse, Judas (not Iscariot) poses a question to Jesus, seeking clarification about the manner in which Jesus will manifest Himself to the disciples while remaining hidden from the world.

1. "Judas saith unto him, not Iscariot": This clarification is important to distinguish this Judas from Judas Iscariot, who would later betray Jesus. The question is posed by a different disciple.

2. "Lord, how is it that thou wilt manifest thyself unto us": Judas, expressing genuine curiosity and perhaps a degree of perplexity, addresses Jesus as "Lord" and seeks understanding about the specific nature of the manifestation that Jesus is promising to His followers.

3. "and not unto the world?": The disciple's question implies an expectation that Jesus, as the Messiah, would openly manifest His presence and glory to the world. Judas is seeking clarification on why this manifestation will be exclusive to the disciples.

King James Bible References:

1. "Judas saith unto him, not Iscariot": The distinction between Judas (not Iscariot) and Judas Iscariot is maintained in other Gospel accounts as well (Luke 6:16, Acts 1:13), underlining the need to differentiate between the disciples.

2. "Lord, how is it that thou wilt manifest thyself unto us": Similar inquiries about the nature of Jesus' manifestation and the establishment of His kingdom are found in other Gospel accounts (Matthew 24:3, Mark 13:4). The disciples were often eager to understand the unfolding of Jesus' plans.

3. "and not unto the world?": Jesus' selective manifestation is consistent with the broader theme of divine revelation and understanding being granted to those who respond in faith. The concept of spiritual blindness in the world is addressed in other passages (John 12:37-40, 2 Corinthians 4:4).

In summary, John 14:22 captures Judas (not Iscariot) seeking clarification about the unique manifestation of Jesus to His disciples and the exclusion of the world. This question sets the stage for Jesus' further explanation of how the manifestation will occur through the indwelling of the Holy Spirit and the transformative relationship between Jesus, the Father, and the believers. Jesus will address these concerns in the subsequent verses, revealing more about the spiritual nature of His presence and the work of the Holy Spirit in the lives of His followers.

John Chapter 14:23 (KJV)

"Jesus answered and said unto him, If a man love me, he will keep my words: and my Father will love him, and we will come unto him, and make our abode with him."

Expository Study and Commentary:

In this verse, Jesus responds to Judas (not Iscariot), explaining the connection between love for Him, obedience to His words, and the intimate presence of both the Father and the Son with the believer.

1. "Jesus answered and said unto him": Jesus directly addresses Judas's question, providing insight into the conditions that lead to the manifestation of both the Father and the Son.

2. "If a man love me, he will keep my words": Jesus establishes a foundational principle—genuine love for Him is demonstrated through obedience to His teachings. Keeping His words is a tangible expression of devotion and allegiance.

3. "and my Father will love him": In response to the love demonstrated through obedience, the Father reciprocates with His love. This emphasizes the harmonious relationship within the Trinity and the unity of purpose in acknowledging and rewarding genuine love for Jesus.

4. "and we will come unto him, and make our abode with him": The consequence of both love and obedience is the intimate presence

of both the Father and the Son with the believer. The language of making an abode implies a permanent, indwelling presence, signifying a close and enduring relationship.

King James Bible References:

1. "If a man love me, he will keep my words": Similar sentiments about the connection between love and obedience are expressed in other passages (John 15:10, 1 John 5:3). Obedience is presented as an outward expression of inward love.

2. "and my Father will love him": The reciprocal love between the Father and those who love and obey Jesus is a consistent theme in the New Testament (John 16:27, 1 John 2:5).

3. "and we will come unto him, and make our abode with him": The promise of the Father and the Son making their abode with the believer underscores the transformative nature of this relationship. This is in harmony with the concept of believers as temples of the Holy Spirit (1 Corinthians 3:16, 1 Corinthians 6:19).

In summary, John 14:23 reveals the interconnected dynamics of love, obedience, and the indwelling presence of both the Father and the Son. This verse emphasizes the transformative nature of a relationship with Jesus, where love expressed through obedience results in a profound and abiding presence of the divine within the believer.

John Chapter 14:24 (KJV)
"He that loveth me not keepeth not my sayings: and the word which ye hear is not mine, but the Father's which sent me."

Expository Study and Commentary:

In this verse, Jesus contrasts the actions of those who do not love Him, emphasizing the direct connection between love for Jesus and obedience to His teachings. He clarifies the origin and authority of His words, attributing them to the Father who sent Him.

1. "He that loveth me not keepeth not my sayings": Jesus draws a clear link between love for Him and adherence to His teachings. Lack of love is manifested through disobedience, suggesting that genuine affection for Jesus naturally results in a desire to follow His guidance.

2. "and the word which ye hear is not mine, but the Father's which sent me": Jesus establishes the authority and source of His teachings. While He is the messenger, the content of His words originates from the Father. This reinforces the divine unity between Jesus and the Father and underscores the significance of His message.

King James Bible References:

1. "He that loveth me not keepeth not my sayings": This correlation between love and obedience is consistent with Jesus' teachings elsewhere in the Gospel of John (John 14:15, John 15:14). Obedience is presented as a tangible expression of love.

2. "and the word which ye hear is not mine, but the Father's which sent me": The notion that Jesus' words have divine origins aligns with the broader theological concept that Jesus is the Word made flesh (John 1:14). His teachings are not arbitrary but are rooted in the divine plan and purpose of the Father.

In summary, John 14:24 underscores the integral connection between love for Jesus and obedience to His teachings. It also emphasizes the divine origin and authority of Jesus' words, reinforcing the unity between Jesus and the Father. This verse serves as a reminder that authentic love for Jesus naturally results in a desire to follow His teachings, recognizing them as expressions of divine wisdom and guidance.

John Chapter 14:25 (KJV)
"These things have I spoken unto you, being yet present with you."

Expository Study and Commentary:

In this verse, Jesus addresses His disciples, indicating that He is sharing these words while still physically present with them. The statement lays the groundwork for further revelations and preparations for the disciples concerning the coming events and the role of the Holy Spirit.

1. "These things have I spoken unto you": Jesus refers to the teachings, promises, and insights He has shared with His disciples during His earthly ministry. This encompasses His instructions, assurances, and prophecies about the future.

2. "being yet present with you": Jesus emphasizes the immediacy of His communication. He speaks these words while still physically present, but there is an implication that there will be additional guidance and understanding to come, particularly after His departure.

King James Bible References:

1. "These things have I spoken unto you": This phrase echoes Jesus' frequent statements about His purpose in coming to reveal and explain the will of the Father. It aligns with His broader mission of teaching and preparing His disciples (John 15:15, John 16:25).

2. "being yet present with you": The temporal context of Jesus' physical presence is significant. The impending departure of Jesus and the subsequent sending of the Holy Spirit will mark a shift in the disciples' experience and understanding (John 16:7).

In summary, John 14:25 reflects Jesus' acknowledgment of the ongoing dialogue He has with His disciples, emphasizing that these teachings are given while He is still physically present. This verse sets the stage for the upcoming revelations about the role of the Holy Spirit, the events leading to His departure, and the continued guidance that will be provided to the disciples even after His physical absence.

John Chapter 14:26 (KJV)

"But the Comforter, which is the Holy Ghost, whom the Father will send in my name, he shall teach you all things, and bring all things to your remembrance, whatsoever I have said unto you."

Expository Study and Commentary:

In this verse, Jesus introduces the role of the Holy Spirit, referred to as the Comforter, and explains the functions the Spirit will perform in the lives of His disciples.

1. "But the Comforter, which is the Holy Ghost": Jesus promises the coming of the Holy Spirit, described as the Comforter or Advocate. This term signifies the Spirit's role in providing comfort, guidance, and assistance to believers.

2. "whom the Father will send in my name": The sending of the Holy Spirit is an act initiated by the Father, emphasizing the divine unity and cooperation within the Trinity. The Spirit comes with the authority of Jesus, operating in alignment with His purpose.

3. "he shall teach you all things": The Holy Spirit is portrayed as the ultimate teacher, guiding the disciples into a deeper understanding of truth. This teaching role extends to all areas of knowledge relevant to the disciples' mission and spiritual growth.

4. "and bring all things to your remembrance": The Spirit will have a unique function of reminding the disciples of Jesus' teachings. This ensures the continuity and accuracy of the message, preventing them from forgetting crucial aspects of Jesus' words.

5. "whatsoever I have said unto you": The Holy Spirit's work involves bringing to remembrance and illuminating the disciples' understanding of everything Jesus has communicated during His earthly ministry.

King James Bible References:

1. "But the Comforter, which is the Holy Ghost": The term "Comforter" is also translated as "Advocate" or "Helper" in other translations (John 14:16, John 15:26, John 16:7). This emphasizes the supportive and guiding nature of the Holy Spirit.

2. "whom the Father will send in my name": The cooperative sending of the Holy Spirit by the Father in Jesus' name is a consistent theme in the New Testament, highlighting the unity of purpose within the Godhead (John 15:26, John 16:7, Acts 2:33).

3. "he shall teach you all things": The Holy Spirit's role as a teacher aligns with other passages emphasizing the Spirit's function in guiding believers into all truth (John 16:13, 1 Corinthians 2:13).

4. "and bring all things to your remembrance": This aspect of the Spirit's work ensures the accuracy and preservation of the apostles' teachings, contributing to the writing of the New Testament and the transmission of Christian doctrine.

5. "whatsoever I have said unto you": The promise that the Holy Spirit will remind the disciples of Jesus' teachings underscores the reliability and continuity of the Gospel message.

In summary, John 14:26 introduces the essential role of the Holy Spirit as the Comforter, emphasizing the Spirit's functions of teaching and bringing to remembrance all that Jesus has said. This verse lays the foundation for the disciples' future understanding and transmission of Christian doctrine under the guidance of the Holy Spirit.

John Chapter 14:27 (KJV)
"Peace I leave with you, my peace I give unto you: not as the world giveth, give I unto you. Let not your heart be troubled, neither let it be afraid."

Expository Study and Commentary:

In this verse, Jesus imparts a profound message of peace to His disciples, distinguishing the peace He offers from the world's understanding of peace.

1. "Peace I leave with you, my peace I give unto you": Jesus bestows a unique and divine peace upon His disciples. It's not merely a worldly tranquility but a spiritual serenity that originates from His own being.

2. "not as the world giveth, give I unto you": Jesus contrasts His peace with the superficial peace offered by the world. The world's peace is often contingent on external circumstances, while Jesus' peace transcends worldly conditions, rooted in the assurance of His presence and salvation.

3. "Let not your heart be troubled, neither let it be afraid": Jesus encourages His disciples to embrace this divine peace and reject fear or distress. The call to remain untroubled and unafraid is an invitation to trust in Him completely.

King James Bible References:

1. "Peace I leave with you, my peace I give unto you": This declaration echoes earlier statements by Jesus about bringing peace (John 16:33) and connects with the Old Testament concept of the Messiah as the Prince of Peace (Isaiah 9:6).

2. "not as the world giveth, give I unto you": The contrast between divine peace and the world's understanding of peace aligns with Jesus' teachings about the transient nature of worldly comforts (John 16:20, John 16:33).

3. "Let not your heart be troubled, neither let it be afraid": Similar encouragement regarding fearlessness is found in various parts of the Bible, including Jesus' words in John 16:33 and other passages like Psalm 27:1 and Isaiah 41:10.

In summary, John 14:27 communicates Jesus' parting gift to His disciples – a profound and enduring peace that transcends worldly circumstances. This peace, distinct from what the world offers, is rooted in the presence of Christ. Jesus encourages His followers not to let their hearts be troubled or afraid, inviting them to embrace the assurance and tranquility that come from trusting in Him.

John Chapter 14:28 (KJV)
"Ye have heard how I said unto you, I go away, and come again unto you. If ye loved me, ye would rejoice, because I said, I go unto the Father: for my Father is greater than I."

Expository Study and Commentary:

In this verse, Jesus addresses His imminent departure, emphasizing the significance of His return to the Father and providing insights into the relationship between the Father and Himself.

1. "Ye have heard how I said unto you, I go away, and come again unto you": Jesus refers to previous statements He made about His departure and eventual return. This likely alludes to earlier discussions about His upcoming crucifixion, resurrection, and the promise of His return in a spiritual sense.

2. "If ye loved me, ye would rejoice": Jesus links the disciples' love for Him with their response to His departure. True love, He suggests, would lead to a rejoicing attitude rather than sorrow or distress. This indicates an understanding of the redemptive purpose behind His departure.

3. "because I said, I go unto the Father: for my Father is greater than I": Jesus explains the reason for rejoicing – His return to the Father. The statement "my Father is greater than I" is often understood in the context of Jesus' earthly ministry, where He willingly took on human limitations.

King James Bible References:

1. "Ye have heard how I said unto you, I go away, and come again unto you": References to Jesus' departure and return are found throughout the Gospel of John, particularly in passages discussing His impending crucifixion and resurrection (John 13:33, John 16:16-17).

2. "If ye loved me, ye would rejoice": The connection between love for Jesus and the joy that comes from understanding His redemptive work is emphasized in other teachings of Jesus (John 16:22).

3. "because I said, I go unto the Father: for my Father is greater than I": This statement has been the subject of theological discussions regarding the relationship within the Trinity. The affirmation of the Father's greater role is understood in the context of Jesus' earthly incarnation and mission (Philippians 2:5-11).

In summary, John 14:28 addresses Jesus' departure and return, calling for a rejoicing response from the disciples based on their love for Him. The statement about the Father being greater than Jesus is contextualized within the specific mission and incarnation of Jesus. This verse reflects the deeper spiritual understanding that true love for Christ includes rejoicing in His redemptive work and His return to the Father.

John Chapter 14:29 (KJV)
"And now I have told you before it come to pass, that, when it is come to pass, ye might believe."

Expository Study and Commentary:

In this verse, Jesus communicates to His disciples the purpose behind foretelling future events, emphasizing the role of prophecy in strengthening their faith.

1. "And now I have told you before it come to pass": Jesus highlights that He has provided forewarning to His disciples about future events. This aligns with His role as a teacher and prophet, revealing knowledge of things to come.

2. "that, when it is come to pass, ye might believe": The purpose of foretelling these events is to build and strengthen the disciples' faith. Jesus aims to establish a connection between His foreknowledge, His ability to fulfill predictions, and the disciples' trust in Him as the Son of God.

King James Bible References:

1. "And now I have told you before it come to pass": The theme of Jesus foretelling future events is recurrent in the Gospel of John, especially in relation to His impending crucifixion and resurrection (John 13:19, John 16:4).

2. "that, when it is come to pass, ye might believe": The concept of prophecy and its fulfillment as a means to inspire belief is found in other parts of the Bible, reinforcing the authenticity of God's revelation (Isaiah 42:9, Isaiah 48:5, John 13:19).

In summary, John 14:29 underscores Jesus' role as a revealer of future events for the purpose of strengthening the disciples' faith. By foretelling specific occurrences, Jesus connects His words with subsequent events, providing a tangible demonstration of His authority and divine knowledge. This verse highlights the intersection between prophecy and belief, emphasizing the credibility of Jesus as the Son of God and the significance of trust in Him.

John Chapter 14:30 (KJV)
"Hereafter I will not talk much with you: for the prince of this world cometh, and hath nothing in me."

Expository Study and Commentary:

In this verse, Jesus communicates a change in His interaction with the disciples, alluding to the approaching influence of the "prince of this world" and asserting His own innocence against any hold that the prince may claim.

1. "Hereafter I will not talk much with you": Jesus anticipates a shift in the nature and frequency of His communication with the disciples. This may be a reference to the impending events of His arrest, trial, and crucifixion, during which His direct discourse with them would be limited.

2. "for the prince of this world cometh": The "prince of this world" typically refers to Satan or the forces of evil. Jesus acknowledges the imminent arrival of a challenging and dark period, marked by the influence of evil powers.

3. "and hath nothing in me": Jesus asserts His moral purity and resistance to the influence of the prince of this world. This phrase suggests that there is no foothold or claim that evil forces have over Him. He remains untainted by sin.

King James Bible References:

1. "Hereafter I will not talk much with you": The reduction in direct communication aligns with the events leading to Jesus' crucifixion and the subsequent preparation of the disciples for His departure (John 16:12).

2. "for the prince of this world cometh": The term "prince of this world" is consistent with the New Testament's depiction of Satan as the ruler of the kingdom of darkness (John 12:31, John 16:11, 2 Corinthians 4:4).

3. "and hath nothing in me": Jesus' claim of moral innocence finds resonance in other passages underscoring His sinlessness (Hebrews 4:15, 1 Peter 2:22).

In summary, John 14:30 provides a glimpse into Jesus' awareness of the challenging events that lie ahead. It signals a change in His communication with the disciples, anticipating the influence of the "prince of this world." Yet, Jesus affirms His moral purity and resistance to any claim the evil forces might have over Him, emphasizing His victorious and untainted nature as He faces the approaching trial and crucifixion.

John Chapter 14:31 (KJV)
"But that the world may know that I love the Father; and as the Father gave me commandment, even so I do. Arise, let us go hence."

Expository Study and Commentary:

In this concluding verse of John 14, Jesus expresses His obedience to the Father's commandment as a demonstration of His love for the Father. The verse also marks the beginning of the events that will lead to Jesus' arrest and crucifixion.

1. "But that the world may know that I love the Father": Jesus' primary motivation is to manifest His love for the Father before the world. His actions and obedience become a testimony that reflects the profound love and unity within the Trinity.

2. "and as the Father gave me commandment, even so I do": Jesus underscores His complete submission to the Father's authority. His obedience is not only a testament to His love but also a demonstration of the perfect harmony between the Father and the Son in carrying out the divine plan.

3. "Arise, let us go hence": Jesus signals a shift in location, marking the beginning of a significant event – the journey to the Garden of Gethsemane where He will face betrayal and arrest. The words "let us go hence" indicate a purposeful and deliberate step toward the unfolding of God's redemptive plan.

King James Bible References:

1. "But that the world may know that I love the Father": The theme of Jesus' love for the Father and His obedience as a testimony is woven throughout the Gospel of John (John 4:34, John 5:30, John 8:29).

2. "and as the Father gave me commandment, even so I do": The obedience of Jesus to the Father's commandments is consistently highlighted in various passages, emphasizing the unity and cooperation within the Godhead (John 5:19, John 6:38, John 10:18).

3. "Arise, let us go hence": This phrase sets the stage for the events that follow, leading to Jesus' arrest and crucifixion. The journey to Gethsemane and ultimately to the cross is significant in the redemptive narrative.

In summary, John 14:31 encapsulates the essence of Jesus' obedience and love for the Father, highlighting His willingness to fulfill the divine commandments even in the face of the impending trials. The verse serves as a transitional moment, signaling the commencement of the events leading to Jesus' sacrificial death for the redemption of humanity.

CONCORDANCE

Concordance of the Gospel of John

A
- Abide: John 15:4-7, 9-10
- Abraham: John 8:31-58
- Alive: John 11:25-26

B
- Believe: John 1:12, 3:16, 5:24, 6:29, 20:31
- Bread of Life: John 6:35, 6:48

C
- Comforter: John 14:16, 14:26, 15:26, 16:7
- Crucifixion: John 19:16-30

D
- Disciples: John 1:35-51, 6:67-71, 20:19-31
- Death: John 11:1-44, 12:24, 19:16-30

E
- Eternal Life: John 3:15-16, 5:24, 6:40, 10:28

F
- Father: John 10:29-30, 14:6-11, 17:1-26
- Faith: John 1:12, 3:16, 3:36, 6:29, 20:31

G

- Glory: John 1:14, 11:40, 17:1-26
- Grace: John 1:14, 1:16, 1:17, 3:16

H
- Holy Spirit: John 14:16-17, 15:26, 16:7-15
- Healing: John 4:46-54, 5:1-9, 9:1-41

I
- I AM sayings: John 6:35, 8:12, 10:7, 11:25, 14:6, 15:1
- Incarnation: John 1:1-18

J
- Jesus' Baptism: John 1:29-34
- Jesus' Death: John 19:16-30
- Jesus' Resurrection: John 20:1-29
- Jesus' Miracles: John 2:1-11, 4:46-54, 5:1-9, 6:1-14, 9:1-41, 11:1-44

K
- Kingdom of God: John 3:3-5, 18:36

L
- Light: John 1:4-9, 3:19-21, 8:12, 9:5
- Love: John 3:16, 13:34-35, 15:9-13

M
- Messiah: John 1:41, 4:25-26, 11:27
- Marriage at Cana: John 2:1-11

N
- Nicodemus: John 3:1-21, 7:50-52, 19:39

O
- Obedience: John 14:15, 14:21, 15:10

P
- Prayer: John 17:1-26
- Prologue: John 1:1-18

R
- Resurrection: John 11:1-44, 20:1-29
- Righteousness: John 5:30, 7:24, 16:8

S
- Salvation: John 3:16, 5:24, 6:40
- Samaritan Woman: John 4:1-42
- Shepherd: John 10:1-18

T
- Truth: John 1:14, 8:31-32, 14:6

W
- Water into Wine: John 2:1-11
- Way, Truth, Life: John 14:6

Y
- Yeshua: John 1:29, 1:36

This concordance provides a comprehensive list of key themes, events, and teachings found in the Gospel of John, allowing readers to easily locate specific passages and study the text more deeply.

CONCLUSION

Conclusion of the Gospel of John

In the closing verses of the Gospel of John, the author reflects on the purpose of his writing and the significance of the events he has recorded. These verses serve as a fitting conclusion to the Gospel, encapsulating its central message and inviting readers to respond in faith.

John 20:30-31 (KJV): "And many other signs truly did Jesus in the presence of his disciples, which are not written in this book: But these are written, that ye might believe that Jesus is the Christ, the Son of God; and that believing ye might have life through his name."

In these verses, the author acknowledges that the Gospel contains only a selection of the many signs and miracles performed by Jesus. However, he explains that the signs recorded in the Gospel were specifically chosen to serve a purpose: to lead readers to faith in Jesus as the Christ, the Son of God. The ultimate goal of the Gospel, as stated by the author, is to bring about belief in Jesus and through that belief, to impart eternal life.

This conclusion highlights the central theme of belief that runs throughout the Gospel of John. The signs and miracles are not merely displays of Jesus' power, but are intended to lead people to a deeper understanding of who Jesus is and to elicit a response of faith. The Gospel invites readers to join the disciples in their journey of discovery, to encounter Jesus through the pages of this account, and to respond in faith to the invitation to believe in Him.

As we conclude our study of the Gospel of John, may we be inspired by the testimonies of those who witnessed Jesus' ministry, may we be drawn into a deeper relationship with Him, and may we, like the disciples, come to believe that Jesus is the Christ, the Son of God, and in believing, find eternal life through His name. Amen.

Shalom,

Dr. Maxwell Shimba
Shimba Theological Institute